NAGÔ GRANDMA
AND WHITE PAPA

A book in the series
Latin America in Translation /
en Traducción / em Tradução

Sponsored by the Consortium in
Latin American Studies at the
University of North Carolina at
Chapel Hill and Duke University

NAGÔ GRANDMA
AND WHITE PAPA

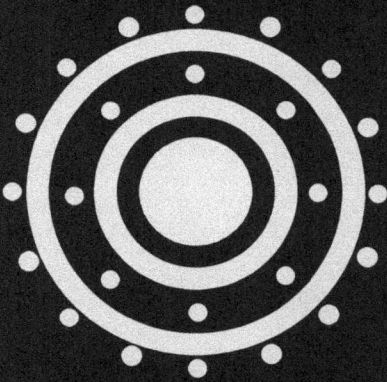

Candomblé
and the
Creation of
Afro-Brazilian
Identity

Beatriz Góis Dantas

TRANSLATED BY
Stephen Berg

THE UNIVERSITY OF
NORTH CAROLINA PRESS
Chapel Hill

Translation of the books in the series Latin America in
Translation / en Traducción / em Tradução, a collaboration
between the Consortium in Latin American Studies at the
University of North Carolina at Chapel Hill and Duke University
and the university presses of the University of North Carolina and
Duke, is supported by a grant from the Andrew W. Mellon Foundation.

Set in Scala and Othello

The paper in this book meets the guidelines for permanence and
durability of the Committee on Production Guidelines for Book
Longevity of the Council on Library Resources.

The University of North Carolina Press has been a member of the
Green Press Initiative since 2003.

Library of Congress Cataloging-in-Publication Data

Dantas, Beatriz Góis.
  [Vovó Nagô e Papai Branco. English]
  Nagô Grandma and White Papa : Candomblé and the creation of Afro-
Brazilian identity / Beatriz Góis Dantas ;
translated by Stephen Berg.
     p. cm.—(Translation of the books in the series Latin America in
translation)
  Includes bibliographical references and index.
  ISBN 978-0-8078-3177-9 (cloth: alk. paper)
  ISBN 978-0-8078-5975-9 (pbk.: alk. paper)
  1. Afro-Brazilian cults. 2. Brazil—Religion. I. Title.
  BL2590.B7D3513 2009
  299.6'73—dc22   2009009197

cloth 13 12 11 10 09   5 4 3 2 1
paper 13 12 11 10 09   5 4 3 2 1

*To the memory of
Josefina Leite Campos,
teacher. With faith and
competence she
initiated me in the
adventure of
anthropology.*

. . . . .

*And to
Bilina of Laranjeiras,
from whom I learned that
initiating* filhos-de-santo
*is also an act of competence
and faith.*

PURITY IS THE ENEMY OF CHANGE,
OF AMBIGUITY AND COMPROMISE.
MOST OF US WOULD FEEL SAFER
IF OUR EXPERIENCE COULD BE
HARD-SET AND FIXED IN FORM.

—MARY DOUGLAS, *Purity and Danger*

Contents

Acknowledgments

I hope this study contributes to enriching the debate on so-called Afro-Brazilian religions, which have not been the object of many publications over the past decade.

People and institutions contributed in different ways to the making of this work. I should like to express my thanks to them:

To the Federal University of Sergipe for having granted me a leave of absence that allowed me to take my degree and to CAPES/PICD for awarding me a scholarship.

To Professors Maria Manuela Carneiro da Cunha, adviser, and Peter Fry, co-adviser, who jointly witnessed the genesis of the idea for this work, believed in it, and supervised its preparation, stimulating me with their enthusiasm, discussions, suggestions, and friendship.

To my colleagues and teachers at UNICAMP's master's program in social anthropology, particularly to Rubem César Fernandes, Mariza Correa, Mauro Almeida, Antônio Augusto Arantes Neto, and Carlos Rodrigues Brandão for their criticism and suggestions, above all in the presentation of the project.

To Gisélia Góis Santana, who patiently deciphered manuscripts that Francisco José Costa Dantas and Rosa Virgínia Bonfim revised in final form.

To the many *pais* and *mães-de-santo* of Laranjeiras and, in particular, to the members of Bilina's *terreiro*, who accepted me and my "wanting to know for study purposes," which was different from their experiential knowledge.

To the many relatives and kin who offered me support at the hardest moments, especially to Ibarê Júnior and Sílvia, my children, who shared with me the discipline and sacrifices entailed by the composition of this work, which were assuaged and dignified by the friendly, stimulating presence of Ibarê, my partner on the journey.

Aracaju, July 1986

Introduction

As an analytical field, the study of so-called Afro-Brazilian[1] religions — and of Candomblé in particular — has traditionally privileged cultural contents and their specificities in addition to the search for their origins. Continuous allusion to Africa and the unceasing search for Africanisms (begun at the start of the nineteenth century with Nina Rodrigues) have taken on various forms, from the simple, mechanical comparison of cultural traits whose resemblance to African counterparts is presented as proof of "survivals" (Rodrigues, 1935, 1977; Ramos, 1951, 1961) all the way to studies that attempt to present the persistence of cultural traits as part of a functional, alternative African religious system (Herskovits, 1967; Ribeiro, 1952) or even as the expression of truly African thought (Bastide, 1971, 1978; Santos, 1976).

It is from this search for Africa that appreciation for the purity of Candomblé emerges. Simultaneously, Nagô tradition[2] is elevated to the height of Africanness and presented as a model cult of resistance in which the upholding of African tradition and values enables an alternative form of being, if not at the level of economic and political relations then at least at the ideological level. This is what Roger Bastide's "principle of scission" proposes — to explain how blacks who became part of capitalist society's labor force possessed an ideological autonomy guaranteed by religious participation in groups of African origin, guardians of a cultural repertory and thought that allude to Africa (Bastide, 1971).

In characterizing Candomblé *terreiros* — above all the purest ones — as havens of Africanness and resistance, authors who adopt this methodological stance implicitly accept that the presence in Brazil of cultural traits that originated in Africa necessarily indicates black resistance. The authentic transformation of Africanisms into proofs of resistance signals acceptance of the given that the meaning of cultural traits is determined through origin, without considering the fact that, whether real or supposedly of African origin, cultural traits may have different meanings in Brazilian society. Not taking this into due consideration leads to a search for Africa within Brazil, and the Nagô model emerges from this incessant search based on empirical data regarding Bahian *terreiros*[3] in which Nagô persists in its "purest" form, said model having been transformed into an analytical category by scholars who, significantly, privilege the most traditional *terreiros* as a field of study.

In dealing with other *terreiros*, the "purest" Nagô is always used as a reference. Inasmuch as they depart from the model, Umbanda, Macumba, and *Caboclo* and Angola Candomblés are considered "degenerate" and "distorted" from this perspective, "less interesting religious survivals"—an assessment that permeates work extending from Nina Rodrigues at the end of the nineteenth century to Roger Bastide in more recent years.

What underlies this logic is that the "pure Nagô" model, which truly represents a continuation of African cultural institutions that were transplanted here and preserved thanks to black collective memory, faithfully reproduced their origins and meanings, thus becoming signs of resistance. In compensation, those who blended with other traditions, degenerating from their original purity, became more integrated. Obviously, integration and resistance came to be judged by degrees of "purity" as defined by cultural traits that were found in the *terreiros* and considered African.

Forsaking this methodological position and gathering clues from research by Yvonne Velho, Peter Fry, and Patrícia Birman (Velho, 1975; Fry, 1977a; Birman, 1980), I became interested in trying to understand the meaning of this obstinate search for Africa and, in particular, the glorification of the "purest Nagô" tradition by an entire school of intellectuals. But I am also interested in examining the problem from another perspective—those who identify themselves as being of African (and specifically of Nagô) descent, and who present fidelity to Africa as a distinctive sign of self-identity.

My analysis attempts to introduce an aspect that has been somehow ignored in studies of Candomblé, to wit: its organizational dimension within the sociocultural and political context of society at large.

As long as the search for Africa was the basic purpose of research on Afro-Brazilian religions, culture was privileged and conceived of as an objective entity, a determinant element in the identification of cults with certain ethnic traditions that, transplanted to Brazil, adapted and perpetuated themselves as best they could in accordance with mechanisms of acculturation. In this type of analysis, culture appears as an autonomous system and the global society in which interethnic contacts and cultural contacts develop is ignored. Even Melville Herskovits—who proposed to study Candomblé as a whole, focusing on aspects of social and economic organization beyond the merely religious (Herskovits, 1967) — somehow isolates the religious unit from the broader context of Brazilian society or considers this relationship only insofar as it concerns syncretism. In attempting to understand black religions as an alternative system, "a subculture which integrates the matrix of general Brazilian culture" (Herskovits, 1954), he emphasizes the idea of a continuity of African tradition even as his perspective is restricted to the cultural level.

In criticizing Anthropology (and culturalists particularly) for treating culture as something abstract that hovers above sociological context, Roger Bastide proposes to study the social conditions of Afro-Brazilian religions. From his perspective, the maintenance of these religious forms should be researched in connection with the dual structure of society, for the "struggle of civilizations is only an aspect of the racial or economic class struggle" (Bastide, 1971: 96).

Thus it would be appropriate to analyze the role of "African" actors who are bearers (according to Roger Bastide) of a pragmatic and utilitarian philosophy within this context in which their interests as dominated groups were antagonistic to the interests of the dominants. However, while it may be true that the interests of structurally inferior black groups appear in the analysis of the historical evolution of religions — explaining, for example, the disappearance of African gods of agriculture who were not worshipped in Brazil and, in compensation, the importance assigned to warrior gods such as Ogum (Bastide, 1971: 97), or even the fact that Candomblé represents a center of support and integration for unprotected post-abolition blacks — on the whole, the author's analysis eventually dilutes the interests of the dominated groups in myriad factors, such as the solidarity between masters and slaves, and, after the abolition, introduces the so-called "principle of scission" to explain why blacks continue to be African even as they are Brazilian. He concludes that Candomblé and other types of African religions have resisted every manner of structural chaos, always finding a way to adapt to new living conditions or new social structures (Bastide, 1971: 236–40), thus inducing the reader to believe that, ultimately, Candomblé endured through African civilization's intrinsic capacity for self-perpetuation.

Authors such as Abner Cohen and Frederick Barth (Cohen, 1969; Barth, 1969) view the relationship between ethnicity and culture from a different perspective, changing the focus from the ethnicity of cultural contents to analysis of the group.

Discarding the traditional view in which ethnicity corresponds to a cultural unit maintained in social and/or geographic isolation, Frederick

Barth sees the ethnic group as a form of social organization in which there is an emphasis on interaction. In spite of this, the group is not diluted, for it maintains an organized complex of behaviors and relationships that mark the ethnic boundaries between "insiders" and "outsiders." In the construction and management of these boundaries, cultural traits are used as differential markers; yet only some of these differences are considered significant by the actors, not the sum total of differences. The central focus of the investigation is the "ethnic boundary which defines the group and not the cultural material it contains" (Barth, 1969: 15).

Abner Cohen considers ethnic groups to be interest groups that manipulate part of their traditional culture as a means of articulating their search for power. Thus, prior to being a cultural phenomenon, ethnicity is regarded as an essentially political phenomenon in which norms, values, and myths are related and used to express organizational functions, operating within a current political context rather than an archaic surviving arrangement undertaken in the present by a conservative people (Cohen, 1969).

For both authors, culture becomes an arsenal generally used to establish distinctions rather than the defining element of ethnicity, which implies a situation of otherness—an affirmation in the presence of others.

From this perspective, contact with others leads to the exacerbation of certain traits of cultural tradition that become diacritical; thus, the original culture (or part of it) takes on a new function: that of marking differences. Manuela Carneiro da Cunha presents the significant example of the Nagô who returned to Brazil from Lagos, Nigeria, in the nineteenth century. Here, they identify themselves as Brazilians, using Catholicism (as opposed to Protestantism, Islamism, and animism) as a basic diacritical sign intensified by other cultural traits, some of which are regarded in Brazil as African (culinary and ritual) and which they present as Brazilian, the better to mark their identity (Cunha, 1977).

This and many other examples lead to the conclusion that ethnicity cannot be defined by culture alone, since culture can be manipulated by the group that, moved by its interests, seeks a space of its own or attempts resistance. If such a position may be criticized for reducing culture to practical interests and reasons (Sahlins, 1979) or, more specifically in the context of ethnicity, to something that "is not posed, but only opposed" (Cunha, 1979), one might well ask to what measure these interests are, themselves, culturally defined. I do not propose to investigate such an intricate theoretical problem, one that Marshall Sahlins locates as the axis of the anthropological debate ever since its origins (Sahlins, 1979).

Rather, I propose to question the validity of comparisons between the cultural repertories of Afro-Brazilian religions, and cultures submitted to different historical and social processes, and to analyze the use of symbols by different social groups; my basis for doing so is the "glorification of the Nagô" undertaken by a chain of intellectuals and by a religious group self-identified as such.

The methodology I have adopted attempts to reflect upon certain aspects of Candomblé's multifaceted reality, aspects that remain unintelligible if analyzed only according to culturalist comparativism. In this regard, my own research experience is significant. When I began my study of the "pure Nagô" *terreiros*, attempting to focus on the historical, economic, organizational, and ritual aspects of a religious center located within a specific social setting (Dantas, 1976a), the insistence with which group members returned to the discourse on the "pure Nagô" in order to attest to their continuity with Africa led me to an analysis of the cultural contents presented as signs of this "African purity" and its comparison with the Nagô Candomblé of Bahia, regarded as the most vigorous African haven in Brazil. The result was disconcerting, for in many aspects there was flagrant disagreement as to the composition of this African heritage. It was understood that there were differences between Africa and Brazil; after all, significant historical and structural differences had been pointed out by Roger Bastide in his examination of the process of interpenetration of civilizations through the persistence of African religions in Brazil (Bastide, 1971).

But how to explain such drastic modifications in the cultural content of Nagô groups in two neighboring northeastern states? To present a cultural content dissimilar to the one found in the "purest" Nagô Candomblé *terreiros* of Bahia as "pure Nagô" tradition was surely an idiosyncrasy of the *terreiro* studied. Thus I resorted to the bibliography on the Xangôs,[4] regarded as the most Africanized in Recife; nevertheless, I remained perplexed. The conclusion appeared to be that there were also differences in the cultural repertories of other "purest Nagô *terreiros*" in the Northeast, differences that, in some cases, involved elements considered central to the religious groups' belief and value systems, such as forms of proselytizing.

In light of this, I began to rethink "Nagô purity" and realize that cultural features called upon to certify it are selected and combined in different ways so as to establish contrasts, and furthermore that, like words, their meanings allow for polysemy and are defined by the social context of the present and in the relationship of forces that involve the structurally superior and inferior.

My field of observation was the Afro-Brazilian segment of Laranjeiras, a small city in Recife's sugar-producing zone and, in particular, a *terreiro* self-identified and recognized by others as "pure Nagô."

From 1970 to 1976, I followed the life of this *terreiro* closely—its rituals, its routine, the *mãe-de-santo*'s relationship with other *terreiros* and with different segments of society at large. The group's acceptance of my presence was facilitated by my previous work on the Taieira, a ritual organized by the *mãe-de-santo* and presented within the Catholic context of the festival of São Benedito. Through it, I became acquainted with many members of the *terreiros* and enjoyed the *mãe-de-santo*'s friendship. One day, she suggested I write a book about the Xangô. This coincided with an idea I had been entertaining for quite some time. I then began to frequent the house with the stated intention of studying the Xangô, in order to write a book as I had done with the Taieira.

To be the focus of a book, to see her name in print and her photograph published as director of the Taieira, was certainly a gratifying experience for the *mãe-de-santo*. Although she let me know that, by making public knowledge what had previously been hers alone, the book had deprived her of a monopoly on information regarding the Taieira, it was obvious that it had been instrumental in raising her status. The idea that I would write a book about the Xangô gave her the possibility of improving that status and increasing her prestige, as well as the opportunity to initiate a new cycle of exchanges in which information regarding the Xangô was repaid with small favors, contributions to the rituals and constant visits that eventually contribute to a *mãe-de-santo*'s position and religious status and that of her religious group. I was aware of the researcher-observer's interference in the lives of those observed and I realized how my own presence in the *terreiros* played into the game of assessing the prestige of houses of worship, and so I interpreted the attempted intensification of my link to the group as a strategy through which to prolong this presence. Its members insistently admonished me against "going from *terreiros* to *terreiros*," arguing that it was "risky for the *senhora* to be walking around these Torés, for *torezeiros* are evil and something bad could happen to you." A behavioral pattern that is part of the group members' code of ethics was thus transferred to the researcher, under the allegation that I was "almost a Nagô." On several occasions, the *mãe-de-santo* warned me: "You have *santo*" or "You are protected by a very strong *santo*," a statement that implied the idea that this protection might be greater if I worshipped it appropriately. However, the proposition remained unspoken. There were clear attempts to get me to establish closer links to the *terreiro*'s life, if not through the *baptism* that would determine my saint, then at least through the establishment of ritual kinship by way of the substitute *mãe-de-santo*'s sponsorship. To be sure, the invitation to serve as godmother when the latter was solemnly invested as group leader was not presented as a mere courtesy, but as a revelation by the deceased *mãe-de-santo* who appeared in a dream to transmit it. Establishing a closer tie between researcher and religious group was not only a means of assuring her presence in the *terreiros* for a longer time, but also of further guaranteeing support by people from the middle class who had relative access to certain institutional sectors. It ultimately meant expanding the group's network of social relations beyond the lower class from which it generally recruited its members, with all of the possible attendant advantages.

When I left to pursue my master's degree in Campinas (1978–1979), although I continued to keep up with the most significant events in the *terreiro*'s life and sent them news of myself, I distanced myself physically from the group. The distance left me more at ease, when I returned to the field, to visit other *terreiros* in regard to which my mobility had, in a way, been restricted because, even though my presence in the Nagô *terreiros* was quite frequent, its expectation was that I, too, respect the boundaries between it and "the others." For some time I had been keeping up with the other *terreiros*' events (and particularly their relations with the Nagô) from a distance, but only now did I feel comfortable visiting them, thus extending my field of observation that I might see how the local Afro-Brazilian group configured itself, the *terreiros*' emic[5] criteria of classification and of attributing status, and the relationship between them and society at large. Chapter 1 is, therefore, a map of the Afro-Brazilian field in Laranjeiras and, in its specificity, an arid, albeit necessary background for the study of the Nagô. This is because ethnicity is a relational concept, and as such becomes operative only through the presence of others with whom the Nagô will dispute adepts and clients in the market of symbolic goods.

In the next two chapters, Nagô talks about itself and others. In chapter 2, based on the *mãe-de-santo*'s representations of herself and of her *terreiros*, I attempt to understand how she seeks to legitimize herself through Africa, to which she is linked by her origins (the "history" of the *terreiros* and the genealogy of their leaders) and by a cultural heritage preserved without "mixture," which would be the mark of her distinction in local Afro-Brazilian groups.

In chapter 3, based on the Nagô *mãe-de-santo*'s representations of other *terreiros* and of the Catholic religion, I return to the Nagô-Toré and pure-mixed dichotomies outlined in chapter 1 in order to analyze the categories underlying this schema of classification (African-Indian and good-evil) and show how the outlines of purity and mixture follow the principles of the dominant and subaltern classes within the social structure through an arrangement (that does not degenerate Nagô purity) with the Catholic Church.

The title of chapter 4 is "The Construction and Meaning of Nagô Purity." In it, I expand my field of analysis, seeking to show that Nagô purity does not result from fidelity to a tradition, but from a construction in which intellectuals play an important role. From this perspective, fidelity to Africa is presented as a distinctive sign of the Northeast and a component of 1930s regionalism. I also show how "pure Nagô" is transformed from sorcery into a "true religion," albeit one that is permeated with exotic-primitive-aesthetic aspects and, also, how in Candomblé's transit from a target of police persecution to glorified Nagô Candomblé, pure Nagô is used as a symbol of the Brazilian nation and cultural democracy.

In the last chapter, I once again restrict my field of analysis to the Nagô of Laranjeiras in order to verify how the intellectual movement of African glorification discussed in the previous chapter is reflected in a small northeastern town and how—having exclusively guaranteed the purest African origin—the Nagô *terreiro* uses it as a survival strategy in the competitive symbolic goods market.

CHAPTER ONE

The Configuration of Prestige in Xangô *Terreiros*

A flourishing city in the state of Sergipe's sugar-producing region during the nineteenth century, Laranjeiras is considered the initial focal point and strongest center of Nagô tradition in the state (Oliveira, 1978), as well as a city in which so-called Afro-Brazilian cults vigorously proliferate.

There are sixteen places of worship in this urban area and an almost identical number distributed throughout the various county villages.[1] The county possesses an area of 161 square kilometers and a population of 13,280, of which 5,150 live within the municipal seat. Although the *terreiros'* network of influence is not circumscribed to municipal—or even state—boundaries, there would appear to be a high concentration of houses of worship in the locality. My research was limited to the municipal seat and I worked with ten *terreiros*, concentrating particularly on one of them.

The way these *terreiros* identify themselves and the way they identify others; the social recognition of the inequality attributed to them by cult participants and by "outsiders"; these are the subjects of this chapter as it seeks to establish the configuration of prestige in a Xangô market.[2]

The word *terreiro* is usually employed both by "insider" cult participants and non-participant individuals—or "outsiders"—in identifying a place and, simultaneously, the religious group. The designations *casa de santo* and *centro* are also used, the latter more frequently in inquiring after the *terreiro*'s name. It invariably appears on licenses granted to *terreiros* registered by the Federations of Afro-Brazilian and Umbanda Cults, and is also used by those that are reluctant to register. As a rule, the *terreiro* contains a leader and his or her followers, generally called *filhos de fé*. The group is sometimes called a brotherhood. The terms *filho-de-santo* and *pai-* or *mãe-de-santo* are infrequently used. Indeed, whenever they were employed by the researcher, they were rejected outright by certain *terreiro* leaders under the allegation that a mortal could never be the father or mother of a saint.

The term *santo* (literally, saint) identifies African *orixás* and *caboclo* spirits alike, the latter being more commonly known as *encantados*.

All visited *terreiros* contained altars with saints to whom feasts are dedicated and carried out with drum *toques* and dances at least once a year. However, some of them do not have congregations (*filhos de fé*) and are almost exclusively dedicated to consultations known locally as *reparos*, or *trabalhos*, a term that includes a series of activities dedicated to immediate problem solving. Such *terreiros* therefore exist for the purpose of catering to individual clients who do not establish ties with the center. Dispensing with congregation altogether, they hold their festivities with the collaboration of *filhos de fé* from other centers who come to dance — something inconceivable in other *terreiros*, where dancing in a *roda* is the exclusive prerogative of members. These and many other differences are emphasized *as* differences within the local segment of Afro-Brazilian religions, differences that express themselves above all in the opposition between Nagô *terreiros* and *caboclo terreiros*.

"OUTSIDERS" CLASSIFY THE *TERREIROS*

In identifying *terreiros*, the terms Nagô and *caboclo* appear as indicators for classification that are employed with a certain familiarity, not only by religious leaders and participants but also by the city's population in general.

Based on informal conversations, interviews with individuals from various social classes and compositions written by [the Brazilian equivalent of junior high school] students, one concludes that, when referring to *terreiros*, non-participants use the Nagô-*caboclo* opposition even though they give preference to employing Nagô-*toré*.

There are several recorded meanings for the term *toré*. It is sometimes used to designate a musical instrument; at other times it indicates a dance; yet it is always associated with Indians. In the lower São Francisco River region of the state of Alagoas, *toré* appears as "a variant of *catimbó*, a ceremony in which *caboclos* or *encantados* manifest themselves in trance — in response to the master — in order to teach remedies, as in a *caboclo Candomblé*" (Cascudo, 1969: 708, the author's italics).

Without restricting this purely curative aspect, the term is used in Laranjeiras as a synonym for *terreiro de caboclo*. At least in this city, however, it presents a pejorative connotation, and is not used by any *terreiro de caboclo* leader to refer to his own religious center, although it is occasionally used to indicate the *terreiros* of others or — above all — of rivals. The negative connotation with which the term *toré* is invested becomes more intense in its derivate *torezeiro*, as applied to *caboclo* cult participants.

As a category, *toré* or *caboclo* stands in opposition to Nagô. The latter is a generic term used in Brazil to designate groups that came from the South and the East of the People's Republic of Benin (formerly Dahomey) and from southeastern Nigeria, including Ketu, Sabe, Oió, Egbá, Ijeshá, and Ijebu. With regard to the word "Yorubá" in Nigeria, Juana Elbein dos Santos reminds us that, in Brazil, the term Nagô was collectively applied to several groups linked by a common language, all of which arrived in Brazil in the late eighteenth–early nineteenth centuries, having concentrated in the states of the North and Northeast, particularly in Salvador and Recife (Santos, 1976: 29). Currently, Nagô indicates a group of practices and beliefs held to be of Yoruba-African origin, according to which a Candomblé nation is defined (Serra, 1978: 37–38).

To the inhabitants of Laranjeiras, a Nagô *terreiro* is opposed to the others, which are considered as *torés*. Classification is, thus, precise: with the exception of Nagô, everything else is *toré*, *terreiro* de *caboclo*. The classification of the *terreiro* leaders is a bit more subtle, as we shall see.

THE *TERREIROS* AS THEY SEE THEMSELVES

Generally speaking, religious leaders are fairly knowledgeable about the city's *terreiros*, and some of them were able to list as many as fourteen *casas de santo*, their locations, leaders, and nations. In classifying the *terreiros*, some employed categories not listed by "outsiders," thus presenting a more highly nuanced portrait of identity that includes different African nations such as Ketu, Ijexá, Jeje, and Angola, in addition to Nagô. However, these specifications always appear in the leader's self-identification of his *terreiro* and nearly always go unnoticed by other religious leaders, for whom that which is not Nagô or *caboclo* or an association of the two is simply mixed or *enrolado* (see table 1).

In table 1, *misturado* (or "mixed") emerges as a category that appears to have a double meaning—it is sometimes a synonym for *caboclo*, although elsewhere it indicates a fusion of *caboclo*, Nagô, and other nations. It is interesting to observe that the adjective "pure" and its correlatives (which are frequently associated to a Nagô *terreiro*) were never used in regard to any *caboclo terreiro*. I shall soon return to the problem of "purity" and "mixture" of Nagô and *caboclo*. For the time being I will attempt to point out existing ties between the *terreiros* in order to establish links between self-identification and identity attributed by others insofar as they would

TABLE I. *Terreiro* Classification according to Religious Leaders

TERREIROS	SELF-IDENTITY	CLASSIFICATION BY OTHER PAIS-DE-SANTO
São Jerônimo 1	Caboclo	Caboclo / Toré
São Sebastião	Caboclo	Mixed
Tupinambá	Caboclo	Caboclo / Toré / Mixed
The Virgin Santa Bárbara	Nagô	Nagô (an adjective signifying "pure," "legitimate," "true," "African")
São José	Nagô	Nagô / Caboclo-Nagô
Filhos de Obá	Obá (Nagô), Ketu, Ijexá, Angola, Caboclo, Jeje	Caboclo-Nagô / Angola-Nagô / Caboclo / Toré / Mixed
Ulufan	Nagô, Ketu, Ijexá, Caboclo	Caboclo / Toré / Confused
Santa Bárbara	Angola	Caboclo / Toré
São Jerônimo 2	Jeje	Caboclo / Toré
Ogum de Ronda	Does not belong to a nation	Toré / Mixed

Translator's note: Both "mixed" and "confused" propose to explicitly render a sense of admixture in the classification of other *terreiros* by *pais-de-santo*; the Portuguese "enrolado" (meaning "confused" or "muddled") is markedly more derogatory than the simple "mixed."

appear to have been elaborated on the basis of a "*terreiro*'s history," in turn closely identified with its leader's life experience and prior experiences with other religious centers where they may have received their training. What is intended is a brief reconstitution of the history of the *terreiros* and their links to one another, to establish the foundation for considering the greater or lesser equivalence between self-identification and attributed identity.

The connection between the various *terreiros* and their identities may be represented in graphic terms by distributing them across two fields separated by a vertical line within which the *terreiros* are situated and interact (see figure 1).

Let us begin with the Nagô *terreiro* of the Virgin Santa Bárbara, where equivalence between self-identity and attributed identity is total. It ex-

pressed the continuity of a *terreiro* of African slaves from whom the recently deceased (1974) female Creole leader was descended, having led it
for over fifty years according to the tradition of Nagô ancestors that she
upholds to the present day.

The history of the Filhos de Obá *terreiro*—self-defined as obá (Nagô)
and, secondarily, as Jeje, Ketu, Ijexá, Angola, and *caboclo*—is similar
to that of the preceding one. But from a given moment on, the person
who led it for over half a century, likewise recently deceased, not only
appeared to have updated the tradition of the Nagô and other African
nations through Bahia but also to have incorporated the cult of the *caboclos* into the *terreiro*. A shift thus took place—from the Nagô field to the
boundaries of the *caboclo* field, and it became "mixed." Its influence in
the history of the city's other *terreiros* is very great. Through the process
of fission that rules religious expansion, its direct derivatives are the *terreiros* of São Jerônimo 1 (self-defined as *caboclo*); the Ulufan (self-defined
as Nagô, Ketu, Ijexá, and *caboclo*); and São Jerônimo 2 (self-defined as
Jeje). It also indirectly influenced two other *terreiros* whose leaders are not
linked to it by membership but who frequented it habitually in the past.
I refer to the São Sebastião (self-defined as *caboclo* and accepted as such)
and the São José (self-defined as Nagô and classified by other leaders
sometimes as Nagô and sometimes as *caboclo* Nagô). The history of the
latter *terreiro* also dates back to Africans who are said to have left *santos
da Costa* under custody of their Creole descendants. These descendants,
under the influence of the Filhos de Obá *terreiro*, are said to have "mixed"
Nagô and *caboclo*. For many years, the *terreiro* leaders who succeeded one
another in kinship[3] followed the double cult tradition until the late 1970s,
under the pretext that the African saints were angry and punishing her,
its leader undertook a "return to [her] roots." She became affiliated with
the *terreiro* of the Virgin Santa Bárbara, the "pure Nagô," and under its
imposition suspended *caboclo* practices. Thus, the *terreiro* is situated at
a threshold and, while some religious leaders accept its return to Nagô,
others continue to regard it as *caboclo*-Nagô.

As for the Tupinambá *terreiro*, it derives from one of the city's famous
and currently extinct *caboclo terreiros*. The Santa Bárbara is linked to a
center from another location, while the Ogum de Ronda presents itself
as dispensing with ties to other *terreiros*, and its leader regards herself as
an *iluminada* who works primarily with consultations. Having affiliated
herself to one of the Umbanda Federations, she has encouraged the cult
of the Umbanda spirits, gathered together in an elaborate sanctuary, as
well as performance of public rituals carried out with the participation of

FIGURE I. *Terreiros* and Their Identities

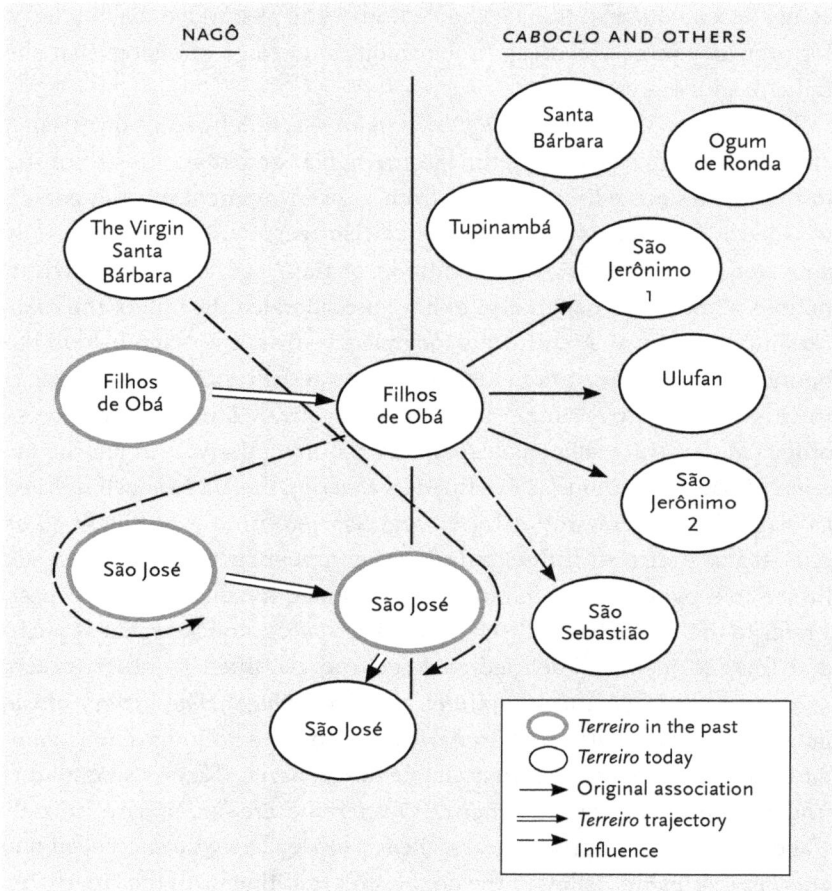

filhos de santo from other centers, in a clear effort to transform what was once a consultation center into an Umbanda *terreiro*.

The outline of *terreiro* histories as reconstructed through information supplied by their leaders shows a correlation between such histories and classifications established by other religious leaders. If we consider the *caboclo*-Nagô duality, we may see that (with one exception) there are greater or lesser correspondences between the self-identity of *terreiros* and the identities attributed to them by others. The only exception would be the São José—which claims exclusive identity with the Nagô—though this recognition is denied it by some of the *terreiro* leaders, certainly in light of its fluctuations along the *caboclo*-Nagô boundary. Thus, the Virgin Santa Bárbara *terreiro* appears as an exclusive identity, recognized not only by "outsiders" but by all local Afro-Brazilian religious leaders. It is regarded as the only "pure," "legitimate," "true," "African" Nagô *terreiro*. Overshadowing the Nagô versus *caboclo* opposition, which is basic for both "insiders" and "outsiders," yet another opposition is thus constructed between "pure" versus "mixed."

In light of the existence of an emic system of *terreiro* classification, one wonders about the possibility of establishing equivalencies between this and other systems of classification divulged by the literature on Afro-Brazilian religions such as Umbanda, Candomble, and so on. How is this subject generally regarded by Laranjeirenses (citizens of Laranjeiras) or by individuals who participate in the services? Unlike Xangô, a widely known term used indiscriminately to indicate *terreiros* and cults, the names Candomblé and Umbanda are practically never used. Significantly, out of a total of fifty-two student compositions, Umbanda appeared only once, having been presented as a synonym for Candomblé. This latter term was used ten times, eight of which as a synonym for Toré (*caboclo*) and in opposition to Nagô, once as "the most appropriate designation to indicate the cults" and elsewhere as a synonym for Umbanda.[4]

Cult leaders do not use these terms either except when questioned about differences between the *caboclo* and Nagô categories. Even so, only three used them. A sampling of statements includes "Toré is *caboclo* business. But my uncle called it Candomblé." Or "Toré is Candomblé by way of Bahia. We use Toré here but Bahian Candomblé is more Ketu. Toré is more Umbanda" (*terreiro* leaders).

In addition to the existence of an independent system of classification centered upon the *caboclo*-Nagô categories, it may be deduced that, when asked to explain this schema, the *terreiro* leaders try to establish equivalencies with another schema of classification that they assume to be better known to the researcher. In this attempt, one notes that there is a tendency to approximate the Toré, at times, to the Candomblé of Bahia and, at other times, to Umbanda. However, there has never been any attempt to establish equivalencies between Candomblé and Nagô. One would expect that, because Nagô was locally considered the depository of "purest African Tradition"—a quality claimed elsewhere by the oldest Candomblé *terreiros* of Bahia—there might be an approximation between the two. However, in the city, Candomblé was associated with the most "mixed" and discredited category—to wit, the Toré. To the Afro-Laranjeiran world, far from privileging the "preservation of African purity," the influence of Bahia over local cults would have acted in the sense of accentuating the "mixtures." In this regard, the history of the *terreiros* is quite elucidative, particularly when seen from the perspective of the Filhos de Obá *casa de santo*, as previously seen.

Insofar as cult naming is concerned, it is worth remembering that, not only in Laranjeiras but in Sergipe generally, the term most often employed by ordinary people to designate them is Xangô, as is the case in the states of Alagoas and Pernambuco. This seems intriguing when one knows about the economic and political dependency that marked the history of Sergipe in relation to Bahia, where the cults are called Candomblé. This denomination, which is usual in Sergipe among the lettered, did not impose itself among the poor, which also indicates that Bahia's influence over Sergipe's Afro-Brazilian segment is not as devastating as students of the expansion of the Bahian Jeje-Nagô cult model would have us suppose (Carneiro, 1964: 121–126) or as geographical proximity and historically recognized economic and political dependency might suggest. The matter of cult naming will be pursued further in chapter 4.

To return to the question of correspondence between emic categories and those disseminated by the vast literature on Afro-Brazilian cults, one perceives that there is a discrepancy between them and, since my present objective is to understand how differences within the religious field are perceived and presented, I have chosen to analyze the categories of people in cults who make a basic distinction between *caboclo* and Nagô, which, in turn, refers us to another opposition—the one between Indians and blacks.

ABOUT DIFFERENCES

The origin attributed to the cultural tradition disseminated by these *terreiros* is the starting point for the observable differences between them. *Caboclo terreiros* were originally linked to the Indians, and the Nagôs were linked to Africa. This idea is expressed in different ways, as we may see here:

> "My *terreiro* is *caboclo*. My saint is *Caboclo* Rescaíza. (. . .)
> I am of Indian descent. My grandmother was an Indian.
> Horses and dogs were used to capture her in the Amazon and
> she was raised in Simão Dias (Sergipe)." (*Terreiro* leader)

> "In olden days, there was nothing but Nagô and Malé in Laranjeiras. (. . .) It was Manué de Zuína who brought the *caboclos*.
> He was educated in the village. He was raised there and then he
> ran away." (*Terreiro* leader)

If the *caboclo* is to be explained through a link to Indians, it is by recurring to the connection with Africa that the origin of the Nago *terreiros* may be understood:

"Nagô is the nation of the *preto velho*, of Black African slaves. It was their heritage." (Student)

"The Afro-Brazilian cult Filhos de Obá represents the traditional rights and succession of the departed president Joaquina Maria da Costa, of African origin, a daughter of the city of Obá, of the Nagô cults. . . ." (*Terreiro* statute)

"Bilina's Nagô *terreiro* belongs to the old African branch.
[They are] different from us *caboclos* who come from Indians."
(*Terreiro* leader)

According to the locals, the differentiated origin of the cults would be at the base of the differences that separate Nagô *terreiros* from *caboclo* ones.

To "outsiders," or non-cult participants, those differences are found in the entities that are worshipped, in the center's activities regarding good and evil practices and, above all, in rituals. It was around these two aspects that the students worked on the differences in their compositions.[5] According to them, the Nagô worship the dead and the *orixás*, whereas the Toré worship *caboclos* and the devil. As a result of their link with the forces of evil, the Toré "make a living from witchcraft," while the Nagô are less maleficent.[6] But it is above all else with regard to ritual that a greater number of nuanced differences is expressed, although these are restricted to external rituals that are open to the public and known locally as *festejos*. Listed differences refer to the festival season, to drum *toques* (percussion instrument styles), to dances, and to garments. The latter in particular are often considered distinctive: "Nagô costumes are white and the Toré's are colored and have prints."

DIFFERENCES AS SEEN BY "INSIDERS"

To *terreiro* leaders, the fundamental difference between Nagôs and *caboclos* is "working" or "not working" with the "left," which incurs resorting to Exu, identified as the "Hound," the "Enemy," the "forces of Evil." Significantly, with the exception of one leader who also resorts to differentiating elements within the ritual,[7] *terreiro* leaders, in addition to referring to their real or supposed origins, limited themselves to this opposition:

"*caboclo terreiros* work with the left" while "Nagô does not work with the left." It should be noted that, out of a total of ten cult leaders who were interviewed, only seven resorted to this diacritical sign; of those seven, only two *terreiros* defined themselves as Nagô; the others defined themselves as *caboclo* or *caboclo*-Nagô.[8] Equally noteworthy is the fact that, although they made use of this differentiating criterion, some *terreiro* leaders raised doubts as to its veracity, suggesting that the Nagô also worked with Exu, under the disguise of another name.

> "I can't assure you that Bilina didn't work with the left. But she had Bará *assentado* [seated or enshrined]. And Bará is what the Nagô nation calls Exu." (*Terreiro* leader)

Notwithstanding this, there is general agreement among leaders who compete for prestige and income within the local magical-religious market, one that presents Nagô as opposed to the manipulation of evil and dedicated to the practice of good. The following excerpt from an interview with a self-defined *caboclo* cult leader is significant because of its reference to the leader of the Nagô *terreiro*:

> "He prepared those ablutions with the strength of the *orixás*. He did not need Exu to do his work. He could do *trabalhos* to help but did not set Exu 'on the ground.' He used only herbs and baths. On the floor, we placed offerings of chickens, cachaça, liquor, gunpowder, and farofa which we spread over peoples' bodies." (*Terreiro* leader)

Thus, "not working with the left" does not imply discarding the existence of a clientele that centers around Nagô in search of services rendered. As we shall see below, the existence of such a clientele is admitted, their wishes to be satisfied through the Nagô *terreiro* leader's skills in dealing with the *orixás de frente*, drawing from them the solution of problems without need for resource to Exu. Thus, for the Nagô, with whom, as we have seen, the notion of "purity" is associated, we must also add the idea of goodness.

THE IMPORTANCE OF *TERREIROS* AS SEEN BY "INSIDERS"

In light of the multiplicity of *terreiros* that exist in the city today—some recent, others longstanding, some large, others small, some Nagô, others *caboclo*—which *terreiros* are considered the most important? In the history of the centers, outlined above in general terms, the Filhos de Obá *ter-*

reiro stands out above all as the matrix-*terreiro* from which several others originated. Might this be an indicator of importance? What are the criteria used in the market of Xangô to recognize importance and prestige?

In this part of the work I shall attempt to see how this question is perceived from "within," by the cult leaders themselves. Almost unanimously, they agree that the Virgin Santa Bárbara and Filhos de Obá *terreiros* are the most important in the city. In their assessment, the two are more or less equivalent, while the next ones in terms of importance (the Ulufan, the São José, and the São Jerônimo 2) are very distant from them in terms of having their importance recognized by cult leaders.[9]

In order to justify the importance assigned to the Virgin Santa Bárbara and Filhos de Obá *terreiros*, they used the following arguments: "Those *terreiros* are over one hundred years old," "they are ancient, historical," "they have *fundamento*," "they came from the Africans," "they know how to do things." To which were added: "They are large *terreiros* with many children," many "cars stop at their doors," "they are discussed on radio and television," or even "they have sent dancers to the palace doors in Aracaju."

Criteria employed to assign importance to *terreiros* may be grouped into two categories. On one hand, there are external signs — indicators according to which it is possible to measure a *terreiro*'s success by the number of members it has; unrestricted circulation within certain sectors dominated by the upper classes and represented by the media; government invitations and the presence of the rich in search of magical services. On the other hand, internal reasons that would be at the base of the explanation for success, such as a *terreiro*'s African origin; its age and its leader's ritual abilities; elements linked directly to a *terreiro*'s *força*, an important concept in emic interpretations as regards the prestige of *terreiros*, to which I shall return shortly.

Attention should also be paid to the fact that, in spite of differences in trajectory with regard to their original legacies and to their identity, the two *terreiros* pointed out as the most important have much in common. In addition to the age attributed to them, blacks who knew the last Africans in the city (and were initiated into the cult by them) have remained in the director position of both. Both of them passed away some years ago, while the two *terreiros* were under the tutelage of recently confirmed leaderships.[10] This fact has not engendered (at least until the present) any reorganizing of the *terreiros*' scale of prestige by the cult leaders themselves. This does not mean that they recognize in new leaders the full ritual ability which can only be recognized with time. One of them actu-

TABLE 2. *Terreiro* Seniority according to Their Respective Leaders

TERREIRO	YEARS ACTIVE
São Jerônimo 1	15 years
São Sebastião	8 years
Tupinambá	1 year
The Virgin Santa Bárbara	Over 100 years
São José	Over 50 years
Filhos de Obá	Over 100 years (certainly since 1906)
Ulufan	13 years
Santa Bárbara	15 years
São Jerônimo 2	6 years
Ogum de Ronda	10 years

ally declares that he "still [does not have] permission to perform rituals," which allowed for other *terreiros* to expand their clientele and become more widely known. What happens is that despite the fact there is usually an identity between a *terreiro*'s prestige and that of its leader, in light of the recentness of the successions, the importance of the aforementioned *terreiros* is assessed in terms of former leaders. Indeed, they continue to be referred to as "the late Alexandre's *terreiro*" and "the late Bilina's *terreiro*." The performance of new, recently installed leaderships will only ratify or alter this profile of importance attributed to local Afro-Brazilian cult centers with the passing of the years. Thus, I have worked with the perspective that "insiders" have of *terreiros* under previous leaderships. In the same way, throughout this book I have made use of the historical present to transcribe the discourse of the deceased.

THE IDEAL AND THE REAL

I shall further explore the internal criteria for evaluating the *terreiros*' importance by analyzing them comparatively in relation to the various cult centers (see table 2).

Considered the most important temples, the Virgin Santa Bárbara and Filhos de Obá *terreiros* date back to the nineteenth century, in which respect they differ from the others. What may be observed, however, is that the importance of a *terreiro* is not measured only in years. Far less important than the abovementioned *terreiros* are those of Ulufan (with thirteen years of existence) and the São José (which has existed for over half a century), followed by a *terreiro* that was founded only six years ago. Meanwhile, cult centers with more than fifteen years of activity were considered "weak *terreiros*."

The Nagô or African origin of its leaders was another criterion used by "insiders" in assigning importance to *terreiros*. Considering that direct African ascendency would express itself in phenotype and, above all, in skin color, I present the "racial markers" of the *terreiro* leaders in table 3.

Of the four black leaders, three claim direct connection with Africa and present their *terreiros* as continuations of *terreiros* founded by the Nagô. They consider themselves to be guardians of the *santos da Costa* which they inherited from African ancestors. In particular, the deceased leader of the Virgin Santa Bárbara *terreiro* insisted on the fact that she descended from African grandparents and had been raised by a Nagô.

"All four of my grandparents came from Africa. But my mother was a Brazilian-born black woman. I was raised by my maternal grandmother. Her name was Isméria, a name she was given in Brazil. In Africa her name had been Birunqué. She was truly Nagô." (*Terreiro* leader)

Establishing close ties with Africa and familiarity with Africans are ways of proclaiming knowledge of cult secrets and *força* and thus legitimizing oneself before local Afro-Brazilian groups who consider the *orixá* more powerful than the *caboclo*.

Likewise, the spiritual power attributed to the African or to his descendent was greater than that attributed to whites or mulattos, a fact that might be interpreted as recognition of the "power of the weak," those who are outside the formal power structure of society (Douglas, 1976). According to an emic criterion of attributing importance, this meant recognizing that black leaders who descended directly from Africans had greater *força* owing to their connection with Africa. Here are a few statements regarding the authority of the leader of the Virgin Santa Bárbara *terreiro*, proclaiming her authority as a consequence of her connection with Africa and her roots:

" . . . She used to prepare baths with the power of the *orixás*. She helped people and had no need for Exu." (*Terreiro* leader)

TABLE 3. *Terreiro* Leaders according to Color

TERREIRO	COLOR OF LEADER
São Jerônimo 1	White
São Sebastião	Light mulatto
Tupinambá	White
The Virgin Santa Bárbara	Black
São José	Black
Filhos de Obá	Black
Ulufan	White
Santa Bárbara	Black
São Jerônimo 2	Mulatto
Ogum de Ronda	White

Note: In light of the absence of objectivity in classifying people by color, the author prepared this table and compared it to the classification presented by *terreiro* leaders, no significant difference having been noted between the two classifications.

"That damned woman. She has already robbed me of I don't know how many clients. She has great *força* and she told their fortunes. Small wonder. They say she's African." (Fortune teller)

But the same Nagô genesis and African heritage are claimed by the São José *terreiro*, and although partially recognized by the other cult leaders, the importance attributed to them falls far short of that of the Filhos de Obá and Virgin Santa Bárbara *terreiros*, beneath even that of the Ulufan *terreiro*, which is led by a white man. In and of itself, this suggests that a supposed or real African ancestrality does not bestow importance, not even when it is associated with senior status as is the case of the São José *terreiro*.

Ritual competency is a term I shall use to encompass multiple activities listed by cult leaders when asked about the meaning of "knowing how to do things," an expression they use to indicate the importance of the *terreiros*. Here, following the example of what occurred in discussing the leader's African ascendency, a *terreiro* was evaluated largely in terms of the leaders' *força* and abilities.

Força is a mystical and symbolic power. According to Juana Elbein dos Santos, it is called *axé* in the terminology of Bahian Nagô cults, transmissible through material and symbolic means. Like all powers, ritual activity can serve to increase or decrease it. The leader of a *terreiro* is the highest bearer of its *axé*, and he must uphold its preservation and enhancement, transmitting it to neophytes through ritual initiation (Santos, 1976: chapter 3). To have many *filhos de santo* and to be surrounded by a large number of followers is a consequence or external sign of power. In assessing the city's *terreiros*, all the cult leaders agreed that Virgin Santa Bárbara and Filhos de Obá *terreiros* had the greatest number of members, thus endorsing the statements of their followers (upon which table 4 is based).

Individual membership in *terreiros* is granted according to various ritual stages that lead to a growing connection with spirits and with the leader who initiates the member. The ability to realize all the stages of the process—*lavagem da cabeça, confirmação*, and *feitorio do santo*—is an index of the *terreiro* leader's wisdom and *força* and, consequently, they are criteria for assigning importance to a center.

Regarding *terreiros* whose leaders have no following, one cult leader said: "It's a make-believe *terreiro*. They play the drums for people to dance. He doesn't know anything" (*Terreiro* leader). It should be noted that none of the centers which do not need members figured as important in the assessment of cult leaders. In compensation, as we have seen, the Virgin Santa Bárbara and the Filhos de Obá were unanimously pointed out as the ones that gathered the largest number of followers. Regarding the latter *terreiro*, an informant says:

> "To me, he is the most important one. Alexandre initiated *filhos*, baptized them and led *iaôs* out of the chamber. Here in Sergipe only he and Nanã de Aracaju do that." (*Terreiro* leader).

The Virgin Santa Bárbara's exclusion from this statement is quite significant. There, the membership process follows different lines that generally correspond to the famous Jeje-Nagô model of Bahian Candomblé. I shall return to this difference at the appropriate moment. For now it is important to highlight that other *terreiros* will be assessed by other leaders according to their greater or lesser proximity to this model, which (the Filhos de Obá excepted) they do not follow to the letter,[11] although the "pure Nagô" Virgin Santa Bárbara *terreiro* had its own, different—and therefore legitimately African—model:

> "The Nagô does not perform initiations. The Nagô thing is different." (*Terreiro* leader)

TABLE 4. *Terreiros* and Their Members, according to Their Respective Leaders

TERREIROS	NUMBER OF MEMBERS	LINK WITH TERREIRO
São Jerônimo 1	1	Washed
São Sebastião	None	—
Tupinambá	None	—
The Virgin Santa Bárbara	Over 100	Confirmed and baptized
São José	20–30	Confirmed and baptized
Filhos de Obá	Over 200	Washed, confirmed, and fully initiated
Ulufan	15	Washed and confirmed
Santa Bárbara	11	Fully initiated
São Jerônimo 2	12	Confirmed and fully initiated
Ogum de Ronda	None	—

Recognition of the two different and legitimate models of linking believers to cult centers alludes to the fundamental opposition between *caboclo* and Nagô. The *terreiro* leader's competency also reveals itself in the efficacy of his magic, which attracts to the center a clientele in search of solutions to their problems. In the days when they were led by the old leaders, the Filhos de Obá and Virgin Santa Bárbara *terreiros* were unanimously recognized as the ones who attracted the greatest number of clients.

But a leader's *força* is also measurable by the rites he or she performs on behalf of the deities. Sacrificing oxen is always remembered as an act in which this *força* is vigorously expressed.

Members of the Nagô *terreiro* who attempted to critically rethink their religious practices and beliefs in light of learning absorbed in schools (in one case, in a graduate institution) explained their surrender to Xangô in terms of an acknowledgment of the *força* demonstrated by the cult leader on the occasion of the sacrifice of oxen. Regarding this same *terreiro* leader, it is said that she had been invited by a member to realize some rituals in a nearby town. Sugar refinery owners who were unsympathetic to Xangô purposely let loose a wild ox to break up the gathering, at the exact moment sacred dances were supposed to begin. The furious animal charged the audience but, at a mere sign from the *terreiro* leader, prostrated itself at her feet. The anecdote is still repeated in Laranjeiras as clear proof of the cult leader's *força*. To the city's high priests, only two centers sacrificed oxen to the *orixás*: the Virgin Santa Bárbara, led by Mãe Bilina, and the Filhos de Obá, led by Alexandre. After their deaths, the leader of a center in a neighboring village whose prestige is on the rise is said to have sacrificed an ox, a fact that was reportedly repeated quite recently at the Virgin Santa Bárbara *terreiro* already under new leadership.

According to Nagô theology, sacrifice is part of the general dynamics of *terreiros* as an element of keeping harmony among the components of the system, insofar as it restores and redistributes *axé* (Santos, 1976: chapter 10). Thus, it is directly related to the power system that, in this specific case, manifested itself even in the ability to immolate a large, physically powerful animal that was rendered immobile by the *mãe-de-santo*'s supernatural power.

In short, what we are attempting to show is that the importance of *terreiros* is largely explained to "insiders" by the *força* of its leaders.

THE IMPORTANCE OF *TERREIROS* AS SEEN BY "OUTSIDERS"

The criteria that are used to assign importance to the townspeople are basically the same as those of the "insiders." In referring to seniority, to African origins and to the abilities of deceased leaders, the vast majority of interviewees elected the Virgin Santa Bárbara and Filhos de Obá *terreiros* as the most important, followed by Ulufan, São José, Ogum de Ronda, and São Jerônimo 2.[12] The scale of prestige is very similar to that of the *pais-de-santo*. However, a difference is observed in the ranking of the *terreiros* by "outsiders" as compared to ranking by "insiders." On the scale of prestige presented by the former there is a *terreiro* that, although it is not an old one and does not even have any *filhos de santo*, stands out because of the magical efficacy attributed to its leader. This is the Ogum de Ronda, of which an interviewee declared:

> "Nowadays, Neuza's is the most famous *terreiro*. She is always performing rites. The famous, older *terreiros* have suffered greatly and become decadent with the death of their owners." (A *terreiro* client)

This would be an extreme example, for the *terreiro* indicated as most important does not have so much as a congregation. Nonetheless, the center that comes closest to an actual rivalry for prestige with the "traditional" ones (according to the "outsiders") would be the Ulufan *terreiro*, often claiming its ritual activities and their efficacy as justifications for its importance, which is also presented as a consequence of its origin in the Filhos de Obá.

Thus it is observed that—at least for a minority of "outsiders" who regard the *terreiro* above all else as an alternative agency for the solution of immediate problems—the competency in ritual performance is an important fact to be considered. Assuming the inexperience of recently vested leaders in the old centers, some of the interviewees who make up a *terreiro*'s potential clientele direct their attention to the *terreiros* they deem best equipped, at that moment, to fulfill their needs. It is also possible that the greater emphasis placed by "outsiders" on propitiatory rituals as being indicative of a *terreiro*'s importance may be owed to the fact that they felt that I was actually interested in knowing for my own purposes which was the best *terreiro* to perform a ritual. People who apparently belong to the middle class are usually interested in *terreiros* for this reason.

At any rate, the tendency of "outsiders" to privilege a leader's ability to perform efficient rituals is one way to explain a *terreiro*'s importance, endorsing the perspective of "insiders."

REASONS FOR SUCCESS

Força is a term quite frequently used in *terreiros* to explain that a leader's power is connected to the supernatural. Ultimately, *força* explains the efficacy of magic executed for the benefit of clientele as well as a *terreiro* leader's success in dealing with *orixás*, thus assuring benefits to leaders and followers alike. A *terreiro*'s *força* is demonstrated by its leader's ability to deal with the spirits, which implies knowledge of the cult's traditions and secrets. Even when this *força* resides in *santos de pedra* that is inherited from Africans and is considered to be *santos fortes* whose ownership represents their owners' potential power, not being able to care for them results in a waste of the *força* and brings benefits to no one.[13] *Força* is associated with competency in dealing with the supernatural. This competence may be acquired through apprenticeship or even "revelation," which presupposes attribution of a link with the supernatural (see chapter 2).

Thus, criteria of seniority, African origin, and ritual competence interpenetrate to make up the *força* of group leadership and, therefore, a *terreiro*'s importance. This leads to the conclusion that, for "insiders" and "outsiders" alike, configuration of prestige in the symbolic market of Xangô is closely associated with a leader's connection to the supernatural; on one hand, therefore, it would derive from charisma, and on the other hand from traditionalism.

In short, explanation for a *terreiro*'s success lies in its leader's *força*. Thus, in explaining success, the theological category of *força* assumes the status of an analytical category.

Some authors have drawn attention to the fact that many studies of Afro-Brazilian cults attempt to explain a *terreiro*'s prestige exclusively in terms of the emic theory of cults, a repetition of popular ideology regarding Candomblé more than an explanation of mechanisms according to which *terreiros* reproduce socially (Fry, 1977a, 1977b; Silverstein, 1979).

Even when they consider that *terreiro* prestige is also measured by the wealth exhibited above all in public rituals, many studies suggest that it is the members, recruited from the lower classes, who materially support the *terreiros*, not giving due consideration to the adherence of the middle and upper classes (including the most traditional candomblé *terreiros*) and what their presence represents to the cults in terms of resources and prestige (Carneiro, 1967c; Herskovits, 1958; Bastide, 1971; Ribeiro, 1952).

Recent studies have dealt with the presence of the middle and upper classes in Candomblé and what this means not only to their survival but also to the configuration of their prestige. Taking the *família de santo* itself as the fulcrum of her analysis, Leni Silverstein shows how, in present-day Bahian *terreiros*, the family is expanded to include an *ogã*, normally someone belonging to the middle class who, after being initiated, "begins to relate fictitiously or ritually to the new family, taking on the obligations engendered by such a relationship" (Silverstein, 1979: 157). Thus, in broadening the networks of ritual kinship, the *mãe-de-santo* extends her connections beyond barriers of class and race to recruit material and human resources from the middle class, thanks to which her *terreiro* is able to survive. From this perspective, the leader's power and the prestige of his or her *terreiro* are not circumscribed to *força*, but explained by the "conversion of social and symbolic resources into economic advantages" (Silverstein, 1979: 158).

Without establishing this linearity of effect between the economic and the symbolic, Peter Fry (inspired by Ernest Gellner) analyzes the economy of *terreiros* as a circuit in which attribution of charisma and indexes of success are consequently related through a system of feedback. If a *pai-de-santo* displays exterior signs of success (many *filhos de santo*, clientele, wealth, the brilliance of its public rituals, etc.), he is likely to be a *pai-de-santo* to whom much *força* is attributed. Thus, the exterior signs of a *terreiro* leader's success reinforce the charisma attributed to him which, in turn, leads to an expansion of the *terreiro*'s circle of influence not only among the lower but among the middle and upper classes of society, whence comes the money needed to keep up the brilliance of its religious festivals and, consequently, to magnify the status and qualities of a powerful *pai-de-santo* (Fry, 1977b).

In theory, this ought to generate huge *terreiros,* but in practice such expansion is self-restrained by various factors. In the case of *terreiros* that self-define as "pure" and traditional, for instance, a factor that limits this growth is the need to control its members and, thus, to guarantee standards of morality and ritual orthodoxy to be used in distinguishing them from the rest. On the other hand, the mutual help provided by the *mãe-de-santo*'s direct mediation becomes impractical in very large *terreiros* where one-on-one contact is no longer possible. We must now understand the attribution of status and prestige in cult groups — a process not circumscribed to the world of *terreiros* but one that unfolds in their interactions with society at large. In the chapters that follow, I shall attempt to show how a *terreiro* capitalizes on its fidelity to Africa and to Nagô self-identification in order to acquire prestige.

◦ ◦ ◦ ◦

[Author's note:] Written in the early 1980s and based on field research undertaken during the 1970s and the early 1980s, this chapter, which maps the Afro cults of Laranjeiras, warrants brief reference to the present. Due to the characteristic dynamics of *terreiros* as living social forms, the picture outlined here no longer corresponds exactly to current reality: some of the *terreiros* visited during that period no longer exist, while others have expanded their activities, although the Virgin Santa Bárbara and Filhos de Obá continue to be the city's most prominent *terreiros.* The *caboclo* versus Nagô opposition remains and renewed interest in the African tradition has increased. Thus, *terreiros* that were originally considered to be Nagô and that throughout their history had incorporated the cult of the *caboclos* chose to render their attachment to the African tradition more explicit. The Filhos de Obá *terreiro,* for instance, houses sacred *caboclo* objects and rituals separately from those of the *orixás*, accomplishing a purification of its African side through this spatial separation which thus gains greater visibility. In turn, the São José *terreiro* continues its return to its Nagô roots with the support of important members of the Virgin Santa Bárbara *terreiro*, the "pure Nagô," which helped to rebuild the *terreiro* formerly led by Herculano de Comendaroba, where mãe Bilina of the Virgin Santa Bárbara *terreiro* (and her replacement Lourdes) received the staff that is the symbol of their leadership. However, it is not my intent to reconstruct the recent history of the city's *terreiros* here and now. I want only to draw attention to the fact that renewed emphasis on Nagô tradition shows that my analyses have lost none of their effectiveness and that the discussions that follow continue to be timely.

CHAPTER TWO

Nagô Speaks of Itself

FROM HISTORY TO MYTH

In studies of Afro-Brazilian religions—particularly those concerning the Nagô Candomblé—the history of *terreiros* and the genealogies of their leaders are often presented as proof of a continuity with Africa which attests to the fact that it is a certain set of cultural features experienced in the *terreiros* that constitutes the purest, most legitimate African tradition.

Insofar as it assigns great importance to explaining the present through a tradition that is always associated with the group's past and, specifically, with its African origins, this methodological position is a consequence of genetic orientation and the search for Africanisms that has deeply marked anthropological writing on Afro-Brazilian cults.

From this perspective, the (always oral) "history of the *terreiro*" appears as something *given*, regardless of the fact that what is retained by memory and presented in discourse *as* the "history of the *terreiro*" constitutes versions that, neither necessarily true or false, have been wrought within certain parameters that induce and orient perspectives and selections of what should or should not be highlighted.

Such perspectives are constructed as a result of the interests in the game and objectives, within the social experience of those who tell the "story" today, for that which is presented as simple discourse about the past winds up acting upon it, reconstructing it and evoking identities, in short, a labor of production of meaning that seeks to legitimize actions in the present.

Edmund Leach's study of the Kachin of the Burmese highlands is significant in this respect. By referring to the events of a more or less recent past in order to describe village factions, the author shows how each chief of the Kachin lineage tells a version that reflects favorably upon him and his group in their struggle against the others. Although they signal different elements of particular groups, the different versions grant others the right to have their own stories. Such narratives, which propose to be the history of struggles that took place during the late nineteenth century, were actually used as a specific language through which rival groups sought legitimacy. They point to tensions and contradictions that exist in society. They constitute a "language of dissension and not of harmony." The falsity or veracity of such accounts is irrelevant; what matters is that the account exists and justifies attitudes and actions in the present. In this sense they are the equals of myths, defined as stories about deities. The author says that stories about the gods are also inconsistent:

> "My conclusion is that the ordinary anthropological definition
> of myth is an inappropriate category as far as the Kachins are
> concerned. Sacred tales — that is to say tales about divine beings
> which are widely known — have no special characteristics which
> make them any different from tales about local happenings 20
> years ago. Both kinds of tale have the same function — the telling
> of them is a ritual act (in my sense of the term) which justifies
> the particular attitude adopted by the teller at the moment of the
> telling." (Leach, 1964: 277)

Thus, Edmund Leach breaks with the separation between sacred tales (myths in the traditional sense) and tales that propose to be historical, showing how they, too, are mythological insofar as their narratives justify social relationships in the present.

If, within a single system tribal society such as that of the Kachin, myths are manipulated as political resources in a class society with many competing religions, in the struggle for control of religious space myths are often created and used as tools.[1] In dealing with narratives that are presented as *"terreiro* histories," one does not mean to deny the possible African origin of many of these cult centers that, in some cases, serve as a matrix for the elaboration of myths, but to call attention to the fact that such narratives are marked by the intentions and interests of the *pais* and *mães-de-santo* who seek to establish through them a narrow and explicit link with Africa, thus presenting themselves as depositaries of a cultural heritage that would be the purest and most legitimate African tradition. I would like to suggest that aspects of these accounts which emphasize continuity with Africa would not be so strongly emphasized if, for instance, the "purity" of the African tradition were not somehow prized by certain sectors of society at large so as to use it to advantage in competing for the religious market's place in society.

The fact that groups of blacks seek Africa as a reference, as in this case study, through the assumption of Nagô identity, can only be understood within the social, political, and economic structure within which they are inserted. Regional differences must be taken into account here. If, in the Southeast, religious practice considered to be of African origin is restricted to Quimbanda because of existing white middle class values inscribed in Umbanda (Brown, 1974; Ortiz, 1978), in the Northeast it is the purity of Africa that is valued through Candomblé. Although the meaning of this appreciation of Africa in the Northeast still remains to be investigated, it is obvious that these regional variations in the prestige attributed to certain symbolic repertories will end up influencing the construction of the "histories" of the cult centers. It is in this sense that the "histories of the *terreiros*" would be constructed histories, mythical histories overly laden with meaning. This does not imply that they must be false and consciously forged; rather, those aspects which are highlighted and repeatedly invoked—as, in this specific case, the link with Africa and the purity of tradition—are so because, beyond the cognitive aspect and the affirmation of identity, there is a possible space for manipulation through which it is possible to legitimize oneself or confer advantages.

Before moving on to the account presented as the "history of the *terreiro*," it would be best to examine certain permeating aspects of the *mãe-de-santo*'s narrative because they are insufficiently explicit, making subsequent comprehension difficult. These aspects deal with the coexistence of the communal cult and the domestic cult.

THE DOMESTIC CULT OF THE *ORIXÁS*

Although Nina Rodrigues recorded the existence of a domestic cult in Bahia dedicated to the *orixás* at the beginning of this century (Rodrigues, 1935: 60–62), Afro-Brazilian religious studies have been almost exclusively dedicated to the *terreiros* and the cult developed by the *pai-de-santo* and his followers. This fact led Melville Herskovits (who was concerned with identifying Africanisms in Brazil) to formulate the following question:

"Do the candomblés assumed to be the only valid expression of
African religious retentions in Brazil rather represent special and
restricted forms of organization found in the urban centers of
Dahomey and Nigeria, transplanted to urban centers of Brazil?
This of course leaves unanswered the further question of whether
intensive study of Afrobrazilian religion in the rural areas may not
reveal retentions of more widely spread African patterns organized

in terms of family and lineage worship of the deities reinterpreted as saints, or under African designations as well, with specialists called in to perform more complex and extensive rituals when these must be given." (Herskovits, 1956: 159)

Similarly, the starting point for Roger Bastide's studies of "African religions in Brazil" is a dualism that characterizes the peoples of the Gulf of Guinea (where these religions originated) as a lineage-based and community-based religion. Bastide concludes that, in Brazil—because slavery broke the *orixá*/male lineage connection that constituted the base of Africa's domestic religion—only the community-based form persisted. Resorting, however, to African cultural alternatives more suited to survival under Brazilian circumstances (transmission of the *orixá* through female lineage), the author acknowledges the sporadic persistence of elements of this cult, albeit incorporated into Candomblé, that is to say, into the cult of the community (Bastide, 1971; 86–89).

Because I am interested in understanding its current reality and meaning, and not with establishing genetic connections or even considering them as a survival of African cultural alternatives, what I have found in Laranjeiras and in the *mãe-de-santo*'s account of the past is that, along with the collective worship of *orixás* performed by a *pai-* or *mãe-de-santo* and his or her followers (who pray for blessings for the whole community), there is also a domestic cult dedicated to the *orixás*.

Currently, the basic components of this cult are to *alumiar* and *dar água aos santos*, in other words, to keep them always in light, whether this be the light of the sun, of candles, or electric light, and keeping suitable bowls of water close by them. The accomplishment of these tasks does not require a specialist, nor even direct connection to Candomblé, and there are *zeladores de santos* who do not even belong to Afro-Brazilian cults. Nonetheless, sporadically (almost without fail, every seven years), the presence of a *mãe* or *pai-de-santo* is needed to perform the rites of feeding the saints [*dar comida aos santo*] which include, in addition to animal sacrifices and the proper preparation of foods, *toques* and dances— the reason why the *pai-* or *mãe-de-santo* is always accompanied by his group of followers to perform the *festejo* [ritual cycle], expenses for which are the responsibility of those who are guarding the saints. These domestic altars, the number of which has increasingly diminished,[2] house *santos da Costa*, nearly always in the form of stones which are considered to be family saints, whose ownership and obligations generally succeed one another according to direct lines of consanguineous kinship—parents, children, grandchildren. For those who inherit one of these domestic shrines but are unwilling to embrace the duties of worship or to simply abandon them — the latter being considered a dangerous and reprehensible situation — there are two socially acceptable alternatives:

1. a permanent break with ancestral ties to the *orixás* through the performance of rituals that require the participation of a specialist and result in more or less elevated expenses,[3] or
2. obtaining a *mãe-de-santo*'s acquiescence to bring the saints to the *terreiro*, thus ridding oneself of daily cult obligations which she now becomes responsible for, even though the *dono de santo* continues to be responsible for financial expenses.[4]

For the time being, these facts will suffice to clarify certain passages of the *mãe-de-santo*'s narrative which refer to the origins of the *terreiro*.

ACCOUNT OF THE ORIGINS

"I was born to be the mistress of Santa Bárbara's African colonies. I was destined to own them after the Africans died out. As a little girl, they carried me on their heads in a basket and danced in the *roda*. This was in Ti Herculano's house, where the *terreiro* was. I don't remember this but Grandma used to tell me about it.

Ti Herculano was a Nagô, but the true founder of the Nagô *terreiro* here in Laranjeiras was Ti Henrique, the first *beg*. [The *terreiro*] was passed down from Ti Henrique to Herculano, and from him to me. Meaning I'm not African. I am the grandchild of four African Nagôs — an authentic Creole.

I never met Ti Henrique, the first *beg*. He was my grandmother's *malungo*. He founded the *terreiro* on rua do Cangaleixo. That's where it was first located. Grandma lived there thirty-five years with his wife. Grandma was a slave at the Tanque de Moura farm and then she became a widow and came to Laranjeiras, and lived here. When Ti Henrique died, the *terreiro* was left to Ti Herculano, who took it to Comendaroba. Ti Henrique's saints stayed in the house on rua do Cangaleixo. His widow, the late Caetana, looked after things with my grandmother. After she died, her daughter Judite took care of the family's saints but the *terreiro* went to Ti Herculano.

I never met Ti Henrique, although I did meet Ti Herculano. He was a very wise African. A big, strong Nagô who lived over in Comendaroba. The house was nice and big and located in the middle of a farm. They were wealthy folk. They owned salt mines and raised lots of pigs. We danced inside the house, which had a great hall, large enough to hold everybody. And in those days there were lots of *filhos de santo*. There were still Africans then. I met Tia Lucinda, whose African name was Inã; Rufino, a Nagô who lived in the Baixa do Calumbi; Ti Oxó—lots of people only I don't remember them all. After the celebrations there, after the offering of the new yam, we would celebrate in all the other houses. We'd go to Riachuelo, to Socorro, to Divina Pastora (neighboring towns), for the Nagô people had saints there, too, and it was Ti Herculano who led those celebrations. We would all go. In Riachuelo there was Ta Lucrécia and, in Socorro, Ta Luiza. It was a lot of work. Nowadays it is all gone. We are the only survivors. [As a child,] I often played in Ti Herculano's house. Later I began to work, to seek employment, and then I returned to take care of that place. Because that place was left to me and Manaia, who was Ti Henrique's son—not his son, his *grand*son. Only he didn't want it so I took care of it by myself. He didn't want to look after his grandfather's saints. I brought them here to the *terreiro*. Because when it's time for celebrations they help out, they give money but I look after the saints. All of Ti Henrique's saints, the first *beg*, are here in the *pegê*. They are genuine African saints and they are very powerful." (Bilina, leader of the Nagô *terreiro*)[5]

Figure 2 charts Bilina's account of her origins and records the genealogies of leaders who preceded her, since the founding of the Laranjeiras temple. It allows us to observe that leadership succession of the religious group (community cult) does not follow consanguineous kinship lines, guided by criteria of ritual kinship,[6] whereas family saints (the object of domestic worship) are transmitted according to blood lines. On the other hand, it shows how two lines of succession eventually converge towards the *mãe-de-santo*, thus reinforcing her link with Africa. It is this link that is emphasized in the account I shall now discuss. Through it, the *mãe-de-santo* establishes a direct connection from her religious center to Africa, by presenting it as the continuity of a *terreiro* founded by Nagôs. She presents herself as predestined to succeed the Africans in directing the cult, when the latter pass on. Such predestination would have been recognized and sanctioned by them through rites that destined her to leadership. In a land where there are no more Africans, their Nagô origins, traceable to

maternal and paternal grandparents, are invoked to attest to their genealogical proximity to the Africans.

The presence of Africa is further underscored by the fact that the
history of the *mãe-de-santo*'s ancestors (the history of her family) often
blends with the initial history of the sect itself and of its founders. Links
were established through her grandmother, who came over with the
same group of Africans that included the founder of the center and developed a longstanding relationship with him, participating in the community and worshipping the family saints of the African who founded
the *terreiro*. This connection has recently been renewed through the cult
leader—who not only directs the original *terreiro* but also became the
guardian of the founder's family saints (which were taken to the *terreiro*
due to his descendants' lack of interest in them). The *mãe-de-santo* (who
became the leader of the cult group through predestination) increases
her power and her prestige before local Afro-Brazilians by taking in
the *terreiro* founder's family saints—"very powerful, authentic African
saints"—and thus establishes further ties with Africa.

The narrative thus connects the present to the past and addresses Africa. This is the *terreiro* and its leader's source of legitimacy. "Purity" is
constructed at the very core of the idea of continuity and fidelity to Africa,
the sign that distinguishes her *terreiro* from the city's "mixed" *torés*, currently conferring upon the *terreiro* and its leaders a prominent position on
the scale of prestige around which Afro-Brazilian cult centers are organized. In this way, the "history of the *terreiro*" is not limited to the simple
reconstruction of a more or less remote past situated within the second
half of the nineteenth and the beginning of the twentieth century, becoming instead a myth of African-ness often invoked to legitimize social
situations and relationships in the present.

THE MÃE-DE-SANTO'S "HISTORY"

Throughout her existence, in her struggle to maintain leadership of the
religious group and uphold the prestige of her *terreiro*, she constantly
resorts to elements of this account. Because her narrative always addresses Africa, one must not lose sight of the *mãe-de-santo*'s many connections with the white world—connections that permeate her entire
life story—in order to perceive that her representations of Africa are
constructed within a world divided between dominant whites and dominated blacks.

"White Papa"

Claiming descent from four African grandparents, Umbelina de Araújo, known as Bilina, was born in the city of Laranjeiras, although she is unable to pinpoint the year of her birth. Thus, with no clear sense of years past and intent on demonstrating that she did not experience slavery, she occasionally states (without much conviction) that she is sixty-five years old; sometimes she says she is sixty-eight, an age that falls far short of the one indicated by her physical appearance and the testimony of several members of her group. In referring to her, one of the informants, who declares himself to be her age, expressed himself thus: "One year, slavery came to an end. . . . We were born a year after that."[7] Many other statements corroborate this one, including some by Bilina herself, leading me to conclude that, when she died, she must have been approximately eighty-seven years old, having most likely been born at the end of the nineteenth century when slavery was being replaced by free labor and Laranjeiras was experiencing the final moments of its golden age.

Her mother, Carolina, known as Calu, was a rural slave, having been sold as a wet nurse to a newborn orphan in the city of Laranjeiras, bringing with her a son she had borne her former master. "He was called Mulato and he *was* a little mulatto because he was the master's son." In her new condition as an urban slave belonging to notary Manoel Joaquim de Araújo,[8] she lived in her new owner's house, breast-feeding the newborn child and helping to raise the recently widowed notary's many children. "That was when she began to have relationships with men outside his house. She lived in the master's house but became pregnant with us in the street," says Bilina, thus indicating the absence of a matrimonial link between her mother and Bastião (her father). He was a black Creole, the slave of Padre Manoel Pontes,[9] and would have given Calu four children (of which Bilina was the third). For a while, Calu was thus assured a profession as wet nurse, a guaranteed market in aristocratic nineteenth-century Laranjeiras, initially as a slave for rent[10] and later, when she obtained her freedom, under her own management. The Nagô *mãe-de-santo* continues:

> "Calu did not even know how to shop for groceries. All she knew
> was breast-feeding and taking care of children. She breast-fed
> everyone in this street. People liked her and were always nice to
> her, so that, with her breast-feeding money, she bought that house
> and another one on the street there."

FIGURE 2. Partial Genealogy of Nagô *Terreiro* Leaders

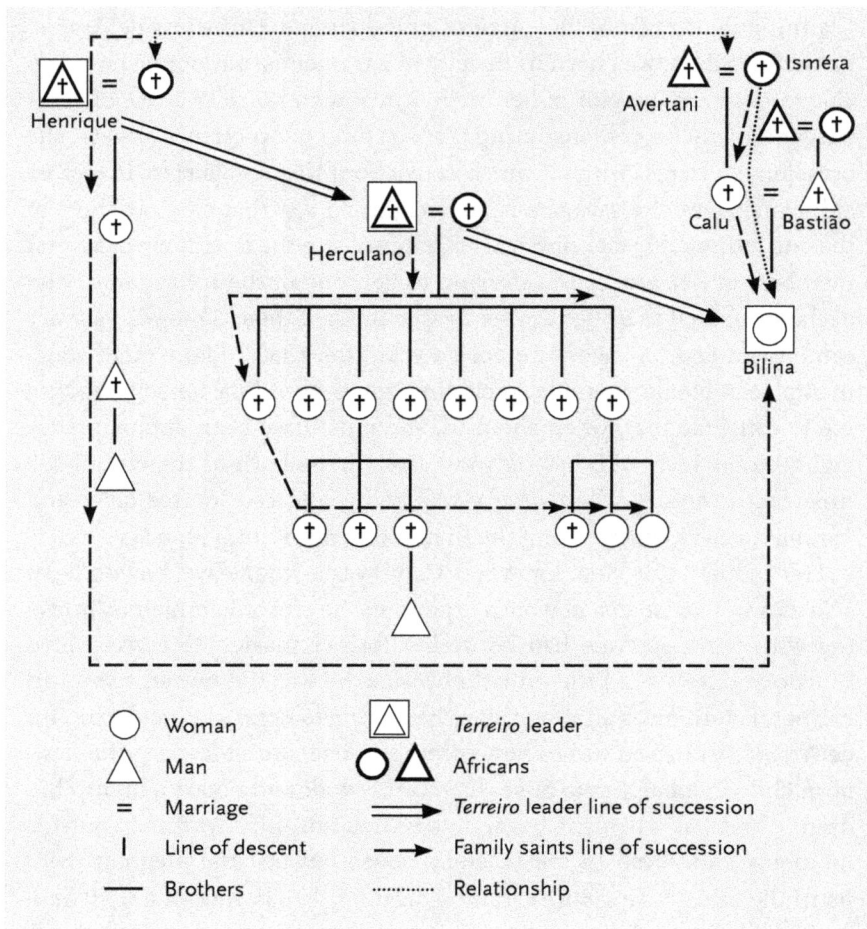

Even so, she continued to live in her former master's house, where her children were born and raised along with those of the notary public himself, whom they called "white papa."

"And the name of white papa's children was our name, too. He gave it to us and we sign our names Bilina de Araújo and Glicéria de Araújo. Their names are Araújo, too, but they belong to the couple and we were foster-children. And we all lived there. Papa put Glicéria, Manuel and Maria [Bilina's siblings] in school. I wanted to go but they didn't send me. The Africans insisted we learn sewing instead of reading." (Bilina)

Thus, due to interference from the maternal grandmother, a Nagô woman who "did not like" studies, Bilina, unlike her siblings, never frequented schools. Later, when she became a domestic servant, she asked her employers to teach her to write and today she says: "I can sign my name, but not much more."

In the case of the notary, Calu lived with her children while he was alive. He was the only father they ever knew for, as Bilina says:

"Bastião [biological father] never spent money on us. (. . .) White
papa gave us everything. I was twelve when he died. And white
papa had set aside some property to give mama but never set
it down in writing, you know? He died suddenly."

So the former master's children would have considered such an adoption invalid and Calu, resentful of the notary's descendents, abandoned the household, refusing to allow one of her children to remain there as an employee, and moving with them to rua da Cacimba, located in the outskirts of city's periphery.

"Then mama put us all to work because papa was no longer there
to give us anything. Papa fed us, clothed us, everything. He died
and that was it." (Bilina)

Inasmuch as Bilina's childhood experience is marked by the individuality of her life history, it becomes sociologically significant because it embodies certain fundamental aspects of traditional Brazilian society at the moment of transition from a slavocratic society to a free society, in which the system of social relations, engendered in the old order, projects itself and persists in the emerging order. The informant's account clearly reflects patterns of social relations in force in the post-slavocratic urban society of the end of the last century, many of which had already been recorded by travelers, in earlier times, and analyzed by various social scientists from different perspectives.[11]

The structure of the patriarchal family, which appears here under the form of an "extended family" and which, in addition to a central nucleus constituted by the white master and his legitimate offspring, aggregates the slave and her children, would have permitted the latter to be raised together with the master's children, to attend schools, and, by extension, to receive the family name, ultimately seeing their master as their father. On one hand, this form of social coexistence, in force above all else among masters and domestic slaves, generated solutions that could result in the slave's emancipation; on the other, it produced more refined forms of dominating the black man, with benign, cordial, or paternalistic treatment presenting itself as the solution when the slave's social behavior expressed itself according to traditionally inherited expectations of obedience, humility, and fidelity (Ianni, 1962: 157–68). It may have been out of fidelity that the former slave continued to live with her children in her former master's house, even after she had obtained her freedom. In this way, in exchange for her work and that of her children, she assured herself and her offspring of a place to live, food, and the protection of her former master.

Bilina never knew slavery; nevertheless, because she grew up in an environment engendered by slavocratic society, she and her family looked upon the master as epitomizing the security and protection that disappear at the moment of rupture with the ruling class, represented here by the notary's descendants. This rupture, brought about by a matter of properties, compels Bilina's family to attempt life at its own expenses, without the support and protection to which they had heretofore been privy. In compensation (and in retaliation), Calu feels disobliged to send her children to serve as employees to the former master's descendants.

There is a break—so to speak—with the system of solidarity that existed up until then and a new phase of life began for the ex-slave and her children.

"Nagô Grandma"

In the first phase of her life, which takes place in an environment dominated by whites, three characters emerge and stand out from the rest: the Creole mother whose profession increasingly drew her closer to the white cultural universe; the father (not the biological father but the foster father), a representative of dominant, official culture; and the maternal grandmother, a Nagô African woman, intent on making her granddaughter a follower of her ancestors' religious traditions. She is presented as a nuclear figure in the making of the future *mãe-de-santo*.[12] She was called Isméria, the name she received in Brazil, for in Nagô she was Birunqué. As a child Bilina, who among all Calu's children was closest to her maternal grandmother, says she heard from her the story of her coming from Africa and, when she recounted it, "she cried as she remembered her land." Separated from her nuclear family, she allegedly embarked on a ship bound for Brazil, being unable to specify the place of disembarkation. Because her grandmother told her this, however, she remembers that disembarkation was fraught with precaution, and blacks were hidden inside barrels, which leads me to conclude that the slave trade was already illegal by the time she arrived in Brazil. She had been sold to serve as a rural slave at the Tanque da Moura, a farm or plantation. Along with her husband, she farmed, for "the Nagô knows how to plant yam," and she witnessed her husband's death at the farm. His name was "Avertani in the language of Africa" and he was trampled to death by a horse belonging to an overseer who sought to intimidate him until he was "broken" and could not work. Later, "the law unearthed the body that had been buried in the husk pit" and, some time afterward, Isméria purchased her freedom and went off to live in Laranjeiras, where some of her *malungos* lived. There, she began to frequent the *terreiro* that belonged to Henrique, the religious organizer of the city's Nagôs, a relationship that lasted over thirty years, at the end of which she went to live with her daughter Calu (Bilina's mother) when Calu left the house of her former master.

From early childhood, Bilina grew accustomed to being with her grandmother, and together with the "other girls, would dance at Xangô rituals." It was to be the beginning of a long apprenticeship that would one day transform her into a *mãe-de-santo*, a function to which she was predestined. Grandmother Isméria spared no effort to live up to the will of the gods and began by keeping the child from attending school. To be sure, many other sources of information acted in the *mãe-de-santo*'s vision of Africa, but her grandmother's reminiscences and information are presented as the most significant.

> "Grandma often spoke to me about the land. She told me
> stories about it. Africa is vast. There are many different places
> and peoples: Nagô, Malê, Jeje, Jexá, Congo. They all came from
> Africa. I mean they come from different places. We have Aracaju,
> Laranjeiras, and Riachuelo, don't we? Well, that's how it is over
> there—they have lots of places. Africa is big and rich. Cowries,
> yams, and all these Brazilian things came from there. The Afri-
> cans knew where to find pearls and gold. And it was in Africa that
> people knew and discovered these things. How comes there is no
> more gold as there once was? Because it was the Africans who
> discovered everything. (. . .) Pearls, gold, diamonds, they knew
> everything. They were people who had lots of gold. Cowry shells
> are money over there." (Bilina)

But the wealth of Africa is not presented as a simple effect of nature; it is not owed merely to the presence of precious metals and stones, but to work. In Bilina's mental universe Africans are, above all else, a working people.

> "They worked there. They had money. They worked with children on their backs, they worked making money. They weren't lazy people. The elderly—the all worked. You see our hoes? They serve to teach us to work, rather than to beg, to ask only when one is not physically able. To teach children and adults. Even in Brazil, the African people knew how to work. And they would die and leave money. (. . .) It was because they knew how to work that the Africans came down to Brazil as slaves. They were smuggled over because the French and the English fooled them over there with tobacco. They were crazy about tobacco because they didn't have it over there. Young and old, they were tricked and captured and put on the boat and sold as soon as they ar-rived in Brazil. That's how slavery began. But that was before my time."[13]

Bilina's representations of work are ambiguously conceived. To be hard-working is a feature of the African and, as such, work is valued as an element of wealth. But the work that ideally allowed the African—whether in Brazil or in Africa—"not to beg" and "to have money" became the very cause of his enslavement and, consequently, of the alienation of the product of his labor and his person, for he worked in penniless servitude. Paradoxically, it is slave labor that is ritually celebrated in the *terreiro*. *Adiborô-pegan*—the rite of the hoe—takes place as part of the ritual cycle of the "cutting of the yam" (which marks the opening of the religious center's liturgical year). Bent over a short-handled, the *mãe-de-santo* does a dance, moving the instrument as if she were tilling the soil. She does this for a while, then passes the hoe to one of the children-of-saint who proceed with a dance that imitates "working," while the *mãe-de-santo* stands off to one side while holding a leather whip. The congregation follows suit and, after dancing, each one returns the small hoe to the cult leader. She then gives it to another member of the group, always presenting the whip as if it were some sort of warning.

The monotonous repetition of this imitative dance—which the entire congregation will eventually perform—is interrupted by some of the faithful whose movements break with the pattern described above. Instead of "working," upon being given the hoe the dancer shows his hands, claiming that they hurt; he grumbles, leaning upon the tool as if tired or handling the tool very, very slowly. In short, the dancer's choreography is a representation of blacks who do not want to work. This draws a reaction from the *mãe-de-santo*, who whips him so that he will return to his labors. Playing the role of "the lazy black" (and always under the threat of the whip), the dancer drags the children into the circle, passing the hoe onto them so that they will continue the work. At some point, coins are tossed on the ground in reach of the "lazy black" and he picks them up. The performance continues for a while, provoking laughter from those present, until the "rebel" black's dance comes to a halt before the *mãe-de-santo* by pleading for compassion under the threat of the whip. Members of the congregation succeed one another inside the circle, nearly all of them without offering resistance. Few of them play the role of "lazy blacks." However, the dance prolongs itself, both entertainment and example.

Although an analogous rite has been recorded in old Bahian candomblé *terreiros* as a rite of purification,[14] in the Nagô *terreiro* of Laranjeiras it is presented as a pedagogical rite:

> "... It is meant to teach [people] how to work. To work until you
> can work no longer. From boys to grown men. To work. To work
> always. To beg only when [one] is no longer able. (...) Remember
> the days of slavery? That's what it's about. I hold the whip because
> that's how it was in the old days. The master held the flail. The
> lazy ones are beaten the hardest so they will learn how to work."
> (Bilina)

The *mãe-de-santo* not only plays the part of the overseer—she also uses the term explicitly to designate herself in this performance of working transposed to the past, to the time of slavery. This role is cele-brated in the *terreiro*, directly transposing the structure of the slavocratic society to the field of ritual: the *mãe-de-santo* conducts herself like an overseer at the service of the whites while the *filhos de santo* represent the slaves. Simultaneously, though, through the motives invoked for the realization of the ritual, slavery is left behind and the rite updated, its stated objective being "to teach [one] how to work so that one does not need to beg" and "to have money," which is not the counterpart to slave labor. At the very least, having money is a form of surviving without having to beg, a greater symbol of degradation and of social disqualification. Work is the way to obtain it in a competitive market,[15] but the concrete way through which it is proposed that people be induced to work alludes to the slavocractic universe—of working for fear of repression—expressed by the overseer's whip. The performance about work is, thus, ambiguously constructed with elements of the bourgeois order and elements of the slavocratic world.[16] That world was crumbling when the *mãe-de-santo* was born, but it was the place in which her grandparents and her mother existed, and their own, succintly recollected experiences indicate two faces of slavery: on one hand, explanations of the lived experiences of her mother, a domestic urban slave, which highlight paternalism; on the other hand, the experience of her maternal grandfather who was murdered by an overseer and buried in the husk pit, emphasizing oppression and violence. Thus, her representations of "slavery" are ambiguous and the adoption of a behavioral pattern or some other standard resembles something that is apparently dependent upon the master's idiosyncrasies: "There were many bad masters who enjoyed tormenting slaves but there were good ones, too." Whereas she resorts to work in order to explain the enslavement of the African, when she explains the abolition of slavery she draws on her personal experience marked by paternalism:

> "Dona Isabel, the king's daughter, was breast-fed by a slave. She told the woman that she wanted to free the *malungos*—her comrades. And Dona Isabel promised to free the slaves and that was the end of slavery." (Bilina)

Slavery had ended but in the exile into which slavery had forced them, the Africans persisted, trying to make their descendants depositaries of the cultural traditions of "the LAND," the land of their ancestors, the land of wealth, the land of work. And, to Bilina and her family, after the death of "white papa," work outside the domestic circle became an imperious necessity, indispensable to survival.

Work

> "So off we went to work. Mama said she couldn't be feeding and clothing all those children so we all took to work. I found employment as a nursemaid. The first money I earned being a nursemaid was two thousand *réis* a month. After that my employer taught me how to cook, and I went off to burn pots, to be a cook."

By the beginning of the twentieth century, Laranjeiras was already in decline. This was reflected in the labor market and in lower salaries:

> "Seeing as how things weren't going well, they called me to Aracaju. I went to work in Aracaju earning ten thousand mil *réis* a month to cook. I spent a few years there and then went to Rio de Janeiro.

While I was there my mother got sick. So I went back because mama said she didn't want to die without seeing me, but when I got there she had already been buried." (Bilina)

She had left her in charge of continuing the Taieira festival, an obligation she took on in order to fulfill a past promise. She returned to Rio de Janeiro, where she lived with and worked for a family that had migrated from Laranjeiras, and remained there until she was called to lead the Xangô.

Close relationships between employees and employers were predominant in the external labor market Bilina entered after the death of "white papa." Employers were usually people raised in Laranjeiras itself and the mutual knowledge of the families of employers and employees created an intimate relationship among them; to this day Bilina remembers the names of her old employers and their relatives for two generations of ancestors and descendants.

Her employers taught her how to write her own name. She attempted to solve the problems that arose in her relationship with the African gods by resorting to her employers. She was in Rio de Janeiro when, in her dreams, an *orixá* indicated the obligation that had to be performed to eradicate the smallpox plague that had befallen Laranjeiras (1911). Her employers served as intermediaries, sending that city's Africans instructions from the deities by telegraph. Understanding her mission, they did not try to stop her when she decided to leave them in order to call off the gods who would have her as their priestess.

Predestination

"I was born to be the mistress of Santa Bárbara's African colonies," and so, during her childhood, under the tutelage of her maternal grandmother, who was very much linked to the religious hierarchies of the Nagô, she developed attitudes that were favorable to the continuation of her ancestral religion. When work leads her away from Laranjeiras, however, she breaks away from that influence.

In Rio de Janeiro, "they told me to go care for my place because my time was coming. I didn't know what time that might be," for, according to her, until the very moment of investiture the person destined to lead the sect was usually unaware of having been chosen by the gods.

When she learns of her chiefdom in the Nagô sect, Bilina is reluctant to submit to the will of the gods. The principal motive for this reaction is her betrothal, trousseau and all—the new position requiring virginity.

"At the start of the yam festival, when our *Pai da Costa* came down,
he sent for me and asked:
    'My child, are you going to marry?'
    'I am.'
    'Do you want to be married?'
    'I do.'
    'Do not want it.'
Other people said:
    'Do not want that, my child, our *Pai da Costa* is asking you
    not to marry.'
    'No. I *shall* be married.'
    As the grandson of Africans, the groom was part of it, too. And
we awaited the decision. And so three years passed. Whenever the
Pai da Costa came down, at the time of the cutting of the yam, a
very special occasion, it was the same thing. And the third time, he
threatened:
    'If you marry you will die.'
And the groom, who was present, said:
    'Don't listen to that *angu* [starch pudding] and *caruru*
    [okra soup] eater. Let's get on with our wedding.'" (Bilina)

But the engagement was broken off, her trousseau sold, and the virgin
dedicated herself to the cult of the *orixás*. From the hands of the last Africans, she received the *exó*, the command stick, symbol of her new status.
So began the new *mãe-de-santo*'s career. Her doubts, though, were many.

"I did not yet know the fundamentals and wondered how I was
going to look after that place without knowing how it is? But I
have everything recorded here [Bilina touches her head]. They
didn't teach me—it was determined by God and Santa Bárbara.
Whether or not it was determined for some special person to stay
in the house, the saints recorded it."

The *mãe-de-santo* recalls the first such premonitory experience during
her sojourn in Rio de Janeiro. The year was 1911 and Laranjeiras was in
the grip of a smallpox epidemic.

"One night I was at home alone when a black butterfly landed
on my arm and I kept thinking it meant a death in the family.
So I went to bed and I was neither asleep nor awake when Omolu
appeared wearing a white robe, holding a Franciscan rosary, two

hanging gourds and a bamboo stick. He had red eyes. He said if I did not perform a ritual obligation, [the *terreiro* of] Laranjeiras would be closed down. He taught me how to prepare the offerings and, after that, no one else in the city died of smallpox." (Bilina)

Bilina insists that this occurred on a number of other occasions, always underscoring the process of transmission of knowledge through direct intervention from the supernatural.

The insistence on revelation (transmission of knowledge by supernatural means), presented as a consequence of her predestination to the position of *mãe-de-santo*, has a clearly legitimizing function insofar as access to the position presupposes possession of special knowledge needed to appropriately performing the functions of a *terreiro* leader. Transmission of this store of knowledge by natural apprenticeship processes was stanched during adolescence when work removed her from coexistence with the Africans to whom she returned to take on leadership of the sect. In this context, revelation and predestination are still presented as sufficiently powerful diacritical signs in the dispute for power, since *terreiro* direction had been claimed by someone else. That person's name was Inácia and she was also of African descent. She looked after the saints of her ancestors, longtime members of the *terreiro* to which she, too, was affiliated. Once leadership was vacated, she is said to have temporarily (with the acquiescence of African elders) taken on the leadership of the cult center. This is the *mãe-de-santo*'s account:

"Ainã and old Lucrécia [two old African women of the *terreiro*] put Inácia in charge until my arrival. Inácia was already there. 'Is this the girl who is going to look after this place?' she asked. Well, Ainã replied: 'Both of you will work, but Bilina will always be the leader because of her God-given gift. [. . .] I was born with the gift and Inácia wanted my position. We stayed but they were two years of ordeals.

Inácia appointed her lover as *patrão*. She left her husband to sleep with that scoundrel. He didn't have any obligations. So I said: what's going on? In order to be a *patrão*, a man has certain obligations. And he was good for nothing. At night, the girls went to sleep and he would [sexually molest] them. How could we have such a man among us in the cult? So we went to a ritual cycle. And Inácia went to the door to greet the saint. And people said: Inácia doesn't greet properly. So I went and greeted. We entered

the sanctuary to arrange things and when it was time for the
Adaru, food was served to everyone but Inácia refused to eat. She
accused me of having brought a basket of sorcery with me from
Bahia. So she refused to eat the food. Everyone else ate and we
formed the dance circle. I started the wheel of virgins with the
girls. After I had finished dancing I called Ainã. She, in turn,
called Inácia, who danced and called the *patrão*. He refused to
dance, insisting that he was Ti Herculano. Inácia went off to fetch
the staff and I said: what's going on? Ti Herculano never used
the staff to dance in that wheel. I seized the staff to put it back in
its place. Later, they took the *tambor mestre* away. And people
said: we'll bring it back. A bloody fight ensued [between those who
wanted the drum present and those who wanted it removed from
the *terreiro*]. Off everyone went to the police station and the 'whites'
decided we were in the right. After this episode, Inácia left us to
organize her own group. She was responsible for this 'disorder'
that reigns in the world." (Bilina)

The "disorder" to which the *mae-de-santo* refers is an allusion to the
multiplicity of religious forms that diverge from the one she considers
the purest African tradition (represented by her *terreiro*). It is interesting to observe how, within the context of *terreiro* leadership claims, she
selects and explores arguments used to defend what she judges to be her
rights.

African ancestry, so often invoked, above all when she is confronted
by [the] Toré and Umbanda or a representative of the white world, does
not add advantage over the other [woman], also recognized as a descendant of the Nagô. Nonetheless, it is in the Nagô and old Africans that she
seeks support for witness of her predestination and right to the position.
Predestination is the key argument. With it, she seeks to reject all the advantages presented by her competitor: to be older, greater familiarity with
the Africans and the consequent claim of having more knowledge about
the cult.

In the previously transcribed account, it may be perceived that youth
was one of Bilina's vulnerable points. There are statements about this in
other contexts:

"When I took over this place they made a lot of noise because I
was young. And people asked: will this girl be able to—with the
responsibility? A *mãe-de-santo* must be very wise" (Nagô *terreiro*
leader)

At the very least, Bilina's early ambition to become a *mãe-de-santo* (she was around twenty years old at the time) struck people as strange, for access to the most prestigious positions in the hierarchy of the most traditional *terreiros* is usually associated with the length of time one has been initiated into the cult structure, configuring something that has been called a seniority system in which elders hold the most important positions.[17]

The argument in favor of predestination-revelation allows her to minimize the importance of age, inasmuch as apprenticeship is not based on coexistence over time (Bilina's account contains frequent allusions to her rival's alleged ritual inadequacies), but knowledge is presented as having been revealed and, therefore, not the result of a cumulative process of observations and experiences, regardless of age. Predestination and revealed knowledge are ambiguously explored in different contexts. In the eyes of the Afro-Brazilian segment and of society at large, it is these things, along with her African roots, that entitle her to direct the sect; simultaneously, though, they do not confer legitimacy upon other leaders who claim "a natural gift," since their apprenticeship was not a result of coexistence with someone who had the knowledge. This expresses itself in Bilina's representations of the city's other *terreiros*, especially with regard to the Toré, as we shall see in the next chapter.

Another aspect to be highlighted in this account of succession to religious leadership is a mutual accusation regarding the practice of witchcraft. Bilina was accused of having brought with her a "basket full of witchcraft from Bahia" and also of accusing her rival of attempting to kill her through witchcraft.

Although it emphasizes community aspects and the internal harmony of the Xangô and Candomblé groups, the literature on Afro-Brazilian cults has often recorded the existence of intergroup rivalries and conflicts that emerge primarily in situations of *terreiro* leadership succession. Such rivalries are usually interpreted as having the positive function of reinforcing certain elements considered "purer" or more acceptable by the others, a perspective that has been modified by more recent studies that analyze accusations and conflicts, particularly in Umbanda (Velho, 1975; Silva, 1976; Mott, 1976), seeing them as strategies in the struggle for power. In his study on accusation and conflict in Umbanda in the city of Marília, Yoshiko Mott demonstrates how accusations of demand — frequent in inter- and intra-group relations — are usually vague, finding specific targets when the parties are in conflict. It also shows how accused and accuser are equivalent; that is to say, because they are a means of struggle for prestige and power, accusations are directed against those who have more or less equivalent power and prestige, against those who are recognized as rivals (Mott, 1976). Thus, Bilina's accusations that her "competition" for group leadership practiced witchcraft against her are a way of reaffirming her *força*, for, after the demand, she consolidated herself as *terreiro* leader and gave continuity to it, while her contender founded another cult group which, even though it worked with Nagô and *caboclo*, did not succeed in overthrowing her.

Just as the *terreiro*'s history, told and retold by the *mãe-de-santo*, had the explicit function of showing the cult center's African origin, the group's current religious practice, its structure, and the collection of cultural traits present there shall be invoked to attest continuity with Africa and especially the fact that, over the years, the original legacy of the Africans had been preserved, making the *terreiro* constitute itself, still today, as "pure Nagô." Thus, not only components of the group's cultural repertory but also its way of organizing itself take on a new meaning, insofar as they are invoked as signs through which "Nagô purity" is expressed. It should be observed that this occurs at the level of internal composition and organization.

NAGÔ DESCENDANTS AND THEIR PLACE WITHIN THE GROUP

Calling itself the "*Terreiro* of the Virgin Santa Bárbara," the sect is made up of approximately fifty followers (those who, by subjecting themselves to the *mãe-de-santo*'s prescriptions, actively and regularly participate in group rituals and, especially, in *terreiro* celebrations).[18] Although flexible enough to include those who have many different types of relationships to the *orixá*, this characterization excludes from the category of the faithful clients who only seek out the *terreiro* sporadically in search of magical services. The group includes men, women, and children who, notwithstanding the differences in which they situate themselves in relation to their involvement with the *orixás*, have in common the faculty of being recognized as apt to participate actively in the cult.

Basically made up of people of color (in a proportion of ten blacks and mulattos to one white) and by women (three women to one man), the group is marked by the presence of the elderly, especially blacks (nineteen people over the age of sixty), a situation that is counterbalanced by the presence of children and adolescents (fourteen in a total of fifty-eight people). Their constant presence in the *terreiro* and their active participation in ritual life represent the principal mechanism for reproduction of the group. Over 50 percent of its current members, blacks especially, participate because their families belong to the Xangô, some of them even having received domestic altars from their dead ancestors, along with the obligation to look after the saints. Pursuit of cures is a strong motive for joining the religious center, accounting for 22 percent of current group membership. Other reasons for joining the group, in order, include the influence of friends and relatives who already frequented the center, an attraction to the beauty of its rites, the *orixá*'s spontaneous manifestation in individuals who were among the present appreciating the dances, and, finally, the search for support to resolve affairs of the heart and/or previous experiences in other centers of Umbanda and Candomblé.

They live in the city and its outskirts, or in the poor quarters of Aracaju. Many were already members of the *terreiro* when they came here from Laranjeiras seeking employment or schools for their children. The majority of them are illiterate or know how to "sign [their] names." Youths attend schools (twelve are fulltime students), at grade-school level and, in one case only, college level.

These are their professions: farm worker (6), Funrural [Assistance Fund for the Rural Worker] retiree (3), stevedore (1), stower (11), military man (1), shopkeeper (1), boiler man (1), washerwoman (5), primary school teacher (1), medical assistant (1), janitor (1), fisherman (1), seamstress (1), domestic servant (18). They have in common the fact that they are all low-paying jobs and nearly all of them require very little in terms of formal schooling.

In short, the group's current composition is mostly blacks and the poor. To this must be added the fact that many current group members are blood relatives and of stated African (specifically Nagô) ancestry. Some of the members maintain domestic shrines inherited from their ancestors in their homes, and the family is the depositary of special emphasis for the continuity of the cult of the *orixás* and, by extension, of the group itself, which is made up of three distinct categories of members: "descendants of the Nagô," "baptized," and "non-baptized" (the latter is a numerically restricted and transitional category). Since the group is primarily a religious group, the manifest function of which is to realize the cult of the *orixás*, the condition of group member is exteriorized through the faculty of participation in the rites, to which members of the various categories have access and the performance of certain obligations is expected of them, ranging from external signs (types of vestments, adornment, etc.) to moral standards. The observance of these rules confers upon them a sense of group unity, expressed by the self-denomination of brotherhood, and some of them function as diacritical signs that delimit their boundaries.

Whereas all "outside" group members possess identical status, internal difference translates into hierarchical difference in which "Nagô descendants"—blacks whose ancestry is supposedly known and places them, through religious participation, within this ethnic group—occupy the highest positions and, by definition, need not submit to aggregation rituals in order to become part of the group. Their condition as Nagô descendants guarantees them a continuity with Africa and with the *orixás* and makes them natural group members, fit to occupy the highest positions of its hierarchy, for which they need only submit to a ritual purification. This cleansing is simultaneously a confirmation of their connection with the *orixás*, a connection inherited from their ancestors—the transmission of a deity according to lineage. In this category, which encompasses nearly half the group members (twenty-four people, out of a total of fifty-eight), kinship lines cross in various directions and their members are basically reduced to three extended families made up of descendants of old Africans and people associated with them by marriage. However, relatives-in-law submit to an aggregation ritual in order to become part of the group.

Thus, by organizing themselves internally according to principles that privilege recognizably African ancestry, the reconstitution of royal or supposedly Nagô genealogies takes on great importance for members of the *terreiro*. Through it the nucleus of the cult group is constituted, the nucleus that will be frequently invoked to certify its continuity with Africa. If this nucleus is renewed through the family, with the children of "descendents of the Nagô" (hence the importance of children in the ritual life of the *terreiro*), the group recomposes itself from its losses through the incorporation of people whose ancestors had no links with the Nagô *orixás*, links that will now be established by the ritual of baptism.[19]

Baptism—the local name for the rite of incorporation to the group—generates the category of the "baptized," composed of whites, mulattos, and blacks not considered Nagô-descendants. It is a mechanism for furnishing them with abilities that are inherent to those who "do not need baptism because they belong to the race" or because "they are already blood kin" or "because they have already been baptized by God."

The way of aggregating members is one of the aspects underlined by the Nagô *terreiro* to mark its difference with regard to others and constitutes one of the elements of that which is presented as African heritage.

Frederick Barth and Abner Cohen, scholars who have analyzed ethnicity as a form of organization in the present, insist that because ethnicity
is a relational category, the culture of the group in contact with others
does not disappear or simply fuse, as theorists of acculturation believed;
rather, it will be utilized to establish contrast. Culture as a whole will
not be preserved under these circumstances, although some of its traits
will be highlighted precisely to show its distinction. Choice of the types
of cultural traits that will guarantee group distinction as such depends
upon other groups with which it is in contact and the society to which it
belongs, for diacritical signs must (by definition) be opposed to others of
the same type (Cunha, 1979: 37).

Thus, in presenting the Nagô's African cultural heritage, I am not proposing a complete ethnography of the *terreiro*—which, in this case, would
be irrelevant—nor testing (through comparisons with Africa) whether
what is presented as legitimate African tradition has a parallel among
the Yoruba peoples. For the purposes of this work, it matters little if the
cultural repertories presented as such really are African. Ultimately, they
might even be forged. What matters is that the group considers them
as African and that they were chosen by the group itself as meaningful,
being used as signs of difference in function of which "Nagô purity" is
declared. I shall now present the cultural traits elected by the group as
markers of their difference and affirmation of their African-ness.

MARKERS OF AFRICAN ORTHODOXY

The mechanism for incorporating the congregation to the sect is one
of those elements that, according to my observation, may be thus described:

A candidate for baptism, a black woman who has been seeking out the
terreiro for six months for health reasons and has been regularly attending its celebrations, arrives in the morning from Aracaju, where she lives.
During the day her routine in the *terreiro* has been the same as during
other previous ritual cycles. At night, most of the congregation continues
to dance to the sound of drums, while a few prominent *terreiro* members
gather in the sanctuary to assist the *mãe-de-santo* in the rite of baptism.
The candidate and her godparents (one man and two women who were
members of the sect) stand before the altar. After successive prayers and
songs to the sound of a *xerén* (a small rattle played only during the most
important moments of rituals), the candidate lies face down, her head

uncovered, remaining in this position for a time, while the *mãe-de-santo* sings with the others. Holding a lit candle, the initiate rises to her knees as the *mãe-de-santo* places the Xangô [the *orixá* to whom she is being dedicated] stone on her head, sprinkling her with water from a branch of green leaves dipped in the water used for the "washing of the *pedra de santo*." Access to this rite is restricted and it takes place some days earlier, with the exclusive participation of some of the more prominent followers (and especially of virgins). Next comes an oath of perseverance, in which the initiate promises to follow ritual requirements and other obligations. This oath is taken in the form of the candidate's replies to questions posed to her by the *mãe-de-santo*, even as her godparents, along with the initiate, hold a lit candle, in a gesture reminiscent of commitment made by them in the fulfillment of these promises. Bowing down, the initiate greets the *orixás* by touching the ground three times with her forehead before the *pegê* and then asks her godparents for their blessing.

Next comes the ceremony of *dar contas*—the saint's necklaces. Previously prepared by the *mãe-de-santo*, they are placed around the initiate's neck, along with a cross and a sign of Solomon. Water from the *pé do santo* is offered to the initiate in a small gourd. The new initiate is led out of the *pegê* under a white sheet, the extremities of which are held by old *filhas de santo*, flanked by her godparents, and they all move to the dance area. There are manifestations of joy. Accompanied by her godparents, the *filha de santo* dances. But there is no possession by the *orixá*. She then retires to the *quarto dos santos*, at the door of which she receives the greetings of the other members of the group into which she has just entered, having become a Nagô by baptism.

If we were to proceed to a genetic analysis of cultural traits that are part of the rite of aggregation to the *terreiro*, one would certainly find traits to which African origin might be attributed, as well as others stemming from Catholic Church ritual or from other sources. Considering the proposed objectives, this is irrelevant. It is more important to notice that the *mãe-de-santo* speaks selectively of the rite and to ponder the meaning of her omissions. Certain elements are omitted, either because they are not considered important or because they are common to both traditions ("pure" Nagô and "mixed" toré), and thus cannot be considered as markers. Other elements are highlighted and listed, at times through negation (that is, by virtue of their absence in "pure Nagô" tradition).

"Here, initiation does not require confinement to a room nor having your head shaved. Here, one achieves brotherhood as in the

Church. One only goes to the *quarto de santo* when one is going to become possessed. Only then and that's it. The business of being confined to the initiation chamber, head shaving, getting all dirtied up with chicken blood, that's an invention of Alexandre and the baianos. But Nagô isn't like that. Baptism is what we do: we give the beads and candle. That's how things are in Africa. It's those Toré folk that do the head-shaving business and confine people to the initiation chamber. Not the Nagô." (Bilina)

It is interesting to observe that, insofar as purity and mixture are polar opposites [as concepts], when she lists the signs of her Nagô *terreiro*'s purity the *mãe-de-santo* is simultaneously speaking of elements of impurity that supposedly characterize other *terreiros*, for possessing a certain set of cultural traits, doing things another way, not flaunting the signs of purity, is a betrayal of Africa, a sign of mixture. Thus the process of aggregation to the Nagô cult group is described by opposition to the Toré, with explicit references to Alexandre's *terreiro*. This is the Filhos de Obá *terreiro*, with whom the "pure Nagô" rivals for prestige and to which it was closest in the past in terms of their origins. Having formerly housed a dissident faction of the "pure Nagô" *terreiro*, the latter was said to have become the locus of the origin of "disorder" by betraying Africa, adulterating original traditions with unorthodox practices imported from Bahia. Thus, the purity of African tradition is emphasized through allusions to the Toré's impurity and mixture, particular emphasis being placed on elements that, from her perspective, constitute an African-based difference.

NAGÔ (PURE)	TORÉ (MIXED)
1. Fidelity to African tradition	1. African tradition adulterated by Bahia
2. Baptism	2. Initiation
3. Absence of initiate reclusion	3. Initiate reclusion
4. Absence of head shaving	4. Head shaving
5. Absence of spilling animal blood on the head	5. Spilling animal blood on the head
6 Giving beads (saint's necklaces)	—
7. Giving candles	—

Although the aggregation ritual adopted by the *terreiro* is much more elaborate and includes many other cultural traits that might have been used as diacritical markers, circumscription of Nagô purity was based, above all, on the absence of certain traits: the initiate's reclusion, shaving of the head, and spilling of the blood of sacrificed animals upon it. These were supposedly not part of the original African legacy, and were indicative of an adulteration of primitive "Nagô purity."

Three considerations must be made here:

1. Traits listed as signs of "mixture," a distortion of original purity, integrate that which, in Bahia, is considered to be the Jeje-Nagô model most faithful to African tradition (Rodrigues, 1935; Carneiro, 1967a; Bastide, 1978).
2. That which is presented as legitimate Nagô-African tradition in the Laranjeiras temple is purified of elements that might be redolent of primitivism (for instance, soiling the faithful with the blood of animals). Such elements were highlighted so as to constitute the mark of the repertory of the Toré's symbolic goods.
3. Although the construct of Nagô purity is African-based and represents fidelity to its traditions, execution of the rite of baptism is compared to the homonymous Catholic rite and, therefore, to another cultural tradition, without representing an adulteration of "Nagô purity." I shall return to these problems in good time.

Further ritual differences are also highlighted—not specifically aspects of a given rite (as was the case with baptism), but elements that generically integrate the ritual cycle known as *festejo*. Conceived as an aggregate of specific rites, conjugated so as to form a unit, one that is expressed by the *mãe-de-santo* in the terms "one must open and close the *terreiro* in order to perform the *festejo*," *festejos* necessarily includes animal sacrifices, collective meals, and dancing to the sound of drums, allowing the *orixás* to possess the bodies of the faithful. A *festejo*'s duration is regulated by the kind of animal sacrificed as an offering to the deities. The slaughter of lambs entails the realization of mortuary rites (the *iguê*) and, consequently, ceremonies are prolonged for seven days, whereas other types of animals allow for the closing of the festivities on the third day.

The *festejo* ritual sequence may be summed up thusly: opening rites (*lavagem dos santos*, obligation to *Lebará*, *levar o ebó*, distribution of holy water to the congregation, permission-giving by the *orixás*, purification of the ritual space and renewal of the congregation's *força*; central rites that include the following sequence: animal sacrifices (*matança*), exclusively

56

vegetable-based collective meals (*adaru*), and dances, including the circle of the virgins, the first circle (both characterized by the absence of possession), and the circle of the *orixás*, in which dancers are possessed by saints. The latter circle is interrupted by yet another meal of both animal- and vegetable-based foods; and closing rites: the procession of the *orixás* (*fereguim*), leave-taking of the saints (*bebemiô*), and yet another collective meal (*guengué*).

To these are added ritual series that only occur during other ritual cycles, such as the offering of the first yam crop to the *orixás* (the cutting of the yam), the representation of agricultural labor (*adiborô-pegan*), the rite of the dead (*iguê*), and the invocation and feeding of ancestors (*fereguim*) that occurs only at seven-day festivities.[20]

Although there are a great variety of rites, many of which are realized inside the *terreiro* and which may only be attended by the faithful, the elements invoked to establish the *terreiro's* distinction, ostensibly based on fidelity to Africa, are, in this case, traits primarily noticeable to "outsiders," for they are clearly visible in the dances that take place in a tent raised on the street in front of the *terreiro*, and they are accessible to anyone. The following differences are pointed out by the Nagô *mãe-de-santo*: the color of the vestments, the shape of the drums, and the rhythms themselves [*toques* or different modalities of percussion].

"Nagô garments are all white because that's how they were in the time of the Africans. These Toré folk wear prints—red, blue . . . a hell of a mixture.

Alexandre [the Nagô who supposedly betrayed his origins by adhering to the Toré] has a long drum there. That's a *terreiro de caboclo* drum. This here is a Nagô drum [barrel-shaped].

Toré rhythms are different from ours. We play in the old African style. All the other styles are inauthentic inventions." (Bilina)

Another element of differentiation pointed out by the Nagô is ritual frequency. Like garments, rhythms and instruments, it functions as an external sign of difference, a diacritical sign which (to the eyes of the "outside" world) is able to mark the differences between African and non-African traditions.

Of her *terreiro*, the Nagô *mãe-de-santo* says:

"We're not like those people who beat their drums every day. The Nagô only beat their drums twice a year—for the cutting of the yam and to celebrate the festival of Ogodô. That's how African things are. Not playing the drums every day, making a ruckus and bothering people."

The limited number of ritual cycles that are considered African markers refers to the question of the religious calendar and the motives for celebrations. In this regard some differences are also emphasized.

The cutting of the yam is the rite that marks the beginning of the liturgical year at the cult center, and it coincides with the time of the harvest of the yam, which occurs in September. The opening of the festivals coincides with the time of the harvest and, for congregation members, it has the explicit function of lifting the alimentary taboo that prevents them from consuming the tubers of the new crop.

> "Nagô folk can only eat the new yam after the [ritual] cutting. If they eat it before then their bodies break out in sores. Those folks aren't like that. But we are. First we have to offer it to them [the *orixás*] and only then we can serve ourselves. When the time comes we don't eat. We wait and offer it to them first." (Bilina)

In fact, the high point of the yam-cutting ceremonies is the offering of the new harvest yam to the *orixás*, an occasion on which the group members also help themselves ritually before the altar to small pieces of raw yam dipped in bee's honey (a symbol of peace) and dendê oil (a symbol of plenty). The extremities of yam tubers are used in divinations that will reveal relevant events for the community for the coming year, and, during the final stage of the festivities, there are dances that mimic agrarian activities.[21] Thus, the ritual action developed during the cutting of the yam indicates the agrarian nature of the liturgical year's inaugural festivities which are structured according to agricultural activity. Thus, the *festejos* begins at harvest time and ends when the yams sprout and their vines begin to climb the wooden stakes used to facilitate the plant's growth. This occurs in May and, from then on, festivities are proscribed until the new crop. Three festivals regularly take place during the period extending from September to May: the cutting of the yam in September; Ogodô in October; and Insã, at Carnival time, a time for worshipping the saints of the deceased, kept in the *terreiro* because the deceased had no descendants to care for them in their own houses. Circumstantially, another ritual cycle may be held during this period, but never during Lent, which is part of the Catholic ritual calendar but was also included in the agrarian-based calendar ruled by the phases of the cultivation of the yam. During Lent "one cannot perform rituals. Even the other folks stop singing, let alone we who belong to Santa Bárbara." Nonetheless, during Lent, not only ritual cycles but all rituals involving *orixás*—consultations included—are suspended. The same thing occurs during thunderstorms, for "the saints don't respond when the thunder claps. You must wait three days. Those other folk—they can do it. But not we who come from Africa, from Africans."

The mixture of the different calendars represents various ways of codifying time, but the differences with regard to the Toré reside in the agrarian-based calendar that regulates the time of the few ritual cycles and the prohibition against consulting the *orixás* during thunderstorms. In fact, prohibition is a recurrent subject used to outline African purity.

It is stated in various ways that the orthodoxy of the Nagô implies many prohibitions, which makes it more demanding with regard to its members' conduct than the Toré. The latter's permissiveness is contrasted, at the level of participation in the *festejo*, with the strict observance of rules imposed by the Nagô.

> "Anyone can dance in the Toré *terreiro*. Sometimes they don't even belong to the *terreiro*. Not here. We don't allow just anyone to walk in and be part of our wheel. This here is for members of brotherhood only and, even so, it's not for everyone. If any of them are *de corpo sujo* they can't come in. They can't be part of the ritual cycle. In order to *festejar* you have to have a *corpo limpo*." (Bilina)

Thus, in the Nagô *terreiro*, participation in dances is forbidden not only to "outsiders" but also to "insiders" whose bodies are *"limpo."* A body's "impurity" is primarily determined by the non-observance of sexual abstinence for a period that varies according to the individual's position within group hierarchy and by his proximity to the supernatural. For an ordinary *filho-de-santo* this period lasts one week, but for animal sacrifices, for instance, this period may be prolonged to forty days. In this sense, R. Bastide is right to affirm that the "hierarchy of Candomblé is more a hierarchy of obligations than a hierarchy of rights" (Bastide, 1978). Menstruation also makes the body impure and prevents women from taking part in certain rites.

Thus, yet another difference is constructed between the Nagô and the Toré. The latter is the place that gives shelter to the "unclean." In referring to one of the *terreiros*, the *mãe-de-santo* says: "The ladies of the evening, the prostitutes, they're all from over there." By opposition, the Nagô is the place of the "clean ones," and great importance is attributed in the *terreiro* to virginity, there being rites in which they are exclusive (or preferential) participants (the circle of the virgins and the washing of the saints). Thus, the "purity" of tradition marries the "cleanliness" of the bodies of the faithful, whereas the "mixture" of the Torés blends with the "dirtiness" [absence of cleanliness] of its adepts.

The prohibition against "outsider" participation in Nagô dances also serves to prevent the purity of African tradition from being (even momentarily) adulterated by the possible manifestation of *caboclos* and spirits (entities) not linked to Africa.

> "We can't allow just anyone to take part in our dance. Sometimes there's someone from one of those *torés* and, the next thing you know, people are being possessed by *caboclos*. Such things cannot be. We deal with the African Santa Bárbara. You could sit here for the rest of your life and never see a *caboclo* spirit. Only *orixás*. African saints. Those other folk are rabble. You'll see *caboclos* and Exus there. But not here." (Bilina)

More than thirty spirits are worshipped in the temple and, consequently, considered African; however, not more than ten of these effectively manifest themselves through trance. Despite the fact that their "stones" are collected at the altar and praised, the others do not "manifest themselves," for their owners have died and there was no one to replace them. Some of the spirits mentioned[22] in the list of *orixás* are very well known to Afro-Brazilian cults; about others it was not possible to obtain information in the literature consulted. Because these were nearly always "saints who no longer manifest themselves though possession," the *mãe-de-santo*'s information is also incomplete.

Orixás associated with lightning, thunder, and storms are very popular in the cult center. No less than seven entities were said to be related to these phenomena. The importance attributed there to these entities is reflected in the hierarchy of the *orixás*, in the myths, in the calendar of activities, and also in the designation of the *terreiro*. So it is that "Ogodô is the greatest devotion" and that one of the year's three ritual cycles is accordingly dedicated to him. Thunderclaps determine the suspension of consultation to the *orixás*, and the myth about Santa Bárbara-Xangô[23] is the only account I have been able to obtain regarding the *orixás* in this *terreiro* that has named itself Virgin Santa Bárbara—a saint who, in the Catholic tradition, protects against lightning bolts and storms.

If the cast of deities worshipped is a form of indicating the exclusivity of the African tradition claimed by the Nagô temple, Exu's presence in the Toré is the trait most often and most vehemently invoked to attest to impurity and infidelity to the heritage of Africa. At the level of discourse about the entities (spirits), it is the figure of Exu that will establish the decisive difference between Nagô and Toré, between the "pure" and the "mixed."

In referring to the Filhos de Obá *terreiro*, the Nagô *mãe-de-santo* declares: "Alexandre has the house of Exu there, the house of the enemy. Whoever heard of such a thing? We cast Exu out and he calls him into his house. He makes a house for him."

The accusation extends to the São José *terreiro* and to the torés in general:

"Nini has seven iron spikes that represent Exu inside Ogodô's
shrine (or *levas*—the group of things that make up the shrine).
She has a house for the Enemy. Those Toré folk are the ones who
work with Exu. Not us, though—we cast him out." (Bilina)

With regard to Exu, the opposition between "pure African Nagô" and "mixed Toré" may be established thus:

NAGÔ	TORÉ
Absence of a house for Exu	House for Exu
To cast out, to be rid of Exu	To embrace (or welcome) and work with Exu

In the *mãe-de-santo*'s discourse, Exu is identified with the Devil, a spirit whose existence cannot be ignored but whose presence and proximity one should avoid. Attitudes of avoidance with regard to Exu manifest themselves in various ways. He is a spirit about whom group members prefer not to speak. When asked about him, they avoid answering and when they refer to him they call him "the Enemy," a name generally used by the local folk to designate the Devil, a name (like that of Exu) one must try never to pronounce. Being identified with Evil, the very utterance of his name may endanger the speaker. Exu's identification with the Devil has thus proscribed him (at least at the level of manifest expressions), which generates certain dissimulations at the ritual level.

The explicit attitudes of cult members toward Exu (presented as exclusively linked to Evil) and attitudes toward other spirits (considered to be directly linked to Good and/or to Evil) are worthy of further attention. In the *terreiro* being studied, two other spirits are presented with this explicit association besides Exu: Lokum (Olokum), considered "a strong saint, [who] dwells in the waters and shares both goodness and badness."

He is therefore an ambivalent spirit who differs from Exu (always represented as linked to Evil); there is also Lebará (Elegbá, Elegbará). Although Afro-Brazilian studies currently lay claim to a genetic etymological bias regarding the names Elegbá and/or Elegbará, they are Dahomeyan names for the Yoruba deity Exu. However, the *terreiro* which is the object of our attention here fiercely refutes it. Lebará is presented as not only different from Exu but as his antagonist. It is said that "Lebará casts out Exu" for Exu is the Devil and "Lebará is an African saint who oversees house and world and [keeps them] free from evil-doing and wickedness."

There are two Lebarás in the *terreiro*. One is located in a shrine in the yard outside the house; its function being to "mind the house and the world. He keeps watch to nip evil gestures in the bud and generally to avoid nuisance." There is another Lebará in the sanctuary, along with the *orixás*, also intended to "rid [the *terreiro*] of wickedness and evil. Evildoers must answer to him. But he is a peace-loving saint."[24]

As long as he is satisfied, he will foster peace. So he must be appeased the night before the ritual cycle begins. The ritual known as *levar o ebó* is performed at midnight of the day before the rituals, when an *acaçá* [a sort of cake made from cornmeal or rice] is placed near the indoor Lebará. Another is taken by men to a crossroads (the place of *Exu*) and yet another one to a river for *Lokum*. The *mãe-de-santo* explains the rituals: "Reverence must be paid them the night before so there won't be any trouble." It is also to ensure peace that the honey of bees is spilled at the entrance that gives out onto the street, for honey symbolizes peace and offering it to Lebará ensures a peaceful ritual. It is with the same purpose that, at the beginning of a slaughter, the first animal to be sacrificed is Lebará's rooster, whose blood is spilled over a mound of earth topped by a wooden stick kept inside the *pegê* and which represents him, and some of the bird's feathers are glued behind the door to the street. Later, when the *orixás* are being served, Lebará will also receive his share. Wrapped in a banana leaf, a small portion of food will be placed next to the saint. Exu must also be appeased. Two *filhas de santo* who are responsible for serving him receive bits of food at the door to the sanctuary, after which they go to the doors that open onto the street and at the back of the yard while repeatedly chanting the words "Exu bá, Exu bá, guia, guia" as they throw the food outside the house. Although they are said out loud, the words are so hushed (*xubá*) as to hardly recall an actual invocation of Exu, yet they "come get the food outside the house, for he has no right to be among us."

The declaration that Exu should have no access to the *terreiro* is a recurrent one and appears in a ritual series in which Lebará is the principal honoree. It is nearly always performed after midnight and involves food and dancing. The food (Oô) is made from yams and offered to Lebará. The dances that follow are also dedicated to him. In the first of these, people dance in a circle and perform a movement with their hands pointing to the street, in a gesture that evokes banishment. The *mãe-de-santo* explains that such dancing is intended to "keep the enemy from disturbing us." A remarkable feature of this ritual series is that its choreography is completely different from the preceding ones, characterized above all by disordered jumping and the movements of several people dancing simultaneously, providing a sharp contrast with the coordination and body language of other dances (nearly always performed solo).[25] The last of these is performed by women who beat one another while some of them throw themselves upon their colleagues in a movement that recalls the *umbigada* [a belly-bumping dance]. At some point, a man is chosen and led almost by force to the middle of the dance circle. With great animation, the women beat him until he manages to escape. The dance suggests intentionally disguised licentiousness and, asked its meaning, the *mãe-de-santo* explained that "Exu could not stand up to the women. The women fell all over him, so he left. He couldn't take it. He's strong but the women are too much for him."

The quality of inversion proposed by a ritual during which possession has never been recorded is more or less explicit and expressed through a shift in the dancing and by women beating men in an atmosphere of furtive eroticism. This suggests the intrusion of chaos and disorder in the highly ordered world of the *orixás*. However, the attempted intrusion is immediately frustrated, for in the struggle between Good and Evil, between Order and Disorder, Exu is soon defeated and expelled. It is Exu's defeat and banishment that are emphasized in the *terreiro*. This is the difference between the Nagô and the Toré.

It may not be of great interest to know whether Exu is truly invoked to assist in *trabalhos*, above all in works of divination, as admitted by some group members and other "outsiders." Similarly, it is irrelevant to know to what degree the concept of Lebará (and above all the rituals dedicated to him) are a reproduction or negation of the concept and rituals of Exu, according to descriptions of Bahian Candomblé *terreiros* that are regarded as more Africanized (Bastide, 1978; Carneiro, 1967c). It might be thought that Lebará was a specific group tradition, whereas Exu was an entity that came from outside it, transformed by the white perspective. At any rate, it is important to observe that the *mãe-de-santo*'s discourse on Exu depicts him as distant from this entity in African tradition (Bastide, 1978: 171). In Laranjeiras, the dualism of Good and Evil and exclusive identification with evil forces approximate Exu to the Exu of Umbanda.[26] Whereas Exu's integration with Good-Evil dualism corresponds to a whitening of Afro-Brazilian tradition, explicitly defended by writers of Umbanda — a trend that reached its discursive apex in that religion's myth of origin, which is located in India (Ortiz, 1978: 120–48) — in Nagô, Exu's inclusion in Good-Evil dualism occurs in the name of Africa and fidelity to tradition, which indicates the semantic ambiguities of the language of "Nagô purity."

The fact is that, by accepting the discourse on Exu generated by the dominant classes, the *mãe-de-santo* elects him as a basic element with which to distinguish the Nagô from the "others" and, in so doing, present entities and rituals as legitimately African, ascribing meanings to them which, regardless of true or alleged African origins, satisfy the requirements of the "here and now" insofar as they develop survival strategies and advantages in the fight for the religious market.

Here, where the question between Good and Evil is not circumscribed to deities, rather unfolding in the struggle between religious agents and groups, the language of Manichean dualism joins with the appeal of "Nagô purity" and sometimes becomes more powerful than the language of fidelity to origins. This will be examined in the next chapter, in which, by analyzing the Nagô's discourse on the others, we shall return to the problem of the separation between the realms of Good and Evil implicit in the opposition between purity and mixture.

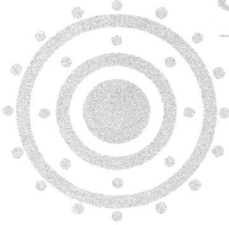

CHAPTER THREE

Nagô Speaks of "the Others"

MALÊ — THE ONES WHO DISAPPEARED
BECAUSE THEY WERE EVILDOERS

Although she initially differentiates cults that came from Africa from those established in Brazil, the *mãe-de-santo* distinguishes different forms of relationship to different African ethnicities among the former.

"In the old days, all you had in Laranjeiras was Nagô and Malê. They both came from Africa. This means they belonged to another class. They didn't celebrate *santo*. They were more like *crentes* [literally, believers or Protestants]. They didn't set their faith in saints. They used rosaries in their rituals, and a stick that they struck upon a table. Ceremonies were held during the month of August. We have ritual obligations and their obligations were performed outdoors. Corn grew everywhere in those roads. Corn and rice." (Bilina)

Other information about Malê ritual is added, always highlighting particularities that distinguished it from that of the Nagô. Yet the greatest difference lay in the connection between the Malês (the ones who disappeared because they were evildoers) and Evil. After telling many stories that seek to demonstrate the extent of the Malês' evildoing, the intensity and efficacy of their practices of sorcery, the *mãe-de-santo* presents these as the very cause of their disappearance:

"The Malê didn't catch on. Xangô (the Nagô) caught on, but the Malê (. . .) they're all dead. One of them survived in the asylum but she died. Zé Sapucari had a daughter who became involved with Alexandre, but they all wound up practicing evil. Their leader was a very bad man. He practiced an awful lot of evil things. When they buried him (. . .) he changed into an animal. So much so that no one has ever been able to open his grave. It has never been opened. He would kill his own comrades to get his hands on their money. Other times he would steal their wives. He died from all that evildoing. When Zé Sapucari was alive, he wanted to mix with Herculano, the one whose group we belong to. But we don't mix. We keep to ourselves. After Zé Sapucari died some Malês came over to the Nagô. They came to dance with Herculano and then they continued to play on with us." (Bilina).[1]

Both the Malê and the Nagô came from Africa, and so Africa is ambiguously represented as the source of Good and Evil. However, it should be noted that the good side of Africa — represented by the Nagô — persisted, while the African component, associated with Evil, is extinct, a victim of its own evildoing.

The stereotype of the Malês as great sorcerers is not restricted to Laranjeiras, having been observed in various other parts of Brazil (Ramos, 1951: 75; Barreto, 1951: 18). It is also known that the accusation of sorcery was not circumscribed to the religion of the Malê, but extended to other Afro-Brazilian cults for, insofar as they were religions of subaltern groups, they also occupied a subaltern position within the structure of the society's power relations (Bourdieu, 1974: 43). Nonetheless, it is intriguing that the stigma of witchcraft that envelops cults of African origin becomes stronger in relation to the Malê, who are always presented as great sorcerers. The term *mandinga*, for instance, which is the name of one of the African ethnic groups that adopted Islamism, is synonymous with witchcraft. This exacerbation of the maleficent character attributed to the Malês may be explained by the distance that the Islamized blacks kept with regard to the dominant Catholicism. During the vogue for etymological explanations, the term Malê has been seen as a derivate of the contraction of *má lei* [Portuguese for "bad law"]. Rather, the Malê were those who did not follow the good law — Catholicism, the true law of God (Amaral, in Ramos, 1951: 69). Nonetheless, I tend to relate intensification of the stigma that weighs upon the Malê to the constant revolts led by those blacks during the first half of the nineteenth century, revolts that constituted a threat against the order of the slavocratic society and to white domination. Identifying the Malê with evil was one more strategy of control at the service of the whites who, detaining positions in the formal structure of power, felt threatened by the uncontrollable magical power attributed to those who, being in relatively unstructured areas of society, become difficult to control with the habitual mechanisms of control (Douglas, 1976: 127). In this context of confrontation between various powers, the accusation was a form of exercising control, for, if there are powers that are exercised in the name of the social structure and protect society, there are powers that are dangerous to it; those who use them are evildoers and must be persecuted. Thus, ideological representation was associated with police repression in order to contain the Malê uprisings; nowadays, their disappearance is explained, at the level of the *mãe-de-santo*'s imagination, as a consequence of their association with Evil.

Equally significant is the fact that the attempted fusion of the Malê (Evil) and the Nagô (Good) is resolved through avoidance of "mixture," the Malê's disappearance as a group and the eventual aggregation of survivors by the Nagô. From this perspective, the dynamics of the relationship between the two groups represents a double victory: that of purity against "mixture" and that of Good against Evil. Celebrated at the level of myth, this victory appears to have its ritual equivalent in the Chegança, annually performed in the city. Like the Congadas and Cavalhadas of South-Central Brazil, the local Chegança basically consists of a struggle between Moors (Evil) and Christians (Good) and is always resolved by the latter's victory over the former.[2] If, in the history of Afro-Brazilian religious groups in Laranjeiras, the dispute is between the Malê (Islamized blacks) and the Nagô, in the present-day Chegança the struggle is between Moors and Christians. Thus, there are common elements between the mythical story of Nagô-Malê relations and the ritual performance of the Chegança (and also of the Cavalhada and the Congada):

1. The realms of Good and Evil are divided in such a way that Nagôs and Christians occupy the same field, that of Good; while Malês and Moors are located in the place of Evil.

DOMAINS	GOOD	EVIL
Myth	Nagô	Malê
Rite	Christians	Moors

This sharing of a common dominion that places Christians and Nagôs side by side does not appear to be fortuitous. It is said that, in the past, Africans linked to the Nagô *terreiro* performed the leading role of Christians in the Chegança. Even today, although that link no longer exists, the Christians of the Chegança usually put on a courtesy performance before the Nagô *terreiro*.

2. Another commonality to be emphasized is that the plot of the Chegança ritual consists of a repetition of the development and outcome of the "history" of the Nagôs and Malês in Laranjeiras: the confrontation

between two irreconcilable, irreducible beliefs does not allow for a "mixture" of symbolic universes, although the passage of individuals from one universe to the other is permissible.[3] Yet their movement is always in the same direction and, thus, the rite of the Chegança—which evokes a historical struggle between Moors and Christians—and the "mythical history" of the Nagôs and Malês of Laranjeiras express different forms of celebrating the victory of the Good that does not "mix" with Evil, but overcomes it.

This "mixture" results in confusion, and the general order of the world (as expressed in the scheme of classification) must be maintained. But it is not always possible to prevent certain undesirable "mixtures" that introduce anarchy and, in this case, it is not only the types of prejudice-laden mixtures that must be identified; a place for hybridity—that which confuses the general scheme of the world—must be established. This is this task that lies ahead with regard to so-called "mixed Africans."

FROM AFRICAN TO TORÉ— THE TRAJECTORY OF THE "MIXED ONES"

There are currently two *terreiros* in the city to which the Nagô ascribes a remote link with Africa. They are the *terreiros* of São José and Filhos de Obá (see figure 1). To the history of those centers, the *mãe-de-santo* adds her own version. She admits that, in days past, there was some link between them and the Nagô. Since they were all African Nagôs, they visited one another and jointly developed certain rituals. But the others strayed from African purity, a process [of separation] that began with Inácia, who vied with Bilina for *terreiro* leadership. Vanquished, "she separated from us to form another battalion. It was she who introduced the anarchy that reigns in the world today. She became involved with Alexandre [leader of the Filhos de Obá *terreiro*] and created this damned mixture."

The Filhos de Obá *terreiro* and the Nagô *terreiro* constitute two of the most prestigious *terreiros* in the city and develop an intense rivalry in which Africa is often invoked. Although he does not deny his *caboclo* component, the leader of the Filhos de Obá *terreiro* proclaims himself the most legitimate heir to African traditions and the one most entitled to give information regarding the Nagô, for he considers himself to be the only *pai-de-santo* in Sergipe to know the Nagô language, a statement always accompanied by a demonstration limited to the cult's most basic vocabulary.

A victim of the 1930s and 1940s police persecution that befell the city's *terreiros* (see Chapter 5), he attempts to escape the violence of the repression, registering his center as a civil organization. Thus, in 1947, under the name of "Filhos de Obá Afro-Brazilian Cult Society," he registers his *terreiro* with a notary public. According to its statutes, its main purpose was

> "to practice charity for the general well-being of humanity and the spiritual development of its members within the concepts of Afro-Brazilian ritual and to distribute benefits to all those in need whether inside or outside its social headquarters."

Although at that time he already worked explicitly with *caboclos* and included them among the *terreiro*'s guides and protectors,[4] in this official document (through which he seeks legality) he resorts to Africa, presenting himself as

> "rightful heir to the tradition and succession of deceased president Joaquina Maria da Costa, of African descent, a daughter of the city of Obá's Nagô sects; he has held the present position since the age of five, through hereditary matrilineal right. . . ." (*Diário Oficial do Estado de Sergipe*, 1947)

The emphasis on African tradition and specifically on Nagô ascendency—strategically invoked in certain contexts and moments of the group's history—does not, however, lead to attachment to an exclusive tradition. He says: "I work in various nations: Nagô, Jeje, and Ketu on the African side and [on another side?] *caboclo*. *Caboclo* is an open language and to learn other languages is to evolve, to grow" (Alexandre).[5]

In presenting different religious traditions as languages, the *pai-de-santo* refers to the idea of communication associated with different cultural forms. If the diverse religious traditions are languages, the question is choosing whatever language is appropriate in speaking to whosoever one wishes to speak to, at the right time. As an "open language," *caboclo* tradition allows for wider communication (not only with the supernatural but with men), affecting broader segments of society and, consequently, enabling the growth of the *terreiro*. If [the] *caboclo* is an "open language," by deduction Nagô is a "closed language," access to it circumscribed to a limited number of people. Thus, on one hand, exclusive mastery of that language obstructs "progress" and "evolution" while, on the other hand, it allows for the establishment of adequate communication with the formal power structure, agents of repression and representatives of law and order.

Nevertheless, the Filhos de Obá *terreiro* leader's wily ambiguity is regarded by the *mãe-de-santo* as a simple betrayal of Africa:

"Alexandre belonged to Santa Barbara, he was Nagô—like us. Later on, he abandoned the *orixás* and embraced the *caboclos*. And then some people from Bahia came along and he left Santa Barbara altogether. He began to build houses for the Enemy [the Devil], to use the enemy to become rich. In no time at all he grew rich. He *is* rich. The Enemy can make people rich. People surrender to him. They offer him blood and soul in order to receive money from him. Whenever the Enemy came to take Alexandre away, he took a member of the brotherhood instead. Many were taken in his place. When he left the Nagô saints, Santa Barbara asked him to dedicate a ritual to her. But he didn't heed her request and went mad. He was institutionalized for a while and when he got better he blessed the statue of Santa Barbara, took it into the *terreiro* and once again began to dedicate festivals to her. But things there are tremendously mixed up and confused. He was Nagô but now he is Toré."

An analogous process of "*toré*-ization" took place with the São José *terreiro*, then intent on retracing its path back to Nagô origins and being admitted to that category. Its history dates back to the "strong, clever Nagô" who owned a *terreiro* in Riachuelo (a neighboring city). When he died, a black man from Laranjeiras is said to have stolen the saints and opened the *terreiro* in this city. But he was a *torezeiro* (linked to the Filhos de Obá *terreiro*) and did not know how to tend to African saints, so "he went off to perform an obligation and died." His sister took over leadership of the group and continued the *caboclo*-Nagô mixture.

"Those were Alexandre's people. She kept to his *terreiro* and was always involved with *caboclo* things. And there she stayed. Later on, she came to us and said she wanted to enter the brotherhood of Santa Barbara; she said she wanted no more truck with any *caboclo* business; she said she wanted to do everything the way we did it. Then I went with the folks to perform the festival. But the lady believed that it would be improper for us to be there. It's a big confusion. She wanted the *dogum* to be sent to her but she didn't know how to manage it. She also made Ogodô with no knowledge at all and put seven crossroad sticks (iron spears representing Exu) inside the Ogodô. She allowed anyone who walked in to play the drum. Unmarried women who lived the easy life, tramps—they

all belonged to her *terreiro*. She introduced all that *caboclo* stuff—
spears, the Enemy, everything. They built a little house for the
Enemy there, and for the *caboclos*, that's the kind of stuff they did.
There was loud moaning going on in the sanctuary when we were
there. We were asked not to return. That much mixture is impossible. That is Toré and we keep to ourselves." (Bilina)[6]

Such a reality is presented as the negation of order. In fact, "anarchy"
is a term employed by the *mãe-de-santo* herself referring to the fluid,
evanescent reality that is not in total accordance with the category of
the Nagôs, such as it is locally constructed. This confounds the general
schema of Afro-Brazilian cults, divided between African Nagôs on one
side and *caboclo* Torés on the other.

In light of this ambiguity and confusion, created by the mixture, order
is restored, and the hybrid (in this case the Toré) is reduced to one of basic
categories of classification. Thus, the Nagô *terreiro* that betrays Africa,
the one that becomes impure, is transformed into Toré.

TORÉ — FROM DEGENERATE INDIGENOUS TRADITION
TO THE ONE THAT WORKS WITH EXU TO DO EVIL

Toré is the category that currently opposes Nagô. This is expressed by a
series of oppositions regarding origins, spirits, values, rituals, and, indeed, the very manner of organization and group leadership that are thus
classified:

NAGÔ	TORÉ
Africa	Brazil (villages)
Black	Indian
Antiquity	Recentness
Tradition	Improvisation
Orixá	*Caboclo* and Exu
Baptism	Initiation
White garments	Colored garments
Barrel-shaped drums	Long drums
Few festivals	Many festivals
Respectable women	Prostitutes
Morality	Amorality
Virtue	Vice (*cachaça*, drinking)
Work for good	Work for evil

Right	Left
Purity	Mixture-impurity
Order	Anarchy

The opposition established between Nagô and Toré leads to inequality and asymmetry, since all the positive attributes are located in the Nagô column and, in this asymmetrical dualism, the Toré is configured as inferior. It shall be interesting to observe that, if Toré currently possesses a negative connotation, with regard to the past or, more specifically, at the time of its appearance as *caboclo*, it is referred to by the Nagô *mãe-de-santo* with a certain complacency and even sympathy.

Caboclo terreiros originated in Brazil—specifically in Indian villages. Although conceived as a local religious form, it began in Laranjeiras sometime after the establishment and organization of the cults that came from Africa.

> "Nagô already existed long before the *caboclos*. They were organized
> by Manué de Zuína. He learned the *caboclo* style of worship in
> the village. He was raised there and eventually fled from there.
> There were two people here who understood this *caboclo* busi-
> ness. Manué de Zuína and Zé Candunga. They knew because they
> learned about it right there in the village. They're both dead. The
> present-day followers aren't like them." (Bilina)[7]

While underscoring the precedence of the Nagôs in comparison with the *caboclos* and, by this means of tradition and antiquity, self-valuing herself with regard to the original *caboclo terreiros*, the Nagô *mãe-de-santo* recognizes their legitimacy as depositaries of a different and not unequal knowledge. Leaders of the old *caboclo terreiros* were initiated in the Indian village, in an unspecified place, albeit one that is vaguely indicated as having been "over by the forest," that is to say, beyond the boundaries of society. This assured them a ritual competency that does not exist in the *caboclo* chiefs of today: "I just don't understand how these folks open a new Toré every day. They don't know anything but they become *mães-de-santo* and *pais-de-santo*. . . . They didn't learn in the village."

Thus, current *torés* are degenerate forms of *caboclos*. Although the terms *caboclo* and *toré* are synonymously employed, the latter possesses a clearly pejorative connotation. The stigma comes from the fact that it is represented as degenerate forms of the original *caboclos*, who are more positively valued as depositaries of "authentic and pure" traditions of the forest-dwelling Indians, which remounts to the Indian as ideologically projected by Romanticism.[8]

Thus, it is the loss of their tradition and original legacy that transforms Indian knowledge and cults from different to degenerate. Therefore, in reflecting the events of society at large, where the Indian expresses original qualities — ideologically constructed as "[the] pure [one]," "[the] savage [one]," "[the] forest dweller" — and becomes disqualified when he loses such qualities, cults based on them also degenerate and become highly stigmatized when they lose their original purity and become inauthentic. Above all, though, Toré's stigma comes from its association with Evil, which may be summed up in the following expression: "working with Exu to harm others."

In a series of accusations against the *torezeiros* made by the Nagô *mãe-de-santo*, harm toward others is exemplified thus:

1. Killing in order to:
   1.1. take a woman
   1.2. surrender one's soul to the devil (pact)
   1.3. appropriate riches
2. separate husband and wife
3. bring about illness
4. bring about misfortune in business, family life, etc.

From a Nagô perspective, the Evil practiced by *torezeiros* through work with Exu especially affects property, family, health, professional activity, and even life. The Evil represented by induced illness or death, family dissolution and attacks upon property, is clearly a distortion of the social order, insofar as it represents transgression of morally approved social norms. Thus, the Evil practiced in the *torés* represents anarchy and amorality, thus bringing about its illegitimacy.

Conversely, Nagô magic basically acts upon the same points, although its basic rule is "not to harm anyone," and may be qualified as the practice of Good and the reinforcement of Morality and Order. Cures, solving robberies, protecting herds of cattle attacked by snakes, bringing husbands and wives back together, neutralizing the effects of envy, and so on are regarded as restoration of an order threatened by the forces of Evil, manipulated by the *torezeiros*. The power that the latter would have to introduce anarchy into the world would come from the fact that they work with Exu, presented as the Devil or the Enemy.

According to the Nagô *mãe-de-santo*'s discourse, the relationship of *tor-*

ezeiro pais-de-santo to Exu varies according to a continuum that goes from "making a house" for him and invoking him for magical works to making a pact with him in which the soul is exchanged for material wealth and success. This extreme accusation is made about one of the *pais-de-santo*, the leader of the Filhos de Obá *terreiro*, the Nagô who would have betrayed the origins and rivals the "pure Nagô" *terreiro* in prestige.

It is interesting to observe that the orthodoxy which, in another context, had been vigorously invoked as a marker of difference with regard to the Filhos de Obá *terreiro*—to which it is closest in terms of origins and the propriety of a certain knowledge bequeathed by the Africans—is converted here into a discourse of morality/immorality, as a result of which the success of the city's most outstanding *terreiros* is differentially explainable: the "pure Nagô" and the Nagô who betrayed Africa. In recognizing the success of the latter, its rival for power and prestige, the Nagô *mãe-de-santo* seeks to explain it through association with Evil, through pacts with the Devil, while the success of her "pure Nagô" *terreiro* is credited to the protection of the orixás and to an association with Good[ness]. In both cases, the explanation for wealth is given by recourse to the supernatural, but what must be emphasized here is how the language of orthodoxy is transformed into the language of morality and possesses an eminently practical meaning that satisfies demands of legitimacy/illegitimacy. As if to say: my power is legitimate because it is "pure" African and works in the name of Good; the power of the other is illegitimate because it is "mixed" and works in the name of Evil.

Acknowledgment of the *torezeiros'* power to produce anarchy in the world through the manipulation of Evil forces raises the question of how the Nagô *mãe-de-santo* conceives this relationship of forces, as exercised by her *terreiro* (representing Goodness) and by the city's other *terreiros* (working, without distinction, for both Good and Evil). Does this not mean that a greater number of allies gives them more power, more *força* than the Nagô? Acknowledgment of the power of others is granted, rather, in terms of a field of activity (that is, of what they can do through an alliance with the Devil); its *força* is greater, however, because it allows it to undo work done by the others, and thus she has more power than the others. This power, however, would be consciously self-contained for moral reasons and through her decision to practice only Good. Finally, the Manichean worldview underlying the Nagô-Toré opposition resolves itself through the victory of Goodness, which is stronger than Evil. In this sense, the *terreiro* not only affirms its superiority over others but also legitimizes itself and produces the illegitimacy of others.

UMBANDA—THE ONE THAT CHARGES
MONEY FROM THE BROTHERHOOD

Whereas, with regard to Malê, Nagô and *caboclo terreiros*, the *mãe-de-santo* expresses knowledge of origins, rituals, spirits worshipped, and other qualities that allow us to characterize them as religious forms, she does not have a "ready theory" to explain Umbanda. She says it is "different from the Nagôs" and that it contains "much invention," yet her discourse soon focuses on Umbanda's organizational aspects, as presented according to the Federations (Federações).

As we have seen in Chapter 1, the term Umbanda is still infrequently used in the city. Its propagation in Sergipe occurred most intensely from the latter half of the 1960s onward, a period in which the Federations of Umbanda begin to be organized and radio programs that seek to disseminate this religious form become more intense.[9] Radio appears to be her principal source of information on the subject.

> "People invent all kinds of stuff. Just listen to all the nonsense
> that comes over the radio. Sometimes I listen in to what these
> Umbanda people are saying. But they don't understand anything.
> Nowadays lots of folks listen to our *toadas* and repeat them over
> there, only differently." (Bilina)[10]

To the Nagô *mãe-de-santo*, in addition to being a different religious form Umbanda is represented above all as an association to which monthly payments must be made. She says:

> "Those people from the Federation are not like us. They've been
> here eight times already to [get us to] mix with them. But that just
> can't be. They do things differently. Every month the brotherhood
> must donate five *contos de réis* [Brazilian currency in use until
> 1938]. Everyone in the brotherhood is poor. We can't afford that
> kind of money. They don't pay me so how can they giving money to
> so-called Umbanda—they can't do that. And we keep our devotion
> to ourselves; we don't go anywhere else."

Taking money from the Brotherhood (a term the *mãe-de-santo* uses to designate her sect, emphasizing its nature of mutual help) is presented as a feature that denigrates Umbanda in two ways:

> " . . . because charging money to the Brotherhood is the stuff of
> the Devil. Who ever heard of *sons* having to pay that much money
> every month, like rent? Everyone in the Brotherhood is poor. They

give money when and as much as they can. Those who can, give more. The poorer ones give less and when you can't give anything at all, you just don't." (Bilina)

To the idea of "giving according to one's means," which prevails in her *terreiro* not only with regard to *filhos de fé* but also with regard to clients, the *mãe-de-santo* opposes the idea of Umbanda's fixed tax, which, compared to "rent," suggests the idea of commerce in religious goods and an exploitation of the poor who would pay the same amount as the rich. These accusations are diametrically opposed to the principle of charity, that is to say, of services freely rendered and disinterestedly proclaimed by Umbanda (Mott, 1976: 90–91). On the other hand, by resorting to the supernatural to the economic success of *terreiro* leaders, the *mãe-de-santo* presents her own success as a sign of the *orixás'* blessing, while the success of her rivals is always explained as a result of transactions with the Devil, whence it results that money and wealth are located within the dualism of Good and Evil. In charging brothers and the poor alike, Umbanda becomes a denial of Goodness, the logical consequence of which is Bilina's condemnation of Umbanda and her refusal to become a member of any Federation.

Among the Federations that are currently active in Sergipe under the denomination of Umbanda or of Afro-Brazilian cults, one of them undoubtedly holds an outstanding position. Supported by important politicians, it is affiliated with the Federation of Brasília and has succeeded in registering a high number of *terreiros* and *filhos de santo*. In spite of this hegemony, which appears to have been consolidated in recent years, the Federations compete intensely not only in the attempt to obtain support from influential politicians (who—in exchange for votes—guarantee them funds for installing their offices, bureaucratic services, social work, and promotional efforts), but also to obtain the adhesion of a greater number of *terreiros*.[11] Federation income derives at least in part from these *terreiros* in the form of monthly dues paid by the centers and their affiliates. Competition for hegemony and control of *terreiros* is intensified whenever they must obtain the adhesion of the most prestigious centers—and not only because of the latter's large numbers of members (whose monthly dues serve to increase the organization's income or obtain votes to elect politicians) but, above all, because of the prestige this will afford them. This is why the various Federations have increasingly targeted the Nagô *terreiro*. Some Federations have made more than one attempt to obtain Bilina's adhesion. This occurred whenever a new director joined the Federation or whenever anyone felt they were influential enough to dissuade the *mãe-de-santo* from her firm proposals of non-affiliation.

Once arguments of persuasion had been exhausted, arguments of force (such as having the police threaten to close the *terreiro*) were frequently employed. Alleging that "no one forbids us [to do anything]" and that "nothing ever stood in the way of Africa," the *mãe-de-santo* refused to be intimidated and saw to it that her *terreiro* remained the only one in the city which never accepted becoming affiliated to any of the Federations.[12]

"WE DON'T GET ALONG WITH CRENTES"

Crente (literally, believer) is the term by which the *mãe-de-santo* generically designates followers of several varieties of Protestantism, visible in the city as Presbyterianism—introduced there in the late nineteenth century—where its activity is identified above all by the presence of a temple known as the church of the Crentes. The *mãe-de-santo* doesn't say much about this religious tradition, but what she does say is enough to exclude it from possible compatibility with Nagô.

> "Protestants and masons alike oppose the Church and don't agree with us either. Remember Corina, the *Taieira* queen? Well, she belonged to the Nagô but she got herself mixed up with this *crente* business—her kids dragged her into it and we didn't want her among us anymore." (Bilina)

In another context, the *crentes* were compared to the Malês, and the common denominator employed for this association was the absence of statues of saints in religious worship. Usually, the presence or absence of statues is the most visible and most exploited opposition used to establish the difference between Catholicism and Protestantism for the working classes, and it is by making use of this diacritic that the Protestants are associated with the wicked Malês and excluded from the field of alliances by the Nagô *terreiro*.

"THE CATHOLIC CHURCH—THE ONE WE MIX WITH"

Unlike what happens when she talks about cults of possession, the Nagô *mãe-de-santo*'s references to the Catholic Church are uttered in tones of respect and acceptance. Her occasional criticisms and accusations are circumscribed to the attitude of certain religious agents, usually priests and nuns, who, present in the city after Vatican Council II, proceeded to the renewal of the ritual and the influence of the Catholic Church.

> "These folks want to destroy the Church. Whoever heard of eating and receiving Jesus Christ? You have to fast before it. Whoever heard of such a thing?" (Bilina)

Xangô's relationship to Catholicism is more ambiguous. In referring to possession cults, she emphasizes her loyalty to Africa and the purity of the Nagô tradition upheld by her own *terreiro*: "We don't mix. We don't mix with Toré or Umbanda or any of that stuff. Nagô has its own place. We only mix with the Catholic Church." On another occasion, in speaking of the same opposition between Nagô and other possession cults, she says: "Among African blacks we are a Catholic religion, but as for this other business—Toré and Umbanda—no. We don't accept it."

Principles of inclusion and exclusion are established here. With the exception of Catholicism, other religions are considered incompatible with Nagô, and it is required of novices that they give up the practice of whatever cult they previously attended. But Nagô and Catholicism are not exclusive. On the contrary, to be Nagô is a condition to be added to being a Catholic.

If we define "Catholics" inclusively as all those who have been baptized, "being Catholic" becomes a demand that precedes "being Nagô," for only those who are baptized in the Catholic Church may be submitted to Nagô baptism and thus enter the cult group.[13] The mode and intensity of Xangô follower participation in the ceremonial life of the Catholic Church is a problem ultimately not defined by Xangô. If many often attend Sunday mass and some even take communion during important Church celebrations, the services sought by the *terreiro* in the Church are necessarily reduced to baptism and mortuary services. This suffices for them to identify themselves as Catholic. Nonetheless, if such services rendered by the priest are considered necessary, they are not considered sufficient for Xangô members who have their own rituals for the same purposes. In the *mãe-de-santo*'s words, "The priests know a great deal, but they don't know everything," whence it results that her knowledge is added to that of the priests, or rather, it is another [type of] knowledge and, in order to explain it, the *mãe-de-santo* often refers to comparisons with Catholicism. In her discourse, Xangô and the Catholic Church are occasionally two parallel systems of knowledge, belief, and organization, and, at other times, Xangô is presented as being subaltern to Catholicism.

For example, in order to explain her belief and symbolic systems to the researcher, she often resorts to comparisons with Catholicism, while Xangô appears as a parallel religion.

"Ogodô is the greatest of all [orixás] in terms of devotion. Because the Church has the Holy Sacrament, doesn't it? So he is present in Santa Barbara's devotion to Africa. Look over there. That's his mortar. Isn't there a chalice in the Catholic Church? Well, that's Ogodô's mortar. (. . .) Here are the little clay water jars. In Church we have the wine. Here, the wine is water." (Bilina)

Ogodô may be further compared to the Holy Sacrament through an examination of its arrangement on the altar. Occupying the highest part of the altar, it is kept inside a small oratory reminiscent of the tabernacle in Catholic churches, while the stones of other orixás repose directly upon the steps to the altar that, it should be noted, does not include statues of saints.

Bilina makes further comparisons to explain the cult of the dead:

"Iguê is a prayer for the dead. All the souls are present. No one goes out into the yard because it is haunted. They can be seen by they don't spook us. They are all around. Don't we pray for the dead during Lent? Aren't all those souls guided by prayers? Well, that's how it is on the day of Iguê. And that's how it is in the choro (another funeral rite), too. (. . .) We pray and asking for Church services helps, too." (Bilina)

Explaining the ritual of aggregation to the cult group, she says: "Being baptized in the Brotherhood is the same as being baptized in church. Only when you are ready for baptism can you enter the sanctuary. (. . .) We baptize, we give out necklaces (of the orixás) and a candle."

Thus, as she explains her religion, in addition to marking its differences from the Toré, the mãe-de-santo's discourse assumes that her interlocutor is knowledgeable about Catholicism and uses that knowledge as a reference to make her religion (which is other) intelligible. This other (which came from Africa and is presented as "pure Nagô," not accepting of mixture with Toré or Umbanda) not only admits mixture with the Catholic Church but, in so doing, puts itself in a position of reverence, if not of subaltern-ness.

"Our devotion was taught to us by God and by Santa Barbara, because Santa Barbara (who belongs to Xangô) is loved and revered by the Holy Trinity, and alludes to the myth of Santa Barbara who is thus transformed into a Nagô myth of origin.

Santa Barbara (Iansã) was a young virgin, the daughter of São Jerônimo (Xangô). As a father, he wanted to bend her to his will. He wanted to harm to her [to deflower her]. She ran somewhere to hide and he ran after her with a sword to hurt her. He was angry with her because she was a spinster. Later on, he was punished. A storm came and he took shelter under the trees and the lightning. The thunderbolt came and broke his leg. The vultures flew over him to catch him but she wouldn't allow it. He was saved. And it was she who saved him. Now he is a saint." (Bilina)

Pointing to a lithograph of Saint Barbara that hangs on the wall, she concludes:

"São Jerônimo is that sword she holds in her hand. He only wanted to hurt to her. She suffered a great deal with that sword. That sword is São Jerônimo. Santa Barbara is beloved and revered by the three people in the Holy Trinity, and so they allowed her to control storms. And to whom did Our Lord give the chalice? Is that not Santa Barbara holding the chalice? The chalice does not belong to the host. It is proof that Santa Barbara is beloved and venerated by Our Lord. He also gave her the palm from Palm Sunday. It is her palm; it is the one we have here [Bilina points to the *mariô*]. Yes, Santa Barbara is loved. She is loved and revered by Our Lord and by the Holy Trinity."[14]

This reverence in "mixing" with the dominant religion is also apparent in ritual. The *terreiro* possesses a ritual calendar ruled by the cycle of the harvesting of the yam. But rituals permitted by the African-based agrarian calendar are suspended during Lent (a period stipulated by the Catholic calendar), as are all consultations with the *orixás*. The *mãe-de-santo*'s explanation for the fact is as follows:

"We cannot celebrate during Lent. It is the time of the suffering of Jesus Christ. The saints of the Church are all covered in purple and we who are devoted to Santa Barbara are not about to enjoy ourselves. Singing during Lent calls forth Satan."

Catholic influence upon supposedly African rituals is further exemplified by animal sacrifice (which is a nuclear element of Xangô). In explaining them, the *mãe-de-santo* says: "Before killing a ram, one must ask Our Lord's permission, for he is the Lamb of God."

In referring to funeral rites, during which the dead are summoned, she says:

"We invoke the spirit of the deceased at a crossroads, taking with us a rooster, a bowl, a needle and a thimble. The bowl is used by the deceased so they may account to Our Lord for all they have done in the world. If they behaved badly, Jesus Christ won't save them." (Bilina)

The comparison between the Catholic Church and Xangô could be used to verify to what degree the religious group's belief system is a re-production or an alternative form of the dominant religion. There seems to be a certain ambiguity with regard to this issue, but what is of interest to us in this case, above all else, is a verification of the outlines of "purity" and "mixture" and the logic that rules them.

THE LOGIC OF THE "PURE" AND THE "MIXED"

In this context, as an emic category, the term "mixture" indicates the connection of religious forms that are considered different. It is by recog-nizing the Catholic Church as "other" that the Nagô admits to "mixture" with it while strongly rejecting "mixture" with other religions. Thus, one arrives at a structure that allows for certain combinations[15] even as it re-jects others. Moreover, the structure presented as "pure" admits contain-ing certain "mixtures" that would not, however, affect its original purity, while others would distort it, bringing about anarchy and impurity.

Schematically, the combinations and results may be represented thus: Given that:

A = Pure Nagô
B = Catholicism
C = Toré, Umbanda, Malê, Protestantism
it follows that

ELEMENTS	TYPES OF COMBINATION	RESULTS
A + B	Permissible	Does not change "purity"
A + C	Forbidden	Transforms "pure" into "mixed"

If not a need to rethink and relativize the opposition between "pure" and "mixed" conceived as a pair of opposites, this at least implies an at-tempt to clarify the logic of the adulteration of purity. Within this context, loss of purity does not result simply from combinations of different things but from certain types of combinations, allowing us to conclude that the very notion of "mixture" is culturally defined and the product of certain perceptions.

It should be emphasized that "mixture" with the Catholic Church permeates not only rituals but certain aspects of Xangô's belief system. It is by recurring to myths about Catholic saints that one explains the origin of the Nagô religion; Catholic baptism is given as a prerequisite for entering the group; rites that, in accordance with the calendar of yam harvesting, would be permitted are instead suspended for reasons that stem from the Catholic liturgical calendar; furthermore, if not completely substituted, the African idea of *força* at least coexists with the dualism of Good/Evil. However, this combination does not bring about the degeneration of "Nagô purity." The authenticity of African tradition is not threatened by it, although it would be if it "mixed" with Toré and Umbanda, notwithstanding that, according to the set of ritual traits (possession, animal sacrifice, the use of drums, dances, etc.), these religious manifestations more formally resemble Xangô than the Catholic religion. In this case, mixture with resemblance would be abominated and with those different from one would be accepted, thus inverting dominant ideas about hybrids, according to which crossbreeding between very different forms would be more degenerative, resulting in disharmonious (and therefore less desirable) hybrids.[16]

The logic of purity and mixture initially observed in the animal kingdom and later extended to man (viewed as a representative of "pure or mixed races" and as a culture bearer — the latter also classified according to criteria of purity, authenticity, and legitimate tradition by opposition to mixture, non-authenticity, and tradition adulterated) suffered an inversion or, to be more precise, a new formulation in this transposition to cults, insofar as the mixture of Nagô with the Catholic religion does not transform Nagô into a better hybrid, but is simply presented as not affecting its original purity.

It seems to me, however, that this inversion is apparent, and may be seen when religions are analyzed according to their external formal differences and resemblances. In the Nagô *terreiro*, the ruling logic of the "pure" versus "mixed" opposition would instead be related to the dualist principle that regulates the division of the world into realms of Good and Evil.

To return to some of the ideas proposed at the beginning of this chapter, I shall attempt here to expand them in order to demonstrate that the combinations permissible to the Nagô are restricted to what they perceive as belonging to the realm of Goodness. So it is that the mythical history of Nagôs and Malês in Laranjeiras, once presented as a victory of Goodnesss over Evil, relived and updated in the ritual of the Chegança, situates Nagôs and Christians within the same field—that of Goodness—in opposition to Malês and Moors, who are situated in the realm of Evil.

With regard to the present, from the Nagô perspective, the structuring of the religious field takes place according to concrete forms of religious agencies that exist in the city today and are also ordered according to the axis of Good and Evil. The latter separates Catholics from Protestants (expressions of the Chegança's Nagô-Christians) and the Nagô of Toré and Umbanda, as may be observed below:

	GOOD	EVIL	
Past	Nagô	Malê	Opposition attributed by the history of the two groups in the city
	Christians	Moors	Opposition expressed in the ritual of Chegança which recalls an event from the past
Present	Nagô Catholicism	Toré-Umbanda Protestantism	Oppositions expressed in the relationship between current religious forms

Historically, the alliances and combinations permissible to the Nagô occur among the elements aligned in the first column, in which Catholicism and Nagô stand side by side, dividing the realm of Goodness between them and thus establishing themselves—in spite of their differences—as elements of the same nature. "Mixture" or hybridity is, by definition, that which "participates in two natures" and in which, as a result, "the confusion of the same and the other is inscribed," the result of which is "an ontological scandal" (Aron, in Poliakov, 1975: 179). If Nagô and Catholicism belong to the same nature because they divide the realm of Goodness between them, then Malê, Toré, Umbanda, and Protestantism (who share the realm of Evil) belong to a different nature.

So that: to "mix" with Catholicism is to produce a combination that does not affect the binary scheme of world classification, inasmuch as this combination occurs within the same realm—that of Goodness—and does not alter the general order of the world. On the contrary, to "mix" with Toré, Umbanda, and other elements classified as belonging to the opposite realm would mean making a combination that, by crossing the boundaries between Good and Evil, would engender confusion and anarchy, damages attributed to hybridity, metaphorically expressed in the breaking of "Nagô purity" and the establishment of the category of the "mixed."

Mary Douglas has shown how the idea of purity is often employed as an analogy for the social order, and how the classificatory pairs "pure/mixed," "pure/impure," "clean/dirty," "order/anarchy" are articulated with the idea of power (Douglas, 1976). From this perspective, the "pure/impure" dichotomy is not only a form of classifying and marking differences but is also (and perhaps above all else) this: a form of marking a place for oneself and others within the schematic set of society's symbolic forces. So it is that the corruption of "purity" does not stem simply from "mixture," but from a given type of "mixture." Impurity and degeneration come from "mixture" with forms socially defined as inferior. The outline of Nagô purity thus follows the lines of that which is structurally dominant and dominated. Although "mixing" with things superior cannot sully African purity, "mixture" with subaltern cults—albeit ones that are apparently similar to them—represents a process of degeneration.

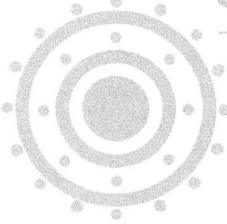

CHAPTER FOUR

The Construction and Meaning of "Nagô Purity"

DIFFERENT FEATURES OF "PURE NAGÔ"

In this chapter, I return to certainly previously stated ideas, to differences in the features of Nagô purity as conceived within the Laranjeiras *terreiro* and in the "pure Nagô" Candomblé *terreiros* of Bahia.

Because the ideology of purity presupposes the existence of an original state, a sort of cultural sanctuary protected from the deforming influences of foreign elements, one might expect the *terreiros* that identify themselves as Nagô and that surely had common origins and a common cultural heritage to define their purity according to a common set of cultural traits. If the original stock of symbolic goods is the same and if the continuity of tradition and fidelity to Africa is the mark of the "pure," it follows that purity should have the same features.

However, we have seen that, by resorting to cultural traits in order to mark the distinction and purity of her *terreiro*, the Nagô *mãe-de-santo* from Laranjeiras presents "baptism"— the rite of aggregation to the group — as a basic characteristic of Nagô and one of its fundamental differences in opposition to the Toré's *feitorio de santo*. In "baptism," demonstration of Africa's purity is based, above all else, on an absence of certain features (the initiate's reclusion, head-shaving and the blood-letting of animals over the head), features she regards as not African in origin but, rather, imported from Bahia and accepted by the local Torés. It should be noted that all such features are part of the *feitorio de santo*, invariably presented by scholars of Bahia's candomblé as a sign of African orthodoxy in the poorest and most traditional Nagô *terreiros* (Rodrigues, 1935: 75–78; Carneiro, 1967c: 115–21; Bastide, 1978). In contrast, a reduction in reclusion time (or its nonexistence) indicates distance from the "pure Nagô" model, and *terreiros* that proceed thusly are classified as distorted or *caboclo*.

Also at the level of cultural features—as a result of which a *terreiro*'s "purity" is internally defined—other differences may be added to further describe this purity. In Laranjeiras, the elongated drums of Bahia's traditional, more Africanized *terreiros* are regarded as distortions of the true

Nagô, whose drums are barrel-shaped. Similarly, instead of the white ritual garb thought to be typical of traditional Nagô, colorful costumes that symbolically reproduce the colors of the *orixás* and help to compose the visual spectacle of Bahian *terreiros* are presented as another example of inaccuracy, as is the presence of a house for Exu, a constant in Bahia's "pure Nagô" *terreiros*, considered one of the necessary elements for reproducing an African village in Brazil (Bastide, 1978: 71); in Laranjeiras, the presence of such a house is seen as one of the signs of African tradition, a characteristic of the *Toré*.

Thus, it may be seen that the repertory of cultural features invoked to attest to African purity and fidelity to Nagô tradition in Laranjeiras is different from that which makes up the Nagô model in Bahia. It should be noted that the phenomenon is not unique to this *terreiro*. It also occurs among the Afro-Brazilian segment of Aracaju where, according to Agamenon de Oliveira, Candomblé with *"feitorio de santo"* was introduced in the 1930s as a counterpart to other, established traditions, including Nagô (Oliveira, 1978).[1] This is not restricted to Sergipe and is also repeated in the state of Pernambuco. According to Waldemir Caldeira Araújo, the "Nagô nation" of Recife is very different from the "Nagô nation" of Bahia. In fact, sect members in Recife regard Bahian Nagô as Keto or Angola, and never as a "Nagô nation"; Araújo adds that certain diacritical signs that identify "pure Nagô" in Bahia are considered Bahian "inventions" in Recife (Araújo, 1977: 139). In referring to the *terreiros* of Recife, Roger Bastide has also noted that the Nagô calendar, considered there as Africanized, "applies to the Yoruba of Pernambuco rather than to those of Bahia," where it is also found, "although in Bantu Candomblé temples preferentially, for they are more permeable to the influence of the outside world" (Bastide, 1978: 86), that is to say: that which is held to be "pure Nagô" in Pernambuco is regarded as part of the "mixed Bantu" repertory in Bahia.

It could be argued that such dissimilarities stem from ethnic differences within the original black groups whose cultural traditions were already diverse even in Africa. But it is worth emphasizing that I am comparing *terreiros* that self-define as Nagô and claim continuity to the same original repertory of African traditions.

The result of this is that "Nagô purity" possesses different features in Bahia, in Pernambuco and in Sergipe. Moreover, it means that the same repertory of cultural features has different connotations in different places, both in terms of origin and in terms of meaning, being used as signs of purity in one place and as signs of mixture with *Toré* in another. This shows how cultural continuity and proclaimed fidelity to an original legacy—they consider themselves to be descendants of the original Nagô, like those of Bahia—do not account for "purity." In fact, studies on ethnicity—and the *terreiros* do closely resemble micro-ethnicities—have clearly shown that culture is not merely baggage that society carries with it and preserves as a whole. It is not a finished thing, but something that is emphasized in different ways to affirm identity and guarantee interests, constantly reinvented and invested with new meanings (Cohen, 1969; Cunha, 1977, 1979).

In an approach in which cultural features are not considered intrinsic proof of Africanness (the meaning of which would be determined by their origins) but as fragments of traditional culture clothed in new meanings, the genetic analysis of features that outline purity in itself has no meaning and may be used for various purposes. However, it is important to analyze the genesis of the ideology of Candomblé purity, the moment in which it appears, the way it is constituted, and the role of intellectuals in this construction.

It seems to me that, like ethnicity, "Nagô purity" is a native category used by *terreiros* to mark differences and express rivalries, which become underscored as the religious forms are organized as agencies in the competitive market of symbolic goods (Bourdieu, 1974).

In transforming this native category into an analytic one—a practice that began with Nina Rodrigues and was consolidated by an entire group of Bahian Candomblé scholars who were fond of Africanisms—anthropologists contributed (especially in Bahia, through construction of the Jeje-Nagô model, considered the "purest") to the crystallization of cultural features that came to be known as the highest expression of Africanness, through which the African would be represented. Neither these representations nor the anthropologists' relationships to their objects of study—the "purest" *terreiros* of which they became *ogãs* and intermediaries of the white world—were constituted independently from the social power structure.

Yvonne Velho draws our attention to the ideological determinations underlying the appreciation of Africa as indicative of prejudice against blacks:

> ". . . Calling these religions Afro concealed a fear of calling them black religions. African origin gave them a 'cleaner,' more 'aristocratic' nature. Africa is faraway, Africans are 'foreigners,' and that confers another status upon them." (Velho, 1975: 14)

Referring to mid-1930s Bahia, Ruth Landes observes that the local middle class used the word "blacks" to indicate merely "the hard-working, poorly paid people who were distinguishable by their dress and songs and other unusual characteristics. They never mean merely people of a certain skin color, and in fact they usually say 'Africans' or 'Afro-Bahians' rather than 'Negro,' which is felt to be insulting" (Landes, 1947: 16).

Actually, it is the transition from "African" (a foreigner with different and exotic customs) to "black" (a dark-skinned Brazilian) that creates problems. It may have been the difficulty in making this transition, with its underlying ideological assumptions, that led authors such as Nina Rodrigues and Artur Ramos to use the (at least apparently) contradictory double model: the evolutionist perspective that required black dilution into whiteness as a condition for progress and the glorification of primitive African purity (Rodrigues, 1935, 1977; Ramos, 1951, 1961).

From this perspective, appreciation of Africa would be an attempt to conceal prejudice against blacks, hiding behind the cloak of glorifying Africa and, thus, making it harder to fight, which would ultimately result in a tactics of domination. Seen thus, the glorification of Africa would be the counterpart (in cultural terms) of the myth of racial democracy, and would have the same controlling function. It seems significant to me that the glorification of African purity—and of Nagô tradition especially—as outlined by Rodrigues at the end of the nineteenth century becomes vigorous in the 1930s, when the move to a "scientific" legitimizing of racial democracy takes place. Thus, I shall attempt to track the development and meaning of this line of thought in connection with a "return to Africa," a back-to-the-roots movement that takes place in the most traditional and glorified Nagô *terreiros* of Recife (and especially of Bahia) during the 1930s, seeking to relate it, on one hand, to the myth of racial democracy and, on the other, to regionalism.

AFRICA AND NORTHEASTERN REGIONALISM

We have drawn attention to the fact that culture was used in the 1930s to make up a cultural nationalism, a modality of vertical integration that superimposed itself on classes, ethnicities, and other forms of intermediate identification, attempting to eliminate differences and highlighting the solidarity expressed by a common cultural heritage. In analyzing the ideological character of "Brazilian culture," Carlos Guilherme da Mota has noted how this concept and its equivalents ("Brazilian civilization," "national culture," etc.) were used to "curb manifestations that extrapolate the interests of the dominant class" and how, in the 1930s (and specifically in the work of Gilberto Freyre), the national and the regional overlap, movement from one to the other taking place without any discussion of mediations, for the "regional" is still "national" (Mota, 1977: 17–73).

Black heritage plays an important part in the construction of this cultural nationalism:

> "It was as if—by following the 'modernist' literary movements which had sought to discover Brazilian originality and cut the umbilical cord from Europe—Brazil had suddenly become aware of the value of cultural features that came from Africa." (Bastide, 1975: 5)

Thus, whereas the glorification of black culture was used to create a national culture, the glorification of things African and, specifically, of Nagô, served to mark regional differences, for it was in the Northeast (and particularly in Bahia) that Africanisms were thought to have been most faithfully preserved. There, as the purest (and in some cases most superior) African tradition, Nagô emerges with a very special meaning, at least since the end of the nineteenth century. Thus, we must return to the period in which the study of black religions begins, even as regionalism appears more emphatically as a theme and the elites used the popular as a distinctive element of local or regional specificities, in their necessary dialogue with the central power, appropriating "ideas of place" to formulate their interests through them and present them as though they were the problems of the region (Almeida, 1977).

Nina Rodrigues (1862–1906) is considered by many to be the forerunner of scientific black studies in Brazil.[2] As a pathologist, his preoccupation with blacks and, particularly, with black religions, is part of a wider frame of reference that is the investigation of Brazilian society, giving it a "certain order and prescribing [practices of social control] based on scientific assumptions" (Correa, 1982).[3]

Unlike abolitionists who emphasized black "humanity" and "equality," Rodrigues was concerned with "deducing general laws and sociological principles" regarding the mental and cultural evolution of societies (Rodrigues, 1935: 21). Considering that, among collective spiritual constructions, language and religion "provide a surer measure of the mental situation of each people" (1977: 121), he analyzed religious sentiment as it is "revealed and survives in the blacks" and in the search for the "African phylogenesis of our fetishism" (1935: 21) as further data with which to prove his basic theory regarding the innate inferiority of blacks and, consequently, the mistake of abolitionists and legislators who considered him equal to the white man.

In analyzing black cultural practice as a doctor who was especially interested in the pathological aspects of *mestiçagem* (or "hybridity"), he feels the need to justify himself, for miscegenation did not "free [us] from an obligation to study the black influence in Brazil (. . .), to collect elements that might lead to a dependable analysis, or to think as men of science and as patriots about correctives with which to oppose the possible negative consequences of such a situation" (Rodrigues, 1977: 7).

With concerns such as these, Rodrigues attempts a quick overview of the past, present and future of Brazilian blacks and *mestiços*, a diachronics underlying the idea that knowledge regarding the social value of Africans and their descendants is a fact to be used in analyzing the country's future.

Convinced of the inferiority of the black race—considered a "product of the unequal march of humanity's phylogenetic development" (1977: 5)—Rodrigues nonetheless admitted differences in ability and degrees of culture between blacks and, after introducing a set of African peoples who came to Brazil, he concludes that the ones introduced here "did not belong exclusively to the most underdeveloped, brutal and savage African peoples," seeing as how white Hamites converted to Islam were also introduced along with the most advanced peoples. Among these were the Nagô, whose predominance and influence in Bahia were evinced not only by language (which became the black *lingua franca*) as by religion.

Using evolutionist models, Rodrigues sought to demonstrate that Nagô religion was superior to that of other Africans, a superiority that affirmed itself not only with regard to the Bantu—who composed above all the black population of the South—but also with regard to the Sudanese who settled in the Northeast. Among these, the most "backward religion was that of the Tshi, the most advanced that of the Nagô, and the most intermediate that of the Jejes" (1977: 230). This Nagô superiority expressed in mythology, in the existence of priesthood and organized religion, not to mention numeric superiority, explained the Nagô's hegemony over the other Africans in Bahia who adopted Yoruban beliefs and cults as intrusions of Jeje. Hence the reason why "Jeje-Nagô rather than purely Jeje mythology prevails in Brazil" (1977: 231).

According to Rodrigues, this cultural superiority of the Nagô should have an equivalent substratum of biological-racial superiority with regard to the other Africans. It was not without reason that, half a century after the slave trade was extinguished, the only organized cult that remained in Bahia was the Nagô, since the Islamism introduced by whites or *mestiço* Hamites and spread among the superior Nagô was being extinguished (1935: 28).

Based on a difference established by blacks themselves (between "people from the Coast [of Africa]" and "people from Brazil"), the author highlights a distinction between the beliefs and religious practices of creoles and Africans. Rodrigues says that the latter, gathered in "colonies and language-based groups," preserved their unmodified fetishist practices, and Catholicism suffered but a juxtaposition with regard to them.

Creole blacks and *mestiços* "of African parentage grew apart from their families because they could not speak their language, and were assimilated by [Bahia's] other, mixed, heterogeneous population. The primitive purity of fetishist practices and African mythology thus *degenerated*, to be gradually forgotten and *bastardized*, and the fetishist worship of *orixás* was replaced by the worship of Catholic saints" (Rodrigues, 1935: 170, my italics).

Thus, the fusion of beliefs was ambiguous, for even as it became a mechanism for a black appropriation of the Catholic religion (presented by the author as superior),[4] it made way for a degeneration of the Nagô religion's primitive purity, elevating it to the condition of a superior African religion, preserved, above all, in Bahia.

It must not be forgotten that Rodrigues was born in the state of Maranhão, although his education and professional activity took place largely in Bahia, a province that stood out in colonial times in terms of economic, political-administrative, and cultural activities and one that, from the Republic onward, saw itself reduced to being a state of lesser importance, one that, furthermore, contained a large black population, perhaps the largest in Brazil. What to make of its destiny, when the "black race" was seen as the cause of Brazilian inferiority? This disturbing question, which affected the nation as a whole, must have been even more disturbing for Bahians, and the solution presented by Rodrigues (a self-proclaimed racist) was rather soothing; black Bahians were descended from the Sudanese, the most highly developed Africans, some of whom were even of mixed (white) Hamitic blood. The Sudanese exclusivity of blacks in Bahia declared by Rodrigues, later relativized by his culturalist disciples who discovered many Bantu "survivals" in it, appears to me to be significant.

In short, by clearly preaching the inferiority of the "black race" in a region that contained a high percentage of blacks, while presenting Bahia's black population as having descended from the Nagô, biologically and culturally superior to other Africans, Rodrigues was attempting to soften the pessimism that resulted from his analysis and claims regarding the innate inferiority of blacks.

To my way of seeing, this attempt to redeem black Bahia through Sudanese exclusivism and the preeminence of Nagô was another way of distinguishing it from southern Brazil, the black population of which was considered to be of Bantu origin and quite inferior from Nina Rodrigues's perspective, although its nefarious influence was counterbalanced by the strong presence of superior whites and, especially, of European immigrants, thus possibly explaining the progress of the South, now transformed into the country's dynamic center.

Although use of the symbolic as an explanation for regional differences is not explicit in Rodrigues, it appears to me that he cleared the brush for the path that would later be traveled by his disciples and other anthropologists who eventually transformed Nagô into a distinctive symbol of Bahia and made the purest African influence an identifying element of the Northeast. This stance is more or less outlined in Artur Ramos and is particularly emphasized in Gilberto Freyre.

Artur Ramos (1903–1949) may be the best-known name in Brazilian black studies. Above all, this may be due to the number of works he published during the 1930s and 1940s, a period during which race, as a model for interpreting the development of societies, was rejected at the level of discourse and gave way to culture. At least in the Northeast his influence was impressive. Without recourse to Bahia's cult of Rodrigues — a cult Ramos himself helped to nurture — the facilities of a much wider dissemination of his countless works (some of which ran to several editions) also stood in Ramos's favor.[5]

Proclaiming himself a disciple of Rodrigues, Ramos declared his aim to reinterpret the master's work, ridding it of erroneous racial interpretations, which he proposed to replace with culture. However, he was unable to move beyond the evolutionist perspective that initially marked his entire work, during the stage in which he made explicit use of psychoanalysis and "pre-logicism," by clearly formulating a "gradual, unilateral and universal uniform evolution," and later, in a more discreet, nuanced manner, or (in his own words) by considering Rodrigues's work "within its respective cultural structures" (1951: 365).

To Artur Ramos, praise of Nagô superiority and the purity of its religious forms contrasts with an evolutionary, Comtean view that the Brazilian transformation of African fetishism into polytheism was a sign of the "perfecting" of inferior religious forms (Ramos, 1951: 130). If, with regard to his scale of syncretisms (which goes from Jeje-Nagô to Jeje-Nagô-Malê-Bantu-*caboclo*-spiritist-Catholic-theosophical), the author explicitly admitted the impossibility of "establishing categories of chronological anteriority and syncretic importance" (1961: 142, v. 3), it would, in fact, appear throughout his work associated to a discourse of praise that refers not only to different African ethnicities, but to black religious practices in Brazil. For example: in characterizing African ethnicities, he uses features that elevate the Nagô to the apex of the scale, while the Bantu are situated well below this. Thus, the Nagô "were tall, big-boned, brave, hardworking, good-natured and the most *intelligent* of all," while "Angolans were physically weaker than the Sudanese. Loquacious and indolent, they were quite festive" (1971: 36–37, my italics).

Bahia benefits from this distribution of superior and inferior blacks, for "the best blacks, Sudanese *aristocrats*, remained in Bahia" (1971: 4, my italics).

In this manner, Ramos, who rejected a race-based interpretation of society, eventually allows his racism to filter through both when he classifies blacks according to degrees of intelligence apparently associated with physical characteristics and according to an elitist stance that classifies Sudanese Africans (a linguistic group that included the Nagô), coincidentally the most intelligent blacks, as aristocratic.

Parallel to this, black cults ranged from "the purest forms" of certain Bahian *terreiros* that safeguard legitimate Sudanese tradition to the most unforeseen alterations of Rio de Janeiro macumba, which originated with the Bantu, the "least interesting of these religious survivals, such is their degree of dilution, their swift transformation upon contact with coastal civilization" (1971: 104). Thus, Ramos, who studied black cults in the Northeast and in Rio de Janeiro, is more explicit in establishing that opposition and in using it as a distinctive regional sign.

For Gilberto Freyre, regionalism is a constant, explicit concern, although he calls upon *mestiçagem* rather than "African purity" in order to make a distinction that is both regional and national. As early as 1926, he wrote: "For this is Brazil: combination, fusion, mixture. And the Northeast may be the principal cauldron in which these combinations, this fusion, these mixtures of blood and values have been processed: Portuguese, Indians, Spaniards, French, Africans, Dutch, Jews, English, Germans, and Italians" (Freyre, 1976: 67).

From this perspective, he is interested in the ingredients of the mixture and their proportion in making up the different pieces represented by regions. In the Northeast, the African ingredient had been quite strong, especially on the coast, and principally in Bahia, where African qualities were most highly praised.

In juxtaposing the "melancholy, quiet, sly and even gloomy populations of the extreme Northeast, especially of the *sertões* [or backlands] with the communicative joy of the Bahians (. . .), their humor, their spontaneity, their courtesy, their honest, contagious laughter," he underscores the positive contribution of "African extroversion" in opposition to "Indian introversion" (Freyre, 1964: 402). If this is praise of the African as a whole, elsewhere he highlights the specificity of Bahia's black population, "shot through not only by the best blood which the slave trade brought to America but by the highest culture it transmitted from Africa to the American continent . . . ," and by virtue of which it became, "during the monarchy, the mother of most of the council presidents and ministers of State" (Freyre, 1968: 660).

Attributing great importance in the explanation of society and of psychological types to black roots—according to a scale of degrees of ethnic and cultural development—the author winds up explaining differences between the "Dionysian" Bahians and natives of Pernambuco who more closely resembled natives of São Paulo, differences that might also be explained by the origins of the African blacks.

In comparing Bahia's black population with that of Pernambuco, the latter is at a disadvantage, for

" . . . African colonization of the extreme Northeast was not as
sophisticated—neither from the European point of view of
aesthetics, nor from that of moral and material culture—as that
of the Sudanese, who enhanced and enriched Bahia (and urban
Bahia especially) in a very special way. But it was dominated by a
strong and malleable type of black, albeit one who was inferior to
the Sudanese in height, in the fineness of his physical features
and in cultural elements." (Freyre, 1967: 130)

Pernambuco blacks were almost predominantly Bantu, nearly always imported to satisfy the demands of farming and industry that required the "physical vigor [of the] laborer," whereas in Bahia they also satisfied "aesthetic and amorous desires" (1967: 129). In short, Pernambuco blacks were physically strong, well endowed for hard labor, while those of Bahia more closely resembled whites, not only in culture but also in beauty. This sounds a lot like the discourse of Rodrigues and so we may see how, in speaking of Bahia, detractors of the black race (or their apologists) appeal to a laudatory discourse that always presents the origins of

Bahian blacks as being related to those of the superior African blacks who, along with fidelity to African religious models, will be presented as their differential marks.

Nonetheless, these differences in the original contingent of blacks who settled in the various northeastern states did not quite undo the region's cultural homogeneity, which of all regions was the one most influenced by Africa, an influence that "softened, sweetened and sentimentalized" northeastern and, by extension, Brazilian character, insofar as the Northeast is the true haven of nationality, where "values which for some time were merely subnational or even exotic were transformed into Brazilian values" (Freyre, 1976: 67).

It is interesting to observe that popular cultures have often been assimilated as sources of differentiating symbols not only for the region but also for the nation, because "in modern States, the legitimacy of power has been based on the idea of a people" (Almeida, 1977: 172).

What does it mean, though, to define a people according to blackness or, rather, according to Africanness, in order to establish northeastern distinction? In transforming the African into a regional or local symbol, would one not be imputing to him responsibility for the region's problems and underdevelopment? For as long as the primitive African was enslaved, the region had been rich. Now that he is a free laborer, a free citizen in Brazilian society, and, above all, in the northeastern region, that region pales in underdevelopment—a sign that, once they were freed, not even "superior African Blacks" were able to provide the region with the progress afforded by the work of European immigrants in the South.

It is symptomatic that the northeastern regionalism of the 1930s (intellectually propagated as ideological expression by the dominant classes) is based on the power of tradition.[6]

We must pause here for a brief analysis of how Freyre works with the opposite pairs of purity versus mixture and tradition versus modernity and how they eventually overlap in his analyses. Freyre does not glorify African purity in itself, inasmuch as mixture is the key element of his explanatory model, which is based upon racial and cultural interpenetration as complementary conditions and a balance of the different ethnic groups that make up the Brazilian nation. Running parallel to this idea of mixture and cultural encounter that would characterize Brazil, though, is another idea—the opposition between past and present, in which the past is idealized through tradition and the present is seen as a form of decadence and distortion of the past's pure and authentic forms. Insofar as mixture is, par excellence, a mechanism that breaks the purity of the past, mixture, which played a crucial role in the making of Brazilian culture in the past, transforms itself in the present into a deleteriously influential element that may corrupt and degenerate the authenticity of the cultural product. Hence the insistent preaching by the "regionalist movement, [which was] traditionalist and modernist in its own way," of a love of tradition which, in the case of Xangô, eventually alluded to Africa. Although Freyre never devoted himself to its systematic study, it is significant that, in his expeditions to *terreiros*, he privileged the ones known for their Nagô orthodoxy, that is to say the most traditional, the "purest" ones, such as those of Pai Anselmo or Pai Adão to which he refers in his work (Freyre, 1959: 185–86; 1964: 435, 547, 648, 671; 1968: 649). Realizing that Brazilian religious traditions had resisted de-Africanization more than "the blood, color and features of men," he concludes that "the substance of African culture shall remain within us throughout [the whole of] our evolution and consolidation as a nation" (Freyre, 1968: 650). From this perspective, the northeastern region would be Africa's haven. In this way, the regionalism that arose as a reaction to socioeconomic transformations which began during the late nineteenth century, representing the dimension of endangered rural aristocratic power (Ortiz, 1980b: 13), by inserting the glorification of Africa and its traditions as an element of the cult to the past would have the ideological function of justifying the region's problems through the high concentration of blacks, or rather, of Africans, in the composition of the people.

Therefore, the responsibility of the local elites and of social structures marked by profound inequalities is exempted, and the region's underdevelopment is explained through ethnic composition.

If, on one hand, glorification of African purity served to justify regional differences, on the other hand it might be regarded as a strategy for the domination of blacks.

THE GLORIFICATION OF NAGÔ AND "CULTURAL DEMOCRACY"

"Nagô purity" having been elevated by intellectuals to the status of a local or regional diacritical sign, one might inquire as to the role played by the elites in the later development of the religions and their possible "domestication" (Fry, 1977a). The 1930s (the period in which the myth of racial democracy was "scientifically" formulated) seem fertile in this respect. Maria A. Brandão signals a coincidence between this fact and " . . . the development of an ethnocentric intolerance against the practices of black culture, later leading to their contemporary folklorization. Additionally, the earliest scholarly statements of the myth also coincide with the suspicion and suppression of black movements from that moment on" (Brandão, 1979: 31).

Repression against Afro-Brazilian cults is recorded in several northeastern states during the 1930s.[7] In Bahia and in Pernambuco, it is known that *terreiros* were persecuted in the name of fighting communists, and it would be interesting to see to what point the movements of the left penetrated northeastern Candomblé during this period in which Brazilian Communist Party activities resulted in riots that affected certain states in that region.[8]

However, there were other reasons for repression against cults, especially a need to control blacks who might use cultural difference (as expressed, above all, in religion) to improve their socioeconomic situation and alter longstanding relations of power. But if potentially dangerous "racial" differences were being harmoniously domesticated by "racial democracy," why not consider a cultural democracy in which black cultural manifestations could be practiced without police repression and, simultaneously, without danger to the dominants?

It should be noted that the 1930s were a particularly fertile period for appropriations by the dominants of subaltern cultural manifestations. Carnival, Samba Schools, popular music (samba in particular), and Umbanda are submitted to a process of symbolic control, recoded and reutilized in another circuit of significations (Oliven 1981). To this we might add the manipulation of dances and popular performances that, under the name of folk amusements, are also selected and presented as elements of a national culture, from a perspective in which the nation appears as the meeting place of opposite pairs in which differences are balanced and harmonious.

Eduardo Diatahy Menezes suggests the existence of three different phases in this process of appropriation of subaltern cultural manifestations by hegemonic culture. The first phase is the initial *rejection,* the moment in which popular culture is regarded as a "misdemeanor" or as "disorder" and thus repressed by the police. This is followed by the *domestication* undertaken by the scientific apparatus of the dominant class, in which, through records, conceptualizations, typologies, theories, and methods, intellectuals establish boundaries between dangerous elements and figurative or merely exotic ones. These elements not only come to be prized but, in a third stage—that of *recovery,* through the si-

multaneous action of the ideological apparatuses and the cultural industry transformed into merchandise—become instruments of pedagogical
indoctrination (Menezes, 1980).

Evidently, such mechanisms do not simultaneously affect working
class culture as a whole, operating through selection and, within certain
historical contexts, appearing to act more intensely than in others. In
this movement of hegemonic culture with regard to subaltern culture,
quite visible during the 1930s and, it would seem, making a selection of
popular culture that closely follows ethnic (or, more precisely, black) cultural outlines (Samba, Umbanda, Samba school, etc.), the "appreciation
of Africa" and of "Nagô purity" is inscribed as a form of controlling black
religiosity and, more specifically, Candomblé.

Selecting African purity from Afro-Brazilian religions to elect it as a
specific field of study and criterion by which to evaluate cults, intellectuals played a significant role in the procedures followed by the repression
and legitimizing of Candomblé. It is worth examining how academically
generated scientific discourse on Afro-Brazlian religions confronts the
law, in whose name the religions were repressed. However, it is once more
necessary to invoke the late nineteenth century, the period in which this
discourse emerges, linked to as yet undifferentiated scientific activity,
and jointly producing Afro-Brazilian studies and concerns regarding the
creation of medical forensic institutes and asylums for the criminally insane, "tying up the elite's preoccupations with social control with a single
knot" (Correa, 1982).

THE CONFRONTATION BETWEEN LAW
AND SCIENCE: NINA RODRIGUES

It is interesting to note that the Criminal Code of 1830—the first one
wrought by the Brazilian state to replace the "repertory of unconnected
laws dictated in times remote" by the Portuguese state—did not include
the persecution of sorcerers. Although black religion was then considered
witchcraft, Brazilian legislators did not feel the need to control it through
general law as long as slavery existed. Freed and consequently (at least
at the level of discourse) subject to political and constitutional equality,
the Penal Code included an article in which black religions might be
criminalized, usually as witchcraft, along with other working class manifestations of religiosity, made potentially more dangerous because they
were followed by millions of free blacks.

The Penal Code of 1890 incriminated not only witch doctors but sorcerers, too, along with other categories such as mediums and fortune tellers.[9] Article 157 established penalties for whosoever ". . . practiced spiritism, magic and its spells, the use of talismans and fortune telling to arouse feelings of hatred or love, inculcating cures for illnesses curable or incurable, in short, to fascinate and subjugate public credulity" (one to six months of confinement to a cell, to be increased if the patient presents "temporary or permanent alteration of the psychic faculties" [in Barreto, 1972: 32]).

Although it does not allude to blacks (which would contradict the newly acquired citizenship and equality assured in the Constitution), the legal repression afforded by this article was an attempt to guarantee the dominants control over free blacks whose places of worship, located above all in cities, would become virtual centers of "danger" and "disorder." To judge by the frequency with which police persecution of Candomblé is reported in the late-nineteenth- and early-twentieth-century Salvador press, one is given the impression that dominant whites felt quite insecure with regard to the subaltern classes, and particularly with blacks who gathered in *terreiros*. The news reported by newspapers that were united in this repressive campaign,[10] and presented by one of them as "social hygiene propaganda," speaks of "African fetishism, which becomes more rooted in this soil with each passing day"; they speak, too, of the growing numbers of "houses in which it is practiced and the appearance of new *pais-de-terreiro*," some of which are called "*caboclo* candomblés." They accuse Candomblé priests and priestesses of exploiting those who "believe in their spells" and of driving defenseless young women into promiscuity and the most diverse "libertine customs." To orgies are added accusations of "a state of dementia stemming from (. . .) initiation into witchcraft," in a demonstration that the acts of sorcerers "enervate and brutalize the spirit of the people which, driven by superstition, can only degenerate rather than raising itself to the lofty destinies to which it is summoned" (Bahia newspapers, in Rodrigues, 1977: 239–250).

Rodrigues positions himself against police persecution of Candomblé, since he felt the persecution to be based on a penal code he considered anachronistic, inasmuch as it considered blacks and whites equally punishable without taking into consideration a "science" that pointed to the inferiority of non-white races. To him, this fact should have been one of the "modifiers of imputability," for blacks could not be judged in the same way as whites.

Thus, at the very moment in which blacks are freed, Rodrigues develops a "scientific" discourse that attempts to establish for him a new inferiority established in the name of "science." Based on "science," he will explain why persecution of cult groups is not only misguided but, in many cases, also illegal.

Drawing attention to the fact that frequent nationwide persecution by the press was proof of the scope of Jeje-Nagô religious practices in Brazil—practices that, having resisted the oppression of slave masters, Catholic conversion, and education, also resisted press campaigns and the violence of police repression—he declared that the religion would "persist as long as the slow evolution of the black race left behind the Negro, the current anthropological Negro" (Rodrigues, 1977: 246).

Regarding Rodrigues's belief in the inferiority black race, "a product of the unequal march of humanity's phylogenetic development" (1977: 5), in his opinion the practices that the police attempted to outlaw represented an expression of the collective spiritual constructions that corresponded to black mental evolution. Thus they were incapable of assimilating the abstract, superior religion of whites. Hence the misunderstanding, since the law considered equal what "Science" proved not only to be different but unequal by nature: blacks and whites.[11] In short, he felt that the attempt to "suffocate the religious beliefs of a race with the same ease with which one might disperse a casual gathering of bystanders" was naïve (1977: 245), concluding that police persecution of the Candomblé would reveal "only a rudimentary state of legal sense, directly applied to the inferior races who colonized Brazil and whose blood still runs hot and abundantly in many of the perpetrators of such violence" (1977: 247).

According to Rodrigues, the illegality of the persecutions did not stem only from the police's arbitrary and violent behavior toward *terreiros*; it also grew out of the fact that the police was infringing the Constitution, which, based on assumptions of equality, ensured freedom of religion to all religions. He argued that, according to studies made not only in Brazil but also in Africa, the Jeje-Nagô cult was "a true religion in which the purely fetishistic stage has been nearly overcome, having arrived at the root of outright polytheism" (1977: 246). As a religion, its practice was not criminal, since only magic was included in the Penal Code.

It is true that the organized cult of the Jeje-Nagôs was not the sole manifestation of black religiosity in Brazil, where the beliefs of the Bantu also persisted, occupying religious evolution's lowest level of "psychological stratification" in early-twentieth-century Brazil, which Rodrigues conceived as being formed by four "overlapping zones" in which race and religion were correlated:

a. official Catholicism or "Catholic monotheism," numerically insignificant but the most elevated of all;

b. popular Catholicism or "idolatry and Catholic mythology of professional saints," a large category that encompasses "*mestiço* whites and more intelligent, educated blacks";

c. "Jeje-Yoruban mythology, the black synthesis of superior animism" that, mixed with the Catholic saints, was experienced by Creole blacks;

d. the "narrow, unconverted fetishism of Africans from the most underdeveloped tribes, Indians, Creole blacks and *mestiços* of the same intellectual level." (1977: 215–16)

It is also true that Jeje-Nagô religious practices would disappear from Brazil, to be replaced by "psychic activities," among which the "curative, criminal activity of sorcery" was already in progress. Even in such cases, though, one would need to examine the psychology of witch-healings and, there, as in religion, science referred to the state of possession, for ". . . it contains the essence of all black religious practices; ultimately, such practices shall be reduced to possession because of the lack of organization imposed upon them by the new Brazilian social environment. As the facts will show, possession is at the irreducible core of sorcery and folk medicine, and of the false Christian practices in which African fetishist religions and others borrowed from the American Indians shall have to survive in the Brazilian population" (Rodrigues, 1977: 237).

Thus, witchcraft ambiguously appears as a stage prior to religion, as a degeneration of true religion. Possession is at the irreducible core of both conceptions, interpreted as hysteria and, therefore, as a pathological state. Consequently, the study of African religions overlaps with that of psychiatry, more specifically a psychiatry based on organicism, one in which hysteria was seen as the result of organic lesions. Thus, the attempted control of blacks (and, particularly, of their religions) was not a problem for the police but first and foremost a psychiatric-medical problem. What the Penal Code proposes to criminalize is, first and foremost, an abnormality, and thus control of blacks is established from within, through the categories of normal/abnormal, healthy/pathological.

In associating possession with psychological instability, emotional unbalance, or distance from normality, a line is drawn that separates blacks as ill and abnormal. In this gesture of division that separates normality from psychopathology, the domain of order is described according to a new discourse—that of medical science—associated with anthropology's discourse on race so as to exercise a more sophisticated control over blacks, one that no longer operates through law but through "Science." With this discourse, Rodrigues not only proposes a need for scientific control over certain social categories[12] but also emphasizes Jeje-Nagô as a special category within so-called Afro-Brazilian religions, establishing the dichotomy of Jeje-Nagô and the others and, thus, inaugurating studies that privilege Nagô and transform it as an analytic standard for the other cults. But this gesture is, simultaneously, one of inauguration and exclusion, for to assume that Jeje-Nagô is a true religion is to assume that others are not. In this way, religion and magic (analytic categories used by anthropology) will be appropriated and used "scientifically" during the 1930s by the followers of Nina Rodrigues in an attempt to focus on the practices of popular religiosity, the true and pure religion of the Nagô and the degenerate practices of witchcraft and magic of other working-class components. There is a similar reactivation of the interpretive theory of possession as a psychopathological phenomenon, the most extreme example of which occurs in Recife, where the local Xangôs would be studied in connection with the Serviço de Assistência a Psicopatas (literally, the Assistance to Psychopaths or Psychiatric Care Services).

DIALOGUE BETWEEN THE LAW AND SCIENCE: THE 1930s

The erosion of myths that preached the superiority of "white races" over "colored races" in the 1930s indicates that the discourse on black biological inferiority needed to be rethought and replaced or, at least, camouflaged, rendered less explicit. It also indicates that the "scientific" control attempted by Rodrigues was still not sufficiently strong and convincing to make legal control disappear.[13]

As established in 1932, the Penal Code retained articles that refer to quackery and magic, and thus the problem between science and law persisted and was thus restated by Câmara Cascudo at the 1934 Afro-Brazilian Congress in Recife:

"Before closing down *macumbas* and arresting *catimbozeiros*, thus making them martyrs of abnegation in the eyes of the people, we ought carefully to study their mechanism in order to countermand their evil, dissolute influence; a series of informative works might simplify the task for psychiatrists and criminalists." (Cascudo, 1937: 75)

Cults were once more regarded as a problem that oscillated between crime and abnormality.

The psychiatric interpretation of possession continued to be in force. It had been revised by Artur Ramos, who, disagreeing with Rodrigues's interpretation that viewed it as hysteria, would expand explanation to "a very complex phenomenon, linked to various morbid states" (Ramos, 1951: 244). He agreed, however, with the master's central idea: possession was a pathological phenomenon. But, whereas Rodrigues deterministically attributed such abnormality to race, Ramos removed it from the exclusive dominion of biology and regarded it as a predisposition that could develop or diminish under the influx of sociocultural stimuli.

Working at a time when the idea of race as an interpretive model for the development of peoples was not, if completely rejected by science, increasingly influenced by culture, Artur Ramos allies the latter concept to an evolutionist perspective that marks his entire work and treats its according to different methods.

Beginning with the duality between primitive pre-logical mentality and civilized, logical mentality, he arrives at the existence of the duality of cultural stages in literate societies, in which the persistence of pre-logical thinking among underdeveloped classes prevented them from having a "true culture." If this occurred in Europe, what of countries such as Brazil, "which were exposed to contemporary aborigines" and to the direct influence of African religions introduced by the slave trade? (Ramos, 1951: 32).

Like Rodrigues, he believed that these "primitive African" religions were at different stages of evolution and here the superior mythical forms absorbed the more underdeveloped ones. African fetishism, already modified today in Brazil in a vast polytheistic system, is the sign that when "inferior religions come into contact with a more advanced religious form [Catholicism], they perfect themselves" (Ramos, 1951: 10). But it would take time for these primitive forms to be elevated to superiority and it was felt that, in Brazil, "we still live in the grip of the world of magic, impermeable, in a way, to the influxes of true culture":

" . . . Our collective mentality is not prepared to understand the true concept of causality. It is impregnated with mystical, pre-logical elements, largely inherited from magic and from religion brought here from Africa." (1951: 353–55)

Recognizing our underdevelopment and attributing it largely to blacks, Ramos nonetheless declares:

"In my studies (in this essay) on 'collective representations' in the underdeveloped classes of the Brazilian population's religious sector, I have not fully endorsed as I have often repeated, postulates regarding the inferiority of blacks or their capacity for civilization. These collective representations exist in any culturally underdeveloped social type. It is a consequence of magical and pre-logical thinking independent of the anthropological-racial problem, because certain conditions of psychological regression may appear in any ethnic group in culturally underdeveloped agglomerations, society's poor classes, children, neurotic adults, in dreams, or in art. . . ." (Ramos, 1951: 27)

There was no reason for patriotism or for inferiority complexes, since exact knowledge of our "emotional substratum" "was the first step on the road to progress" and, through education, it would be possible to "get through to the [human] mass (. . .) and draw strength from its participation" and thus overcome primitivism.

In this perspective, he associated the installation of the Mental Health Service in Rio de Janeiro's schools to research in the "hills," in "*macumbas*" and in "centers of sorcery," and presented them as a "a wide-ranging hygiene and education project" (1951: 27). It was a positivist belief that science would not only reveal Brazil's evils, but would also serve to guide the state's actions in solving them.

Thus, in the name of psychology, intellectuals attempted to rid the cults of police control in order to submit them to "scientific" control. Now seemingly divested of biological-racist features, anthropology also continued to be part of this dialogue through the categories of religion and magic. They take on great importance in this dialogue between the law and science because they establish the boundaries between legality and illegality.

Once more taking up Rodrigues's maxim that Jeje-Nagô was a true religion, Ramos returns to Africa to demonstrate how religion and magic were unified but, in Brazil, under white pressure, the functions of sorcerer and religious agent became dissociated; thus, the *candomblés* (especially the more Africanized ones) concentrated on the religious activities related to *orixá* worship (Ramos, 1951: 163). The idea that the "purest" Candomblé was a religion above all in opposition to *Macumba, Catimbó,* etc. (all of which were dedicated to magic) would later be taken up again and developed by Roger Bastide.[14] But in the 1930s, under the influence of a return to the African and his cultural heritage, it was refined so as to guide intellectual study and practice, neither of which were limited to the mere observation, description, and interpretation of sects; at times they participated as *ogãs*,[15] and attempted to mediate relations with the police.

In Recife, this mediation between *terreiros* and the organs of repression was accomplished with the participation of intellectuals associated with the Mental Health Service, who would attempt a new approach based on the "purest" African traditions preserved in some *terreiros*.

The Case of Pernambuco

In Recife, intellectuals began to approach Afro-Brazilian cults and to study them in the first years of the 1930s on the initiative of psychiatrist Ulysses Pernambucano de Melo (1892–1943), a disciple of Rodrigues who proposed to continue the master's work in Recife, also taken up in Bahia by Ramos. He inspired the 1931 creation of the Mental Health Service (MHS), a division of the Assistance to Psychopaths of Pernambuco.[16] In 1932, at the Mental Health Service, under the supervision of Ulysses Pernambucano, his disciples (Pedro Cavalcanti, Gonçalves Fernandes, Cavalcante Borges, René Ribeiro, Waldemar Valente, and others), many of whom were psychiatrists, began to study local Afro-Brazilian cults as well as popular forms of spiritism and the black pantheist sect, different forms of religious expression in which possession was the common denominator (Lucena, 1978: 165). The Service's interest in studying trance-based religions was not a casual one. One of Ulysses Pernambucano's concerns was the "social face of psychiatry" and thus, alongside biological factors, he sought the "social" factors (living conditions, studies of the environment, *religious influences, fetishism*, etc.) that produced illness, which, once elucidated, "brought about solutions to current mental health problems" (Pernambucano, 1937: 257). On the other hand, it should be remembered that, according to Rodrigues's interpretation, which suited the scholars' medical-psychiatric background, possession was interpreted as a pathological syndrome.[17]

Thus, the MHS was also a study center where practitioners of Xangô were submitted to "rigorous observation" and "mental examinations" that proposed to establish a "scientific control" of cults, one intended to replace police action.[18]

Following the Bahian example, studies of Afro-Brazilian cults were made from a medical perspective and linked to a psychiatric institution, a phenomenon duplicated in other northeastern states, albeit one that appears to have been more systematized and continuous in Pernambuco.[19]

Since *terreiros* were highly stigmatized and subject to violent political repression at that time, the MHS became a way for the Xangôs to obtain licensing to function by the police.[20]

The testimony of Pedro Cavalcanti, one of the pioneers of these studies, is a highly significant wealth of information. It was presented at the Afro-Brazilian Congress of Recife in 1934 and shows how scholars approached Africa and its purity.

> "Three years ago or so, when I was still a technical assistant at the state Mental Health Service, under the influence of professor Ulysses Pernambucano, we came into contact with some of the city's African cults. Those cults lived in a sort of hiding either because the police did not allow them to function freely, or because newspapers occasionally printed complaints from 'the dwellers of such and such a street' who complained of showy *despacho* and noisy black festivals and dances.
>
> The cults were (and continue to be) known by the name of Xangôs; they are also known as *catimbó*. In the Police we had the opportunity to see some registered as *maracatu*. We rarely heard them referred to as *macumba* or Candomblé. At first, it wasn't easy to make contact with them. Understandably so, seeing as how the poor blacks were persecuted. . . . But eventually we managed to connect. Well-meaning *pais-de-terreiro* contributed to this. They realized we meant well and, from the start, they attempted to show us that their cults were serious, even as they *clamored against those who abused the African name and traditions in entertainment and exploitation centers.*
>
> One of our good helpers in this approach was Pai Anselmo and, in part, this Congress thanks him for his good work as diplomatic facilitator and for being the friend he has always shown himself to be.
>
> So it was that, in late 1932, the fathers and mothers of Recife's *terreiros* met with the Board of the Assistance to Psychopaths and agreed upon measures regarding the sects' free operation. We committed to obtaining a police license for this. The *pais-de-terreiros* opened their doors to us and gave us the explanations needed to distinguish those who practiced religion from those who practiced exploitation." (Cavalcanti, 1935: 243–44, my italics)

The opposition between religion and exploitation unfolds into many others that are revealed throughout the text. So it is that, alongside religiosity, the purest African survivals are profiled "in the good *terreiros* [in which] their leader only truly uses his knowledge to worship the African deities and to perform cult obligations" through "toques, noisy parties with dancing and food." These are the "good, respectful *pais-de-santo* who are pleased to be of use to us." Similarly, "they are the ones who are always complaining about the evil deeds of those who are in a cult but are incompetent." Or who have a cult but use it to exploit others.

Not having mastered African knowledge, they "take advantage of their cult to perform *despachos, catimbós*. Those who do so are marginal groups and are brought here to be booked" (Cavalcanti, 1935: 245).

In short, the basic opposition is between religion and magic, understood as an opposition between Good and Evil, the legitimate and the illegitimate use of the Sacred.

In "good *terreiros*," "proper" *pais-de-santo* use their African wisdom to worship their gods and practice religion. Consequently, they are respectful and useful. They pose no threat to social order. On the other hand, those who are "incompetent" or who do not possess true African tradition, perform illicit "*despachos* and *catimbós*," magic for evildoing and exploitation. Such priests are dangerous and considered a "marginal group"; in other words, they are marginalized by intellectuals who use African purity as a criterion for classification according to which legitimate use of the sacred coincides with the greatest fidelity to African (and predominantly Nagô) tradition. Years later, in 1935, it was the Nagô who supplied the model calendar according to which the police should regulate the number of *toques* annually permitted to each *terreiro* (Fernandes, 1937: 10).

Thus, there is an attempt to standardize criteria for inspecting the *terreiros* and penalizing those not classified as African religion, which in turn were defined by scholars according to their fidelity to the "purest" traditions, still preserved in a few *terreiros*.[21] Thus, interference with the sects was standardized according to knowledge and scientific activity that emphasized and promoted tradition even as they inhibit and denigrate modernity (identified as degenerate and bad).

This proposition is also adopted (with variations) by the Recife Center for Afro-Brazilian Culture, a black organization founded by Solano Trindade with the support of local intellectuals such as Gilberto Freyre. Like many others that were active during the 1930s, the aim of this organization was to "morally re-erect the black Brazilian family" (Lima, 1937: 20). Protesting the myth of superior and inferior races, it preached that "it is cultural development which makes us distinguish one from the others"

and invested in black education to endow it with the behaviors and encul-
turation that would result in its "moral elevation." With this objective, in
addition to conferences at places where blacks congregate (which points

to the need for schools), the Center for Afro-Brazilian Culture promotes
studies and publications that seek to present the situation of blacks in
Pernambuco and enable them to overcome their cultural inferiority. The
investigation of Afro-Brazilian religions becomes inevitable and the results appear in a book called *Xangô*, the fruit of observation in the *terreiros*, facilitated by the MHS team at the Assistance to Psychopaths. Its
author, Vicente de Lima, concluded that, in Pernambuco, true African
religion was restricted to a few *terreiros*, and that Xangô was degenerating
and becoming "a faraway, putrefied fragment of its primitiveness, devoid
of Africanisms or religiosity" (Lima, 1937: 8). The following opposition
was established between truly African Xangôs and their distortions:

> "The *terreiro* priests themselves tell us that, with the *pernicious and
> offensive intention to exploit*, distant from all religious purpose, *the
> modern Babalorixás of the present-day Xangô* elaborate suggestive
> beliefs which affect our society in its entirety.
>
> Amid growing decadence, the *terreiro* priests tell us that their
> cult cannot survive at the hands of *the incompetent and the insin-
> cere*.
>
> Deep down, we only want to protect black youth from this
> poisonous, contagious microbe: we want to break the strong links
> of the chain that is the bondage of their eternal slavery.
>
> *We can chart new directions for leaving the right to Xangô priest-
> hood in the hands of those who are sincere and concerned* (and who
> are now practically nonexistent). However, it may be verified that
> everywhere, especially in the city outskirts, where *the proletarian
> masses are concentrated in their shanties*, exiles from the evolution
> of the city and its great skyscrapers, *terreiros are formed and centers
> [for the practice] of low spiritism and worship are opened* which we
> shall consider in the following chapters, giving birth to curious
> (and even police-worthy) cases." (Lima, 1937: 45–46, my italics)

In light of this confused and eclectic sociocultural heritage, it was necessary to select what suited the moral elevation of blacks and discard that
which socially demoralized it. From this pedagogical perspective, the traditional, Africanized Xangô needed to be preserved because it was true
religion directed by "sincere, concerned" priests and did not denigrate
the image of blacks. It was pure, African tradition.[22] However, the mod-

ern, distorted Xangô became an impediment to "moral elevation," often generating "police-worthy cases," and thus needed to be abandoned and replaced by religious forms that were more in keeping with the proposition for integrating blacks into class society.

One of the alternatives was the sect of the God Is Truth Pantheistic Circle, founded by the black priest José Amaro Feliciano and registered in 1935. Said to have been inspired by the "religious sense of the Brazilian black" and rooted in "primitive forms which evolve with their own mythology," independently of Indian pantheisms, the cult retained "traces of Brazilian animist fetishism" (of which the trance state was the most significant example). It was, however, a cult dedicated to black moral uplift. Morality was the basic point of doctrine, which sought to "make a man for his family, ridding him of vices that degenerate him" (Lima, 1937: 60). The need to maintain an organized family life is highlighted and combines well with the intended image of practitioners of pantheism, presented as "an elite of proletarian men, healthy and strong, honest and hardworking." In short, it was the opposite of the modern Xangô, which was "exploitative, pernicious and offensive," "degeneracy and barbarism" that denigrated black image before society at large.

In the final analysis, the central axis of the argument is identical to the one used by Nina Rodrigues and Artur Ramos. True religion is the purest African Xangô. Loss of this purity leads to the modern mixture identified with sorcery, degeneracy, and exploitation, and thus is susceptible to opposition from the police and from those who work for the moral elevation of blacks.

In Recife, therefore, the 1930s attempt to legalize cults primarily through use of the opposition between the traditional and the modern alludes—through another language—to the legitimization of the "pure" and the disqualification of the "mixed."

The Case of Bahia

In Bahia, the concept of the purest African (and above all Yoruba) tradition—classified as a true religion by opposition to the magic of impure *terreiros*—is quite visible in the late 1930s, even as a current ideology in the local Afro-Brazilian segment. The aseptic quality of Nagô *terreiros* becomes clearly visible in Ruth Landes's astute observations regarding Bahian Candomblé in 1938/1939. Visiting the "purest" African and the most stigmatized *caboclo terreiros*, she occasionally expresses the differentiated use of magic.

Of a *caboclo mãe-de-santo*, she wrote:

"I was surprised to hear her order a *despacho* since this was evil magic, supposedly repugnant to the mothers, at least to mothers of the Yoruba persuasion. I recalled having heard Menininha tell, outraged, of a man who had called on her at the town house to request her to prepare a *despacho* against the lover of a young girl he desired for himself. [. . .] He had offered her a good sum of money, but she had refused, saying severely: 'Sir, you know that I am a mother of our African cult, and therefore a friend of people, not a wicked magician. I maintain relations with the gods not with the devil. Surely you realize that. I will cure you of sickness, and I will try to advance your happiness in all ways that the gods indicate but I cannot do the work of the devil.'" (Landes, 1947: 182)

Great evil deeds were attributed to the *caboclo terreiros*, like for example the death of Rui Barbosa. Thus, the non-orthodox traditional African centers appeared as havens of evil and witchcraft whose existence was not admitted in the more Africanized *terreiros*, for the Nagô priestesses were bound by a code of ethics not to practice black magic. Black magic was presented as an activity external to traditional Yoruba *terreiros*, although it was occasionally parallel to them and at times even linked to them, albeit regarded as a thing of the past.

"The Nago cults *formerly* had associated with them certain men who practiced divination and *sorcery* but who were not cult heads. One or two such old men still operate in Bahia, and are called *babala.o* [sic] 'father in godhood.' They were consulted by the whole population, including the *candombles*, though sorcery is forbidden in Bahia." (Landes, 1947: 390, my italics)

One of those famous sorcerers was Martiniano Bonfim, of whom Ruth Landes wrote:

"Édison and I were certain that Martiniano supported himself from the practice of magic, which he had learned in Nigeria, and which he refused to teach people in Bahia. White and black people alike respected him for his talent, and some even believed him to be the devil himself, with his black skin and red eyes, and his devotion to Ifa, the deity of Fate. The police believed he was a professional magician, and watched him. Temple followers thought that he had performed magic for Aninha during his long service at her temple, magic which she needed to have done, but which her priestly vows would not allow her to perform. He was in fact indispensable to

her, unlike any other *ogan*, and her success grew with the association. She was the priestess, he was the sorcerer." (Landes, 1947:
208–9)

This attempt at a clear separation between priest and sorcerer recalls
the effort of intellectuals to depict Candomblé as a true religion by contrasting it with magic (and, particularly, black magic), for it was recognized that "sorcery was illegal under Brazilian law, and also that it had no
proper place in the amiable atmosphere of Bahia's candomble" (Landes,
1947: 208).

The practice of sorcery inside the most Africanized *terreiros* was presented as an excrescence, something related to attempts at subverting the
terreiro's internal order and its power structure:

> "People later told me that Menininha's second in command, Dona
> Laura, did practice black magic, contrary though this was to the
> code of a priestess. But Dona Laura was also said to make it her
> business to go contrary to the wishes of Menininha, whom she
> regarded as a priestly rival, and she could not be halted; in fact,
> she was said to be popular and to have many clients." (Landes,
> 1947: 182–83)

Elsewhere, she adds:

> "Dona Laura, indeed, is supposed to be practicing bad magic,
> which no mother should do; but in that way she draws a following
> that Menininha isn't interested in, and everybody has to reckon
> with her because she's dangerous." (Landes, 1947: 207)

Thus, sorcery represented a danger to the *terreiros'* very order and, from
such a perspective, it reproduced the representation of society at large,
likewise fearful of the powers of Evil, which constituted the strength of
the weak it had attempted to domesticate.

If magic cannot be extirpated from Candomblé, it must be used only
to do Good, although, at any rate, what will stand out in the activity of the
most Africanized *terreiros* is actively held to be religious. In this respect,
the author's comparison of black cults in the South and Northeast is significant. She finds it strange that a *caboclo mãe-de-santo* should "refer so
openly to the magic" she practiced:

> "I recalled too the newspapers in Rio de Janeiro, which several
> times a week carried stories about the bad magic practiced by
> Negro men there, fathers of the temples. The Bahia papers did

not carry such reports, except rarely, concentrating instead on the religious performances of the mothers." (Landes, 1947: 183)

Thus the de-Africanization of religious cults in southern Brazil is opposed to resistance by the "purest" *terreiros* of Bahia (idealized by intellectuals as not containing conflict and magic).

Dealing with a system made up of religious elements (harmony, solidarity, etc.) and characteristics of magic (internal dissent, individualism, political disputes), intellectuals focus on the religious, on the public ritual, on the collective, on that which constituted, so to speak, the onstage activity, even as they omit the private ritual, the individual and the magic, which take place in the wings. This rupture between the interdependent magical-religious activities of the stage and wings is the fruit of an attempt by intellectuals to "cleanse" the *terreiros* of aspects regarded as negative and eventually becomes a romanticized vision of the subaltern.

This basic opposition between religion and magic (which directs scientific work on cults in the Northeast, since the end of the nineteenth century, seeking to legitimize Africa and "purity" and disqualifying *caboclo* and "mixture") also established the forms of organization through which intellectuals and *pais-de-santo* attempted to rid the cults of police control and obtain their freedom.

The absence of a mechanism through which to legalize *terreiro* life led them to be at the mercy of police arbitrariness. As of 1934, a law required them to register with the police department, and so the regulated functioning of *terreiros* became dependent upon a special license granted by the police. In an attempt to counterbalance this imposed police registration and free themselves from the stigma of clandestineness, the *terreiros* registered as civil societies.[23] Organizations that sought to congregate all the *terreiros* followed these isolated attempts to challenge the repressive power of the state. In Recife, the legalization of candomblés was obtained through the Mental Health Service, which—although it did not fully replace police control—functioned as an organization that at least mediated that relationship. In Bahia, recognition of the *terreiros*' legality was attempted some time later, and that movement was spearheaded by Édison Carneiro.

Édison Carneiro (1912–1972)[24] was born in Bahia and in 1930 he participated, along with Jorge Amado and other intellectuals, in a movement of cultural renewal known as the Academy of Rebels. Soon after, he became interested in popular cults of African origin and, following the Bahian tradition of glorifying the Nagô, he began to study the language and the tradition of the Engenho Velho *terreiro*. He did not restrict himself to it, however. He researched the *caboclo terreiros* "here, there and everywhere" and, in 1936, published *Religiões negras*, soon followed by *Negros Bantus* (1937). It was by following the genetic method inaugurated by Rodrigues that Carneiro found Bantu survivals in the *terreiros* of Angola. Thus he sought to demonstrate Nina Rodrigues's exaggerations regarding Sudanese exclusivism among Bahian blacks. Yet he observed that, at least in part, the Angolas copied Nagô ritual, thus surrendering to the interpretive model of their cultural superiority and subsequent transformation in comparison with the study of other *terreiros*. Significantly, by studying *caboclo* candomblés in which he identified a mixture of Bantu and Indian myths, he applied "the same rules of Nagô orthography" to transcriptions of words to chants (Carneiro, 1981: 64). Comparisons with the Nagô model are constant in references to *caboclo* candomblés.

> "*Caboclo* candomblés become increasingly decadent, adapting themselves to spiritist rituals and producing the current *caboclo* sessions which are well known in Bahia. They lack the complexity of *Nagô* or *African* (that is, Jeje-Nagô) candomblés. Extreme ritual simplicity enables rampant charlatanism. . . ." (Carneiro, 1981: 70, the author's italics)

According to him, charlatanism and exploitation reigned in *caboclo* sessions—the final stop on the continuum established by Artur Ramos and adopted by Carneiro, Nagô being at the other end. He says:

> "Influencing Afro-Bantu Candomblé, spiritism produced Bahia's current *caboclo* sessions, the last step on the Candomblé scale, a sort of bridge to black Bantu's total adhesion to so-called low spiritism." (Carneiro, 1981: 235)

And adds: "Magic medicine is practiced in these *caboclo sessions*, the probable foundation for the social phenomenon of quackery in Brazil" (Carneiro, 981: 235, the author's italics).

Quackery was an illegal practice and so, in attempting to create a legality for the "pure Africans," it disqualifies and illegitimates the "degenerate *caboclos*" with their practices of quackery and witchcraft.

This point of view is well explained in another passage in which the author compares Nagô *mães-de-santo* to *caboclo pais-de-santo*:

> "A few of these priests never underwent the process of initiation. They are untrained, spontaneous priests, distant from organic

African tradition—held in contempt by the Nagô (. . .)—these priests are the ones who have contributed the most to the demoralization of candomblés, surrendering to the practice of quackery and witchcraft—for money. Although cases of quackery and sorcery are rare in Nagô and Jeje candomblés, when they do occur, they are limited to innocuous magical practices, at the most medicinal herb teas or a *despacho* (an ebó) for Exu at the nearest crossroad." (Carneiro, 1967: 130)

In short, it is the opposition between religion and sorcery that is reprised and re-elaborated to obtain the legitimacy of idealized African candomblé.

Athough Carneiro's intellectual trajectory led him to other subjects,[25] at least while he was living in Bahia his work and activity on Afro-Brazilian cults were profoundly marked by the influence of Rodrigues and Ramos. By continuing to explore the issues which concern them, Carneiro attempts to legitimize Candomblé, privileging its African features in the process.

In 1936 he was hired by *O Estado da Bahia*, a newspaper that allows him to publicize *terreiro* festivities (Carneiro, 1981: 7).

The following year, along with other black studies scholars, he organized the Afro-Brazilian Congress of Bahia, one result of which was a report directed to the governor, pleading for the acknowledgment of African cults. The text is quite exemplary of my own thesis, and it is well worth transcribing:

"i.—All people have their own religions, their own special ways of adoring God—and Candomblé is *the religious organization of Bahian blacks and men of color* descended from black slaves who bequeathed to them the various *Afro cults* into which African religious forms were subdivided. Even after such fractioning and subdivision, this intellectual heritage has a right to life as the expression of the highest sentiments of human dignity which it awakens among those it influences.

ii. As well proven, the sharpest observers—especially Nina Rodrigues, Artur Ramos, and the Afro-Brazilian Congresses held in Recife (1934) and in Bahia (1937)—there is *nothing* in *African cults* which goes against *morality* or *the public order* (article 113 of the Federal Constitution). On the contrary, without exception both Nina Rodrigues and Artur Ramos and the intellectuals who took part in the aforementioned Congresses have claimed black religious freedom as one of the essential conditions for the establishment of justice among men. Hence the religious freedom enjoyed by Pernambuco blacks and the correlated resolution passed by the Afro-Brazilian Congress of Bahia.

III. Only black religions belong on a lower plane, depending directly upon state police authority for the exercise of their social function. Inequality—which can only be justified, in part, as a result of the previous administration's policy of many years—shall not go unnoticed by Your Excellency's superior, enlightened mind, said inequality being in disagreement with the statutes of the Constitution of July 16, 1934.

Honorable Governor, these reasons lead us to suggest that your Excellency *recognize the coming-of-age of the state's African cults* and their subsequent right to direct themselves." (in Ramos, 1971: 199–200, my italics)

It should be observed that the basic rationale behind this request for the legalization of Candomblé is the fact that it is a religion, an idea that had been developing since Rodrigues with regard to Nagô exclusively and one that Carneiro amplifies to encompass other religious forms imported from Africa. The search for legal recognition was therefore circumscribed by the boundaries of African heritage, above all of the purest tradition. Since sorcery, charlatanism, and the exploitation that—according to him —reigned in *caboclo* candomblés were obstacles to the legal recognition of Candomblé as a religion, it was necessary to supervise and control the orthodoxy of the cults. For this reason, the Union of Afro-Brazilian Sects of Bahia, an organization created by intellectuals[26] with the strong support of the Axé Opô Afonjá to congregate the *pais-de-santo*, had the aim of defending the religious freedom of Candomblé and "maintaining and orienting Afro-Brazilian religion to remain within ritual boundaries bequeathed by ancestors" (Bastide, 1971: 239; Carneiro, 1964: 98–102 and 208; Landes, 1947: 30).

In keeping with the concern regarding fidelity to Africa, Martiniano do Bonfim presided over the organization; according to Vivaldo Costa Lima, it was a sort of "institutional organ for controlling ritual purity and the seriousness of *terreiro* priests and priestesses" (Lima, 1977: 38). Of Nagô descent and a former collaborator of Rodrigues, he had "returned to the primitive lands of his people; to the coasts of Africa (. . .) to study black customs and beliefs in their *initial purity* and *lead this purity to be respected among Bahian blacks*, increasingly threatened with involvement in white beliefs, as their cults were massacred by political repression" (Amado, 1940: 328, my italics).[27]

Struggles against police repression and against the loss of African traditions go hand in hand. Both include the participation of intellectuals who (having made a selection of sects in which fidelity to Africa is a point of reference) eventually interfere with guidelines set by the police. The most "traditional" *terreiros* are studied by anthropologists as centers of "true religion" that they protect, and manage to safeguard against police repression that comes down more violently against the unappreciated "impure."[28] Those whose "strength" is immobilism and traditionalism are first to abandon obscurity in favor of public performances. The 1930s bring a significant participation by "more traditionally Africanized" *terreiros* during the festivities of the Afro-Brazilian Congresses of Pernambuco and Bahia. Xangô performances are held during the former's closing ceremonies at the Teatro Santa Isabel while, in Bahia, more than forty *terreiros* take part in the Congress, and many of them (above all the most traditional ones, such as the Procópio, Engenho Velho, Axé Opô Afonjá, Gantois, and Bate-Folhas *terreiros*) "received congress participants with dazzling festivities" (Carneiro, 1964: 100).

THE AFRO-BRAZILIAN CONGRESSES AND THE POPULARIZATION OF AFRICAN HERITAGE

Two Afro-Brazilian Congresses were held in the Northeast during the 1930s. The first one took place in 1934 in Recife, organized by Gilberto Freyre, who had the unconditional support of Mental Health Service research group led by Ulysses Pernambucano de Melo, proclaimed President of Honor of the aforementioned Congress. Of him, Freyre says:

"It was natural that, having classified Afro-Brazilian cults as religions, thus protecting them against stupid police repression, the idea of holding an Afro-Brazilian studies congress—the first such event to be held in Brazil—in Recife should be regarded with the greatest sympathy, as one of Recife's most remarkable cultural and social anticipations. This was another suggestion I must immodestly claim to have been mine." (Freyre, 1978: 140–41)

Years later, in 1937, the second Afro-Brazilian Congress convened in Salvador. Its organizers (Édison Carneiro, Aydano do Couto Ferraz, and Reginaldo Guimarães) were intent on emphasizing Nina Rodrigues as a forerunner of Afro-Brazilian studies, a pioneer whom Freyre did not challenge and (as Bahian intellectuals might have wished) did not emphasize.

These divergences apart, the two events shared a concern over the search for Africa and authenticity, based on ritual purity and on the presence of the popular, not only in cultural or "racial" traits to be dissected[29] but also in the physical presence of common people among congress participants.

Anthropologists had long been working to obtain social acceptance for Candomblé by presenting it as a religion. Even admitting that, with the passing of time, the ideas developed by intellectuals (and initially restricted to academic and intellectual circles) would be disseminated and incorporated to common sense, it was necessary to expand them, immediately, to society at large so as to reflect a less negative image of African Candomblé, which was then identified with witchcraft, sorcery, and evil deeds. At the core of the movement that emphasizes and appreciates African heritage as an important source of Brazilian social and cultural identity, it was necessary not only to glorify Africa but to popularize the glorification of this heritage. It seems to me that the Congresses would thus have the function of publicly showing alliances between the intellectuals and the people, or, better yet, of conferring popular support to the work of intellectuals, breaking the tight circle to which it had been circumscribed until then and disseminating it among different social classes.

The presence of the general public at the Afro-Brazilian Congresses is, in fact, emphasized by organizers in Pernambuco and in Bahia. In Recife,

> "the collaboration of illiterates, cooks, and *terreiro* priests alongside scholars, gave new strength to the studies, the freshness and the vivacity of contacts with brute reality." (Freyre, 1937: 351)

As for its Bahian edition, in the words of Carneiro (one of its organizers), the "Congress was deeply rooted among black populations," and "that immediate connection with the black people" was "the greatest glory of the Bahia Congress" (Carneiro, 1964: 98–99). The community presented more than celebrations of Candomblé, capoeira, and samba performances; it was also present at the inaugural session of the Congress presided by Martiniano do Bonfim, an African descendant and colleague of Rodrigues. Several *pais-de-santo*, among them Aninha of the Axé Opô Afonjá, "wrote memories for the debate" (Carneiro, 1964: 99). Thus, "men of science and men of the people stood shoulder to shoulder, discussing the same problems which interested some from their theoretical aspect and others from a practical perspective, as part of their lives." (Carneiro, 1964: 102)

This made the Congress a "popular contest, even as it was a scientific one." Thus, the presence of the community supported the activity of intellectuals who sought to legitimize Candomblé through Africa. If, on one hand, the Congresses legitimized intellectual activity through popular support, on the other hand they served to disseminate a less negative image of Candomblé to society at large, which was then regarded as witchcraft and sorcery—the stuff of the Devil.

"Congressional" activities had the advantage of doing away with the "scarecrow that Candomblé still represented to Bahia's so-called upper classes. (. . .) Publicity regarding the Congress in the newspapers and on the radio contributes to create an environment more tolerant of the colored man's religions" (Carneiro, 1964: 100).

Similarly, in referring to the Recife Congress, Gilberto Freyre says it included the "enthusiasm of Recife's best citizens. People who had finally discovered a new wealth of emotion, sensibility, and even spirituality in 'black things'; a great and living part of real Brazilian culture" (Freyre, 1937: 349).

Thus, in two languages—one that highlights class differences and their representations of Candomblé and another that regards black heritage as a basic ingredient of cultural nationalism—the underlying idea of the Congress's organizers is the same: to disseminate the valorization of African tradition—and above all of the "purest" African tradition—to various social classes and to legitimize the candomblés through their connection with Africa, the stigma of which could be measured by the police repression that affected them.

Together with the Afro-Brazilian Congresses which, according to Carneiro, "inaugurated the season of black performances" (Carneiro, 1964: 115), a trend is established that had been heralded in some studies—that of associating Candomblé with exotic spectacle, dance, and celebration. This idea is discussed along with the opposition between religion and magic or, more precisely, between religion and sorcery. Sorcery is traditionally hidden or disguised. Its practices are esoteric and sinister and, as a "true religion," Candomblé must be public and show itself. However, in doing so it must appear as an exotic celebration.

But the exotic is also an aesthetic category.

"Segalen defined exoticism as an *aesthetics of diversity*. That which does not resemble us is therefore seen as *beautiful*. Following this, by our hand beauty becomes reality, the realization of a previous imagination." (Auzias, 1978: 67, the author's italics)

This approach, which links the exotic to the aesthetic, leads certain aspects of Afro-Brazilian cults to be emphasized in studies. Thus, the rhythms, the *toadas*, the musical instruments, the choreography, the color of the *mãe-de-santo*'s garments and ornaments and, above all, the dances culminating in the state of possession are repeatedly described in detail (Rodrigues, 1935; Ramos, 1951; Carneiro, 1967c), and this perspective winds up giving the impression that Candomblé can be reduced to a great celebration. In some writing, this point of view is more or less explicit. Establishing a separation between Xangô—"true religion"—and Candomblé—magic—Pedro Cavalcanti says that in Recife's "good *terreiros*" the "leader only takes advantage of what he knows to worship the deities of the Coast and to fulfill obligations of worship. To this end, he organizes the *toques, loud festivals with dancing and food*, on certain days of the year" (Cavalcanti, 1935: 245, my italics).

There has been an attempt to reduce Candomblé to rituals, open to a lower (and increasingly middle and upper) class. In this context, the Candomblé festival calendar is specified and included among items for negotiation in the operation of *terreiros*, which intellectuals attempted to pursue with agencies of repression. In Recife, for instance, the calendar of (one of the) 1934 Afro-Brazilian Congress organizers Pai Anselmo's Nagô *terreiro* was suggested by intellectuals as a model calendar to be used by the police in order to regulate the number of *toques* annually allotted the Candomblés. In all, there would be eighteen of those and ritual days were determined a priori by the police based on the Nagô calendar, a practice that drew a reaction from the *pais-de-santo* (Fernandes, 1937: 10).

In Bahia, too, emphasis was placed on the "religious spectacles of *mães*" frequently reported in newspapers, as observed by Ruth Landes in the late 1930s (Landes, 1947: 204).

It is interesting to note that the term Candomblé itself (which currently possesses a more inclusive meaning, indicating not only the place of worship but also the very system of beliefs and religious practices as a whole) once had a more restricted meaning. Resorting to its etymology, some authors present it as a ball or a dance (Mendonça, 1973: 126). This is one of the meanings attributed to it by Rodrigues, when he lists it among the "fine arts of [Brazil's] black colonizers" (Rodrigues, 1977: 155).

Seeking a philological explanation for the term that might have a Bantu component, and realizing that it was a designation cult worshippers did not agree with, Carneiro says: "Although we cannot imagine how, we may safely assume that Candomblé was imposed in Bahia by force from the outside" (Carneiro, 1964: 127). Scholarly interest in *terreiros* and the emphasis placed on public dance rituals might lead one to assume that the term Candomblé (which originally designated a dance), was disseminated throughout Brazil as the name for the religion of black Bahia. It is interesting to observe that, in the Northeast, blacks themselves used other terms to designate their religious practices.

Even in Bahia, "it is known that Nagô leaders of yore preferred not to use the word Candomblé which, in the old days, possessed a meaning more ludic than religious" (Lima, 1977: 38).

The white elite's ideologized view reduces black religion to forms of play and dance and maintains that dance is "impregnated in the blood" of Africans, who therefore tend to "reduce all things to dance — whether work or play" (Freyre, 1947: 172).[30] And why not religion, too? Ramos says that, among primitive peoples (Africans included), magic and religion are inseparable from dance and music. "Dance was an institution among the black peoples who supplied America with slaves." Quoting a French author, he adds: "There is feverish dancing everywhere in black Africa. It is an entertainment passionately enjoy by both sexes" (Ramos, 1951: 193).

African passion thus perpetuated itself in Brazil through dances profane and sacred. The latter — of particular interest to us — are extremely discreet and have a marked ideological connotation.

"The total body participation of *filha de santo* choreography is frenetic — arms, hands, legs, and head are violently and tirelessly, and continuously contorted until the final spasmodic possession." (Ramos, 1951: 194)

To its description, the author adds others, not only by pioneer Rodrigues, but of "those of our writers [who] described these Candomblé dance scenes, such is the suggestive effect provoked by them" (Ramos, 1951: 195). Various descriptions by novelists[31] follow, their content indicating that, within this context, the languages of science and art move in the same direction.

Expressions like "sinister writhing," "frenetic shouting," "a muscular delirium possesses the monster," black women who "rock and tumble into the arms of frenzied men," and members compared to "winged boa constrictors" permeate the texts and eventually paint a picture of savagery and lust activated by "black music, with all the atavistic fermentation of hovering apparitions, ghostly forests, feverish swamps, rustling groves, giant snakes and chimpanzees, pack of lost beasts or Sobas spying on cannibal sacrifices, an aura of nightmare and madness" (Herman Lima, in Ramos, 1951: 200).

The idea of the primitive African savage is strongly imposed by this "poetics of the drift," removing him from domesticity and civilization, categories that (as Patrícia Birman demonstrates) appear in Rodrigues and his followers, constructed from the opposition between nature and culture (Birman, 1980: 29). Driven by "instinct, emotion and reflex," Africans and their Brazilian descendents are closer to untamed nature, their primitivism fully revealed in the dances to which primitive black religion appeared to be reduced. The "dirty" gaze of exoticism about which Sartre speaks makes its appearance here, associated to a non-explicit practical project which gradually moves exoticism away from itself to a subaltern place.

The function of exoticism in colonial ideology has been widely denounced and analyzed in studies referring to peoples situated in distant countries, as is the case, for example, of Europeans with regard to Africans and Asians, ultimately to what might be called external primitives (Leclerc, 1973). Yet, as early as the 1940s, Sérgio Buarque de Hollanda had astutely perceived and criticized what it meant to transform the black man — an element of everyday Brazilian social life — into an exotic object of study which, always referenced by mysterious, distant Africa, helped to keep him far from "us," European whites, by supposition or desire, explaining the black "other" as a different stranger, thus rendering him even stranger, more distant, and exotic, *because of* his Africanness. He was a construct of our internal primitive after all. Hollanda writes:

"The error of a considerable number of recent [Brazilian] studies on black influence appears to me to be that they focus too insistently upon the picturesque, the anecdotal and the folkloric, in other words on the *exotic* aspect of Africanism. Not that this is contemptible in itself, but because the exclusive attention paid to such details is only a more intelligent variant of the traditional way of considering the problem — namely forgetting or ignoring it. When black influence ceases to be something hardly confessable in order to become something simply *interesting*, we naturally distance ourselves from it, without truculence and without hu-

miliation, but with a distant, superior curiosity. When his drum-
ming and *macumbas*, his superstitions, his religiosity, his civil and
domestic customs or his mores are met with benevolent scientific
attention, the black man may even be proudly exhibited to foreigners. It is a way of showing that *we, too*, are different from him, that
we regard him as unique phenomenon worthy of contemplation.
Considered in its true, obscure motives, has not the real problem
been avoided and replaced? In studying what it is that distinguishes the black man minutely within our pseudo-white civilization, what it is that ceases to influence it or will influence it only
indirectly or negatively and which consequently makes it more
self-assured, more legitimately distinguished, we do not refuse to
consider him in what he truly means to us and to our nationality."
(Hollanda, 1978: 13, the author's italics)

From this analytical perspective (through which blacks become African and the familiar exotic), appreciation of Nagô emerges in association with the glorification of exoticism, Nagô being considered the purest
and, therefore, the most exotic African. The core of this celebration of the
African is a movement of return to Africa that takes place primarily on a
symbolic level.

THE MEANING OF THE "RETURN TO AFRICA"
AND OF THE GLORIFICATION OF "PURE NAGÔ"

The search for African legitimacy, shaped by intellectuals who often
proved more interested in preserving tradition than the cult leaders and
founders themselves (Hamilton, 1970: 366, in Brown, 1974: 82), is obviously reflected in the *terreiros*, above all on the more Africanized ones,
transformed into paradigms of African heritage to be preserved or even
enriched by new practices brought over from Africa. Journeys to the original land of Candomblé undertaken in the 1930s by some of the most
famous northeastern *terreiro* leaders became an important mechanism
of re-Africanization.

One of Recife's most respected *pais-de-santo*, considered to be of the
"purest tradition," went "to Africa to perfect his knowledge." After his
return, his prestige grew enormously and, contradicting the norms of
succession, he took control of the cult group in which he had been initiated and there introduced "a series of innovation in the practices of that

group which considerably altered the ritual followed until then" (Ribeiro, 1952: 104).

In Bahia, former Rodrigues collaborator Martiniano do Bonfim's voyage had similar effects, reflected above all in the Axé Opô Afonjá, a *terreiro* that in the 1930s, according to Aydano do Couto Ferraz's assessment, executed the "most important organized reaction in Bahia and, perhaps in Brazil" in the sense of "a return to the primitive purity of Afro-black cults" (Ferraz, 1939: 177). In 1937 (the year of the Afro-Brazilian Congress of Bahia), this *terreiro*, in a clear demonstration of return to Africa, introduced the twelve ministers (*obás*) of Xangô into the roster of its ritual organization, "chosen from among the most enlightened *ogãs*, of the highest position within the group, stable and prosperous in their businesses and professions, highly regarded and well-related within Salvador's global society" (Lima, 1966: 9).

Thus, through this Africanizing innovation, protection by the rich (already present in Candomblé through the institution of the *ogãs*) was legitimized by means of a return to African tradition.

The movement back to Africa spread, apparently led in Bahia at the traditional Nagô Axé Opô Afonjá by Aninha, "an intelligent woman who followed and understood our aims, who read our studies and loved our work" (Carneiro, 1964: 208). The prestige of elders and of the motherland grows, and blacks send their children over to learn cult tradition and introduce it in Brazil. Simultaneously, African biological ancestry is glorified: ". . . The finest recommendation that can be made of any person is that they are pure black, the children or grandchildren of Africans, with no mixture of white blood" (Carneiro, 1967c: 339). Ultimately, the mystique of an appreciation and return to Africa resonated within Candomblé and, to those *pais-de-santo* who were unable to make the inverse journey undertaken by their ancestors—following a trajectory that would soon be made by anthropologists who traveled incessantly between Bahia and the western coast of Africa[32]—there remained the strategy of re-encounter with mythical Africa, to be imitated in the works of intellectuals who, guided by the idea of preservation, had recorded the beliefs and ritual practices of the "purest" *terreiros* in their books.[33]

Carneiro refers to Aninha of the Axó Opô Afonjá as a reader of those works (Carneiro, 1964: 208). In the 1940s, during his first trip to the Northeast, Roger Bastide met many *pais-de-santos* who owned those books (Bastide, 1945), a phenomenon also recorded in Recife by René Ribeiro (Ribeiro, 1952: 103). Through the appropriation of those discourses that Marilena Chauí calls "second or derived discourses," which will teach each person how to relate to the world and to men, "competency is granted to those who were able to assimilate them" and thus "the belief that they are subjects" is created "in socio-economic and socio-political objects" (Chauí, 1980: 12).

If, in the Northeast, the use of this bibliography by *pais-de-santo* resulted in legitimate action, above all when it was associated with an account that established historical and genealogical connections with Africa, in the Southeast its use was regarded as exploitation and mystification. In 1938, a Rio de Janeiro newspaper denounced as roguery the use made of "books by Ramos, Rodrigues, Carneiro or Gonçalves Fernandes" in simulating "authentic macumbas," to which tourists and high society were attracted in order to obtain money, negotiating "with things that smell of Africa" (*Diário da Noite*, Rio de Janeiro, October 5, 1938, in Ramos, 1951: 159).

Africa was becoming lucrative merchandise, but for now we must further investigate the meaning of this movement of return to Africa which affects, above all, the northeastern candomblés, and was also detected in the late 1930s by Aydano do Couto Ferraz (1939), and about which Carneiro expresses perplexity:

> "In this step backward, it was possible to detect a sign of the frank decadence of black religions in Bahia currently represented by constant police raids. Yet it is also possible that this return to Africa is a sign of black religion's profound inner strength." (Carneiro, 1967a: 339)

This return to origins has been variously interpreted as the black man's reaction to his socioeconomic situation, "for the nationality and citizenship he had been given were decimating him as an ethnic group and as an individual" (Souza, 1978), and as Candomblé's attempt to resist attacks from the world of white capitalism established after the abolition and continued in the Republican period, to use the very categories so dear to Roger Bastide, it would be "a movement of *purification* for Candomblé in reaction to the *degradation* of Macumba" (Bastide, 1971: 239, my italics).

As regards the existence of a religious market within which many sects competed for "*filhos de santo* and clients," this return to Africa could be regarded as an emphasis upon diacritical signs that allowed the more traditional *terreiros* to better mark their differences from *caboclo* candomblés that (endowed with a much more fluid organizational structure and

better equipped to meet the demands of modern society) multiply rap-
idly and compete with them. Starting with the opposition between native
cults (*caboclo* candomblés) and African cults (traditional candomblés),
the latter reactivate their ethnicity, reintroducing African practices and
using them in the struggle to maintain a space for which *caboclo terreiros*
competed. Thus, there seemed to be a climate of propitiation toward the
glorification of Africa within the cults, and the return to Africa appeared
(among some blacks) to be a distinguishing feature of the struggle for
the religious market. Inasmuch as cults are ranked according to degrees
of purity, glorifying their fidelity to Africa might be regarded as intensi-
fying rivalries within the popular segment.

On the other hand, in privileging the exotic-aesthetic, emphasis upon
"the purest Nagô" favored Candomblé's inclusion within the capitalist
circuit of symbolic consumer goods as merchandise:[34] the more African,
the "purer," most exotic, and most valuable in the market.

But if appropriation of the popular, particularly of Candomblé, by the
white bourgeoisie became economically lucrative, above all in more recent
periods, such as the 1970s, it first interests me to analyze the ideological
functions of this valorization of Candomblé in the multiracial Brazilian
society of the 1930s and 1940s.

Gilberto Freyre had long argued that biological *mestiçagem* (or hybridity) and the apparently free exchange of cultural traits among the various
ethnic groups constituted the specific character of Brazilian society, presented as essentially democratic in nature, which expressed itself, for example, in the absence of any type of racial prejudice. Blacks had entered
as one of the basic ingredients in the Brazilian social *formação* and their
cultural heritage was patiently researched, the conclusion having been
reached that it survived most powerfully in religion — in Candomblé.

Originally black and faithful to Africa, this religion was thus doubly
exotic and could constitute itself in a strong distinguishing feature so
as to affirm the specificity of the Brazilian nation within a universal
concert. Significantly, in the late 1930s, Ruth Landes observed that, although other northeastern states possessed large, dense black populations, "Bahia is known for the unique quality of her Negro folk life. What
the Negroes do in Bahia is 'typical' of Brazil. [. . .] Out of Bahia come
forms and symbols for national chauvinism to cling to" (Landes, 1947:
7).

But as a popular black religion, Candomblé could also be a sign of
Brazil's "cultural democracy," giving the impression that there would
be room here for the most varied and contradictory articulations of val-

ues. Thus, beyond its use as a national symbol (and therefore destined to identify us in the group of nations), the valorization and legitimizing of Candomblé, one of the signs of such a "cultural democracy," had its counterpart of internal use, allowing the dominant classes to conceal intolerance not only against black movements but also against the black man himself, as ethnic category.

Landes (who had so perspicaciously perceived the use of the Bahian black as a national symbol) ends up proclaiming our racial and cultural democracy.

> "I was sent to Bahia to learn how people behave when the Negroes among them are not oppressed. I found that they were oppressed by political and economic tyrannies, although not by racial ones. In that sense, the Negroes were *free, and at liberty to cultivate their* African *heritage.*" (Landes, 1947: 248, my italics)

Thus, racial democracy had its counterpart in cultural democracy, myths that, by disseminating a false idea of black equality, masked racism and cultural intolerance, making them hard to combat.

But in the "Brazilian racial-cultural democracy" certain divergent forms of the dominant culture, originally linked to blacks, are not only tolerated but praised and glorified. This is what happens, for example, with Nagô Candomblé. One might well inquire as to the meaning of this praise of the cultural forms of the oppressed.

In an article by Bertrand Russell, exhumed by Szasz (1978), the English philosopher suggests that compensatory, idealized images of the inferior's superiority are generated in the power relations between the dominant and the dominated.

> "A rather curious term of this admiration for groups to which the admirer does not belong is the belief in the superior virtue of the oppressed: subject nations, the poor, women and children. The eighteenth century, while conquering America from the Indians, reducing the peasantry to the condition of pauper laborers, and introducing the cruelties of earlier industrialism, loved to sentimentalize about the 'noble savage' and the 'simple annals of the poor.'" (Russell, 1937: 731)

The author further observes that this glorification of the oppressed is a passing and unstable phase:

> "It begins only when the oppressors come to have a bad conscience, and this power only happens when their power is no longer secure.

The idealizing of the victim is useful for a time: if virtue is the greatest of goods, and if subjection makes people virtuous, if it is kind to refuse them power, since it would destroy their virtue. [. . .] It was a fine self sacrifice on the part of men to relieve women of the dirty work of politics. And so on. But sooner or later the oppressed class will argue that its superior virtue is a reason in favor of its having power, and the oppressors will find their own weapons turned against them. When at last power has been equalized, it becomes apparent to everybody that all the talk about superior virtue was nonsense, and that it was quite unnecessary as a basis for the claim to equality." (Russell, 1937: 732)

However, the way in which part of the Brazilian intelligentsia of the 1930s (and even today) treats blacks, above all in Bahia, is symptomatically celebratory. As for the late 1930s, this is how Ruth Landes characterizes the position of Bahia's intellectuals and upper class regarding blacks: "Brazil's social scientists devote themselves to these Negro citizens as completely as Mexicans do to the Indians, and in a similar mood of gallant appreciation and of expiation for the past" (Landes, 1947: 7).

She further observes that "upper class people, who are usually well educated and in professional occupations, like the Negroes enormously and enjoy showing them off" (Landes, 1947: 16).

The current glorification of Candomblé, above all of the "purest Nagô" has become a theme ubiquitously explored by singers, painters, sculptors, and writers, usually the *ogãs* of important candomblés. In using its themes as inspiration for works of art,[35] whether consciously or not, these artists contributed to disseminating the task initiated by anthropologists of drawing nationwide curiosity to Candomblé.[36]

This glorification of black symbolic production—an attempt by the dominant classes to appropriate aspects of traditional culture and incorporate them into romantic nationalist ideologies—presents itself as a mechanism behind which the dominant attempts to hide the domination he exercises over the black man by masking it with the mantle of equality and cultural democracy. Symptomatically, the celebration is selective, limiting black identity to spectacle as it transforms (whether involuntarily or not) his symbols into folkloric merchandise stripped of its cultural and religious meaning. To Édison Carneiro, this is the "logical fate" of African-originated cults in Brazil and if, on one hand, it contributes to the disaggregation of cults as religious units, on the other—he says—it empowers them by "rendering them more comprehensible and acceptable, a general predisposition which helps its maintenance and multiplication in a given region" (Carneiro, 1964: 140).

From this perspective, without dismissing the subaltern's abilities to create their own forms of counterbalancing domination, the legitimacy of Candomblé and, particularly, of the purest African occurred through a process that celebrates and reifies it.

AFRICA DENIED VERSUS AFRICA GLORIFIED, A PARALLEL BETWEEN UMBANDA AND CANDOMBLÉ

The legitimacy sought for Candomblé in the Northeast, particularly in Bahia and in Pernambuco during the 1930s, depends upon the glorification of the purest African heritage. This search for legitimacy through Africa contrasts with what happened to *Umbanda* in the Southeast. There was an attempt to purge Umbanda of African cultural heritage, explicitly identified as inferior and pejorative. The role of Umbanda's codifiers was to rid it of the negative influences associated with its African past. This mission is explicitly formulated by the first Umbandist leaders who proclaimed a need to "purify Umbanda of its essentially African rites" (Brown, 1974: 130). By denying Africa, Umbanda would become "clean," "white," and "pure," identified with the practice of Good for charity and free of cost, and thus worthy of broader social acceptance.

In contrast, African heritage in the Southeast is represented as barbarian and considered to be dangerous and subversive, as well as a constituent element of *Quimbanda*, a haven of Evil, of sorcery and exploitation (Luz & Lapassade, 1972; Ortiz, 1978; Brown, 1974).

In short, within the symbolic field of religion Africa is glorified in the Northeast and negated in the Southeast. Considering that different cultural forms are not simply expressions of particular ways of life, revealing, rather, "manifestations of opposition or acceptance which imply a constant repositioning of social groups in the dynamic of class relations" (Durham, 1977: 35), this inversion of Africa's value becomes interesting when one compares it with the specific mode of black inclusion into the structures of different regions, the background of which are racialist ideologies. Ever since the nineteenth century, Brazilian racial and racist ideologies were expressed in the proposition of whitening as a solution to national problems and, simultaneously, as a rationalization of the country's advanced *mestiçagem*. Although whitening was a national ideal, it is interesting to note that regional differences permeate the ideological constructions of the southeastern and northeastern elites. It is significant that the idea of transforming blacks into an object of study should have come from Sílvio Romero, a northeasterner, and that it was in the Northeast that it was most vigorously imposed. Black physical and cultural visibility imposed itself as a fact of reality to be studied. So it is that, while lamenting the absence of studies on African religion and languages in Brazil in 1888, Sílvio Romero wrote: "We who have the material at home, who have Africa in our kitchens, America in our jungles, and Europe in our parlors—we have produced nothing in this sense!" (Romero, 1888: 10, in Rodrigues, 1977: xv).

The empirical field is, therefore, imposed upon theoretical reflection that, by focusing on the analysis of differences, would seek them in Africa and present them as the result of a specific and irreducible nature. Thus, through a process that repeats on a smaller scale the very construction of the object of anthropology as a discipline generated by the West, focused on the study "of the primitive" (Copans, 1974: 15–44), northeastern blacks are transformed into our "internal primitive" and erected as objects of science, subjects for study.

Guerreiro Ramos has interpreted this position as a social pathology of whites (and above all of northeastern whites) who—while suffering from "unstable self-esteem" as a result of judging themselves inferior to the European archetype—initially systematize blacks and later glorify them in an attempt to disguise his ethnic origins (Ramos, 1957: 117–192).

It is also significant that the substitution—for appreciation and glorification—of the idea of subverting the canons of black racial inferiority so widely disseminated among Brazilian intellectuals in the late nineteenth (and first quarter of the twentieth) century also occurs in the northeast. It appears to me that the high concentration of blacks in the region is an element with which to study the constant regional intellectual preoccupation with this problem and to think about a possible differentiation, within the nation, in addressing the problem of race, a differentiation articulated with the demographic, historical, and economic variations of the regional structures and the specific mode of black presence within those structures.

In suggesting European immigration as a path for fulfillment of the whitening ideal, the government and elites of the South and the Southeast not only attempted to legally prevent the entry of "native Asians and Africans" but also made an effort to present a more positive image of Brazil in Europe. One way to do this was to minimize Africa's influence on the country. Although the practical result of these promotional efforts was reduced by the statements of European travelers who were always impressed with the powerful black presence in Brazil, it is important to note that, since the nineteenth century, the local southeastern elite had been willing to dilute African influence in the more practical and immediate interests of obtaining European labor for economic development as well as the more general ideological interests of whitening (Skidmore, 1976: 142–62).

In the Northeast, where, for historical and economic reasons, colored peoples have concentrated more intensely throughout the twentieth century (Hasenbalg, 1979), it was easier not only to disguise black presence but also to promote a short or mid-term whitening of the region.

If Brazil's problem was to "rid itself of its fifteen million blacks" or, in Afrânio Peixoto's sugar-producing metaphor, "to purify all this human brown sugar," would there be starch enough to refine all this scum"? (Peixoto, in Skidmore, 1976: 215).[37] In light of the drop in European immigration to the Northeast, there certainly wasn't enough of the white ingredient to purify the "human brown sugar," in other words, to dissolve the black African stain. In light of this, without renouncing the ideal of whitening, the solution found by northeastern intellectuals was the rehabilitation of the African, recognizing the participation of European, African, and Indian "races" as "equally valuable" to the making of Brazilian society.

The new scientific consensus that blacks were not intrinsically worse than whites was born in the Northeast and disseminated from the 1930s on. However, far from promoting racial equality, it served principally to "reinforce the whitening ideal by showing graphically that the (primarily white) elite had gained valuable cultural traits from their intimate contact with the African" (Skidmore, 1976: 211).

In the Northeast particularly, culture became the central focus of interest in blacks. The study of black culture, protested by Romero and begun by Rodrigues, is consolidated by the culturalism that marks 1930s Afro-Brazilian studies and has its greatest exponent in Artur Ramos. The latter is interested in "black cultural personality" and sees blacks, above all, as "culture bearers." Beyond the historical problems and anthropometric variations among races, it is ethnological problems (above all those of genetic orientations) that absorb white intellectuals who study blacks. Similarly, the few Bahian intellectuals of color who write about blacks are attracted by "the African, by his customs and traditions, especially by the survivals of African culture" (Pierson, 1971: 261).

Placing blacks within this "cultural ghetto," social agents, their living conditions, and their insertion within class society are ignored. The fact that free blacks had been absorbed by the region's traditional labor structure, characterized by servile relations of dependency and a strong paternalism (Hasenbalg, 1979), led to the false idea that the vicissitudes of blacks were simply the result of cultural differences.

Paternalism presents itself as an efficient mechanism to inhibit black collective identity and political solidarity, and blacks are politely kept in their place. This reinforces the false impression that the situation of blacks in the Northeast is more benign and that the social inequalities between whites and blacks smaller than in the Southeast.[38] White paternalism is replaced and recreated at the level of culture. Significantly, religion was liberated by the protective intervention of the ogãs, which may be regarded as mediation through the "ideology of favor" (Schwarcz, 1977).

In the Southeast, the emergence of movements of black non-conformity and racial protest in the 1920s and 1930s — movements that resulted from a process of economic transformation and modification of the urban social structure, accelerated by the solid presence of immigrants who competed seriously in the black labor market, quite flagrantly exhibiting the "winners" and "losers" of economic development and prosperity (Hasenbalg, 1979) — imposes the black man's presence as a person, the debate on his inclusion, and his place within the socioeconomic structure.

Not even after the modernists discovered the African aesthetic and Mário de Andrade researched black dances and popular autos, seeking to link them with Africa, was a continuity of studies established, the investigative fulcrum of which is African culture, with the vigor and permanence of what is recorded in the Northeast. Among the black population, Africa also appears not to have become a motive for glorification. Analyzing the Afro-Brazilian press of the Southeast, Roger Bastide says that "the appreciation of blacks does not go as far as Africa." It is never the African that is glorified but the Afro-Brazilian, and this glorification never extends beyond the period of African presence in Brazil. There is a fear of introducing Africa to the discussion, for it is considered barbarian and savage (Bastide, 1973: 149). In this context, the black attitude toward traditional culture is to discard it, because it is seen as an impediment to social integration and ascension.

Even when Africa is brought up, problems of integration and improvement of black social, educational, and professional status are not neglected.[39]

It is significant to observe how religion becomes a locus in which the problem of emphasis upon African culture or upon blacks is reflected.

Northeastern Candomblé is a mythical celebration of African culture. The history of *orixás* alludes to African places and geography. Ritual proposes to be an orthodox reproduction of ancient African practices. Meanwhile, southeastern Umbanda rejects African cultural heritage and incorporates the figure of the Preto-Velho. This is interpreted by Diana Brown to mean that Umbanda may be regarded as a metaphor for acculturation, one in which Afro-descendants are accepted insofar as they themselves accept modifications in their cultural heritage. It is important to note that the African is being symbolically appreciated as a slave, and thus as socially inferior (Brown, 1974: 136).

In the Northeast, the glorification of African cultural heritage (and of "purest" heritage above all) did not deny the racist hegemonic project engendered by the dominants, expressed also in the theory of acculturation, albeit with regional adjustments. The high concentration of blacks points more strongly to the direction of Africa as a subject of potentiality for ideological manipulation. On the other hand, the theoretical frame of reference of acculturation that informs the largest part of studies on Afro-Brazilian cults allows for the methodological validation of this fixation in studies of the purest African heritage. Artur Ramos, who appears to have been the great propagator of the theory of acculturation in Brazil, systematically applying the American terminology and concepts of the early 1930s, presents a study plan that begins with the "community of origin," moving on to "cultural contact," and from there unto an analysis of the acculturation of "psychological mechanisms of cultural contact," the results of acculturation and the "current community." Origin and "purity" are initially sought. Given the origin, the next step in studies would be its modifications, which would account for the totality of the phenomenon. He writes:

"The reconstitution of Africanisms is therefore the anthropologist's first task, necessarily followed and completed by the study of the successive cultural transformations engendered by acculturation." (Ramos, 1961, 1: 245)

Analysis would target the original "African" version behind different religious forms such as Candomblé and Macumba, the one from which everything began. And, even if the general direction of the process leads to cultural syncretism — "the final, peaceful stage toward which people and cultures of different origins tend . . ." (Ramos, 1961, v. III: 153) — it must be remembered that "reaction" is one of the possible results of acculturation. Thus, the almost pure forms of some old candomblés would be closer to reaction, while Rio de Janeiro's Macumba, which "contains the most unpredictable alterations," would be an example of the greatest syncretism. The realization that the predominant movement of fusion made the precise ethnic identification of African survivals—that is to say, of the "purest origins"—increasingly difficult resulted in the need to preserve and glorify the forms closest to the "original versions," scarce and exotic products of a distant Africa, ideally transformed into a haven of Goodness. Emphasis on even the purest African heritage did not deny acculturation; on the contrary, it evinced the validity of the theoretical-methodological model that predicted different results or phases of the process.

These results, however, pose no threat to the general order of society or to white hegemony, given that the "conservatisms of Africa" glorified in the Northeast are standardized and kept under the control of science, which, by establishing boundaries between religion and magic, includes the purity of African religion within the territory of religion. But through science's alleged neutrality, what had been identified as religion is eventually transformed into morality and into politics when African Candomblé is presented as the realm of morality and of order. Thus, in the Northeast, where the highest percentage of blacks is concentrated and where racial inequalities are more marked, the glorification of Africa is presented as the re-elaboration of a logic destined to ensure the continuity of domination. By culturally appreciating blacks and denying them conditions for social equality, the continuity between culture and life is broken and inequalities are hidden behind an emphasis on symbolic forms of integration. Notwithstanding this, given the polysemy of the word (about which Mikhail Bakhtin has written), there is still a possibility of removing Africa from the "cultural ghetto" to which it had been confined by intellectuals in their culturalist reveries and replacing it in the flow of life, where blacks would not be regarded as mere "culture bearers" but as living, active beings in a society that sees itself as effectively democratic.

CHAPTER FIVE

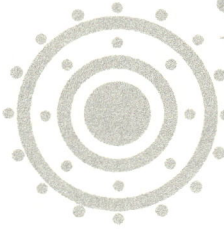

Uses of Africa
by the Nagô *Terreiro*

In this chapter I propose to analyze how the intellec-
tual movement that glorified the African is reflected in a small city of the
Northeast and how the Nagô *terreiro* of Laranjeiras, having established its
exclusivity of pure African tradition, uses such glorification in the competitive market of symbolic goods. At a more restricted level, I propose
to see how this process develops within the local religious field and, at
a more inclusive level, how it occurs in the broader segment of symbolic
goods that make up what might be generically called "the traditions of
the city." This alludes to its past.

TRADITIONS AND THE CULT OF THE CITY'S PAST

During the nineteenth century, Laranjeiras became one of the most important urban centers of the province of Sergipe. Its wealth came primarily from the sugar produced in the plantations of the Continguiba valley, hence the concentration within that area of a large black population,
including the highest percentage of Africans existing in the province at
the end of the century.[1] The influx of slaves to the city, accompanying
their masters—a movement that occurred in the Northeast during the
nineteenth century (Freyre, 1968)—not only made Laranjeiras a place
for the storage and commercialization of sugar. It also transformed it into
a city in which the diversification of professional categories attested to a
social differentiation[2] reflected in its cultural life through reading rooms,
schools, French lessons, clubs, theaters, and newspapers that disseminated the important economic, social, and political issues of the second
half of the century.

Substitution of the slavocratic order for free labor had a repercussion
on Laranjeiras's economy and, in 1897, a chronicler of the day wrote of
the city: "It was the most commercial location in the state [and it lost its
importance that] quickly decreased so that, currently, it finds itself in a
state of complete decadence" (Lisboa, 1897, in Dantas, 1976a). The displacement of the commercial axis to Aracaju affected the life of the city,

the decadence of which grew during the following decades when the capital, situated only a few kilometers away, absorbed the urban functions of the cities of the Cotinguiba valley.

The sugar mills and partial substitution of the cane fields for cattle raising did not restore its greatness. The city government is rich. It has one of the highest tax collection rates in the state. But the community is poor. The local population currently has very high expectations that recently established production units of ammonia and urea might restore its past greatness.

Wealth is an important element in the representations that the natives of Laranjeiras make of their own city, its present nearly always contrasted with its past.[3] There is a common nucleus of representation between the different ethnic and social groups of Laranjeiras natives that make Laranjeiras an *old city*. Educated individuals claim it was founded during the sixteenth century, information that is repeated in leaflets edited for tourists by city hall. Referring to the "times of the city," they establish two categories: "olden days," currently referred to also as "the old days," and "the time of today." "The olden days" may have some derivations such as "the time of slavery," always uttered when the speaker is talking about the black man, his work, and his presence in the city. In general terms, the "olden days" are referenced by the cultural life that seems to be associated with the city's wealth.

> "There was a great deal of partying here in the old days — lots of rich people. See all those mansions falling apart there? They all belonged to rich people. Now there are only common people, poor people. The great ones, the really great ones, have all left. What you have nowadays is a lot of poor people. Poor and black. Have you seen how many black people there are in Laranjeiras, ma'am? That's on account of the Africans from the old days." (Teacher)

> "In the old days, Laranjeiras was a rich city — rich and cultured. We produced illustrious citizens here. João Ribeiro was one of them. We even have the Casa João Ribeiro [named after him]. In my opinion, the Laranjeiras of olden days was sort of the Athens of Sergipe. (. . .) There were lots of blacks here, too. There were then and there are still. . . . " (Public servant)

The Laranjeiras of "olden days" is a *rich, black, cultured city*, a time which contrasts with "the time of today," where it is represented as a *poor city, albeit rich in traditions*.

It is for the attributes surrounding representations of Laranjeiras's "olden days" that the city is celebrated. To mythically celebrate the glories of the past is a form of redeeming and compensating for the poverty of the present. Overcharged with meaning, this cult of the city is more accentuated at certain moments of its history. During the 1930s, following the vogue for cultural nationalism, the city's cult of the past is expressed by laudatory historical "reconstructions"[4] and by the valorization of its erudite and popular traditions. The title "Athens of Sergipe" attributed to it on account of the cultural effervescence of its elite during the second half of the nineteenth century is insistently highlighted. But it is not only the cultural tradition that is exalted; popular tradition is, too.

THE NAGÔ AND THE "WHITES":
APPROACHES TO POPULAR TRADITION

It is interesting to follow how, during a single historical moment, selections from the popular culture are made that allow some "aspects" of this culture to be ignored; while others are destined to be repressed by the police and others, still, glorified and presented as the city's traditions, to be identified as folklore, as manifestations from the past.

Strongly supported by local government and by intellectuals, these samples of popular culture are recorded in the local press. During the 1930s, newspapers not only reported on the many dances — *Cacumbis*, *Cheganças*, *Reisados*, Taieiras, and *Lambe-sujos* versus *Caboclinhos* and *Maracatus* — and their rehearsals and performances, but also praised some of their organizers or congratulated their mayor for his enlightened vision in appreciating and reviving local folklore, restrictively understood as dances, entertainments, and popular festivals. During the same period, the attitude toward Afro-Brazilian cults was quite restrictive. The attention of "our diligent municipal police" was directed to an inconvenient Candomblé set up in a street and articles violently attacking macumba were transcribed from Rio de Janeiro newspapers (*Vida Laranjeirense*, 1932, 1933, 1935, 1936).[5]

In the city, strong police persecution was moved against the *terreiros* of Xangô, and those who challenged the prohibition of celebrations were arrested and had their ritual objects apprehended and "burned behind the public jail."

In this strongly repressive climate, the Nagô *terreiro* enjoyed preferential treatment and was allowed to function — a fact that can only be explained by the *mãe-de-santo*'s relationships with members of the ruling class and the significance attributed by it to African tradition in a time when intellectuals glorified the cultural contribution of the black man. The category "the whites" used by the *mãe-de-santo* to indicate "racial" (skin coloring) and, above all, social (individual position in class society and its power structure) features permeates her discourse when she talks about herself and her *terreiro*. Present in her life story as "white papa" and as "boss," they reappear in her narrative about the dispute for religious group leadership, now explicitly associated with upholding an order represented by the police commissioner and by the police (see Chapter 2). Because of a quarrel between factions vying for *terreiro* leadership, "everyone was summoned to the police station but the whites said we were right." Defeated and without "white justice," her rival had started the "disturbance" by opening another "mixed" place of worship. The Nagô *mãe-de-santo*'s account continues:

> "Our brotherhood continues to this day. Nothing ever stood in its way. Everything was proscribed in the time of Lieutenant Maynard and Dr Chico, but not us. Nothing ever stood in the way of Africa." (Bilina)

The time of "Lieutenant Maynard and Dr Chico"—the federally appointed governor of Sergipe and the federally appointed mayor of Laranjeiras, respectively—dates back to [Vargas's] *Estado Novo* [dictatorship], a period in which the city's *terreiros* were targeted by violent police repression.

According to the *mãe-de-santo*, the "whites" (who commanded repression against the Toré but respected the Nagô) spared it because of its African heritage and because they appreciated it.

> "The whites like Nagô. Important folks sometimes come to see the dancing, they appreciate our performance. Father Filadelfo himself and Miss Zizinha the schoolteacher held us in high regard. I mean, the Father didn't attend the Nagô but no one ever bothered us. They insisted we perform at Saint Benedict's Feast." (Bilina)

The Taieira (through which the alliance between the priest and the Nagô is expressed) is a dance organized by the *mãe-de-santo* to be presented within the context of the Catholic Church (that is, at the Feast of Saint Benedict). It is linked to the so-called *Reinado dos Congos*, an institution widely disseminated within Brazilian slavocratic society. Elected by black religious brotherhoods and endorsed by the police and the Church, the *Reis do Congo* had the function of mediating relationships between

masters and slaves, inducing them to work and containing their uprisings, an instrument of domestication which blacks, however, used more
than once to oppose themselves to the dominant group.[6]

For the coronation of these kings, whose mandate was annual or life-
long, festivals were organized and grand processions accompanied them
to the church where there were crowned by the priest. Like other dance
processions, the dance of the Taieira was said to derive from these royal
retinues (Carneiro, 1965: 12). With the passing of the years, the Congo
Kings were incorporated to the group of dancers and, currently, like the
Queens of the Taieira, they still today attend church during the Feast of
Saint Benedict, where they are crowned by a priest who places the crown
of Our Lady of the Rosary on the heads of the queens. Having worshipped
the protector saints of the blacks, the Taieiras leave to visit the houses of
important people of the city or of those who are associated with the organization of the feast by ties of friendship, or who have nativity scenes
in their homes. They present their dances and are repaid with lunches or
amounts of money (Dantas, 1972).

Bilina, who organized the dance for more than fifty years, was said
to have inherited this charge, independently of the *terreiro* leadership,
from her mother, who performed the dance in fulfillment of a promise.
However, she makes no attempt to link the dance to Africa, as she does
insistently with the Nagô, although the Taieira chants often mention the
Congo Queens and include various words thought to be African. According to Bilina: "Nagô and Taieira are two different things: the Taieira is
performed for Saint Benedict and the Nagô for the saints of Africa." But
the observable differences in manifest ritual functions and forms are at-
tenuated—and even diluted—whenever it is a matter of activating the
network of social relations through which she will obtain the necessary
resources for the realization of both. White sectors that might prove in-
different or even aggressive with regard to the Xangô—still subject to
stigmatization in those days—are "domesticated" by the Taieira. The
latter is part of the city's popular traditions—that is to say, those parts
of culture deemed worthy of appreciation. It is included among the so-
called *folguedos* [entertainments or amusements] and folk dances, and
was very often highlighted by the local press during the 1930s and 1940s,
in which the Taieira was always featured, its organizer frequently mentioned and praised as "deserving of a prize for the lovely contribution
paid to our poetic and popular tradition" (*Vida Laranjeirense*, 1932).

It is as a guardian of popular tradition—then regarded as a true depository of nationality—that Bilina is presented to Laranjeiras society of

the day, not as the *mãe-de-santo* of a Xangô *terreiro*, the *terreiro* of a spurious religion (rather, of a superstition) and witchcraft subject to repression.

Within this ambiguous context of representation and symbolic activity, the Nagô *mãe-de-santo* situates herself strategically and ambiguously at the intersection of the permitted and the glorified, the forbidden and the stigmatized.

The context supplies her with frames of reference and categories of language (Bakhtin, 1979) and thus not only reinforces Nagô ethnicity as a form of expressing its difference in relation to the expanding *torés* but also guarantees room for survival amid repression. Xangô could improve its image in society at large if presented as "the tradition of the Africans," a legacy that, at this moment, was eagerly rehabilitated by an entire group of intellectuals who were conceiving Brazilian culture and the role played in it by the various ethnic components of nationality.

THE PRIEST, TRADITIONS, AND NAGÔ

At a local level, such ideas were primarily disseminated through priests and teachers,[7] characters who often figure in the *mãe-de-santo*'s discourse whenever she refers to her relations with the dominant classes. The role of these intellectuals in the dissemination and polarization of official worldviews in force among the educated class has been analyzed by Antonio Gramsci, who, similarly, draws attention to the heteroclite, fragmentary, and incoherent character of subaltern class conceptions of the world and of life (Gramsci, 1978: 183–90).

In Laranjeiras, Zizinha the schoolteacher and Father Filadelfo were considered great enthusiasts of the "city's traditions," among which they attempted to fit the Nagô, a symbol of African tradition. A native son of Laranjeiras and its vicar from 1904 through the mid-1960s, Father Filadelfo's attitude toward the Afro-Brazilian cults that flourished in his parish was significant.

A member of the Academy of Letters of Sergipe, the father participated in the gatherings of the local intellectuals and wrote the "History of Laranjeiras" in which, after presenting a history of the city's Catholic *terreiros*, he refers to Candomblé in the following terms:

"Devotion to Saint Barbara
Candomblé
Because of its agricultural development, Laranjeiras was a com-

mercial hub for the importation of African slaves. For this reason, the survivors of this race live on with all their *traditions and superstitions. Devotion to Saint Barbara has endured the challenge of the years* and the destructive ravages of time. Africans and Creoles gather to invoke Saint Barbara offering her the blood of lambs and roosters sacrificed according to specific rites, eating the innocent victims with *acassá, angu* and *fubá*, after which the Candomblé dances begin and continue for seven or eight days.

Sad, monotonous African songs come from breasts homesick for African sands. Suddenly a member of the company faints. Imagining herself to be possessed by a saint, she is taken to the foot of Saint Barbara, whence she later returns to start up the Candomblé once again.

This martyred, suffering *race* slowly *disappears* from Brazil because of the destructive action of death and the *purifying absorption of the white race*, leaving behind only the dark shadow of a sad past." (Oliveira, 1942: 49–50, my italics)

His narrative is based on two intercrossing axes: that of inferior race (which disappears through the purifying action of the white race) and that of culture (made up of "traditions and superstitions" that have resisted time). Among such "traditions and superstitions" is "devotion to Saint Barbara," that is, the Candomblé which time was unable to eradicate. Thus, although he regards it more as the territory of another belief (or rather, of superstition), he has no reason to declare open battle against it. In fact, such action would be innocuous. History teaches this lesson. It would be more viable to act upon the superstition, divesting it of aspects considered inconvenient or incompatible with dominant Catholic values that also ratified the very order of society, and presenting the divergent religious form as mere "African tradition," embedded in the lives of Laranjeiras natives. This might explain the priest's tolerance in light of the accusation that a schoolteacher (who belonged to the Pious Union of the Daughters of Mary) frequented the Nagô *terreiro*, having soothed her when, in distress, she justified her sporadic presence at the Candomblé as an obligation inherited from her parents (who worshipped African saints): "You go because you are a Laranjeirense."

Thus, in making "superstition" a "tradition," the priest allows himself to coexist peacefully with Candomblé, a permissiveness expressed in the Nagô *mãe-de-santo*'s affirmation that "the priest never bothered us, Santa Barbara's people."

Cordial relations between the Nagô *terreiro* and the local agent of the Catholic Church are based on a sense of compromise in which the absolute exclusivity of the Catholic Church is not threatened by "African tradition"; on the other hand, the Nagô do not consider Catholicism as a rival tradition but rather as a religion that must belong to everyone and to which the Nagô is added. In this respect, the requirement of Catholic baptism for those who propose to embrace the Nagô cult is quite significant and, through its agents, recognizes the dominant religion's exclusivity to "perform rites of insertion of individual biography within civil society."[8]

It should be recorded that, through tradition, many other cultural manifestations of the common people, some of them considered African, were already integrated into the rituals of blacks who, through the Church, are included in the order of white society. Referring to one of the city's *terreiros*, whose patron saints are Benedict and Our Lady of the Rosary, the priest says:

> "Men of color concentrate all their devotions in this *terreiro* where, over one hundred blacks perform (in costume, representing the *Reisados, Cheganças, Congos,* Taieiras, *Mouramas, Marujadas* and *Maracatus*) in the famous and traditional Twelfth Night, celebrating the wars between Christians and Moors and singing songs to the Virgin of the Rosary, victorious at Lepanto." (Oliveira, 1942: 49)

Insofar as they preach the victory of Catholicism over other beliefs and thus propagate the ideological values of whites (who control their performance spaces and have tribute paid them in their rituals), such traditions (or *folguedos,* as they are generally called) are placed as elements for upholding order and social legitimacy, and thus incapable "of reserving for the black man, at least symbolically, an identity and an attitude [with which] to oppose the ethnic dominancy of the white man" (Brandão, 1977: 170).

By this I do not mean that "pure" Nagô candomblé is situated at the same level of ideological manipulation as black rituals performed at Church festivals. I am saying that, in the specific case of Laranjeiras, the contours of "Nagô purity" were not constructed independently from the pressures of the dominant religion expressed, for example, in the language used by the Nagô to speak of their "African purity," which often takes on the language of the Catholic religion, its rites, its liturgical paraphernalia, and its values.

Within this context something must be said about the languages of the "pure," for the rhetoric of purity takes on different expressions. It seems to me that the language used to draw its outlines has a great deal to do with education and the intellectual's specific area of activity (priest, judge, teacher, doctor, scientist, etc.) that, at the service of upholding the hegemony of the dominant classes over the common people, plays a more important role at the local level (Gramsci, 1978).

Whereas, in Laranjeiras, signs of Africa take on the language of the dominant religion, in Bahia (where the search for "African survivals" became a scientific concern at the end of the nineteenth century and the comparison of cultural traits in Bahian and African candomblés became a habitual practice), "Nagô purity" is expressed through the language of science, which, in studying the differences between whites and blacks—that is, between dominant and subaltern classes—ranks these differences by transforming them into inequality and attempts to conceal domestication through an appreciation of primitivism.

The ideological function of highlighting primitivism—or rather "Africanism"—within a "civilized," "modern," or "capitalist" society is to keep blacks in their place, in the place destined to them by whites—the place of the subaltern—inasmuch as blacks internalize the elements of their own domination (Birman, 1980: 20).

In the Nagô *terreiro* of Laranjeiras, the signs of Africa, at least in the initiation of *filhos de santo*, are stripped of representations that might recall savagery (for example, bloodletting over the head, cuts to the body of the initiate, and head shaving). The ritual language is that of the Catholic Church, with whom they mix with no loss to African purity.

It seems to me that, in both cases, "purity" is the dominant characteristic of Afro-Brazilian religions according to a moral and evaluative criterion (pure/impure), and that this operation comprehends the concepts of "domestication" and "danger."

THE LANGUAGE OF AFRICA AS SURVIVAL STRATEGY

The identification (by dominant sectors) of the Nagô with Africa and recognition of African cultural heritage as tradition appreciates the Nagô in proportion to fidelity to its origins. Along with the idea that the Nagô practices only Good, this appreciation creates a privileged space for them in competition with the *torés*.

One of the advantages is the establishment of temporary monopolies with regard to services normally rendered to the population by various centers. This occurs during the periods in which the police close down the *terreiros*, yet allow the Nagô to remain open.

In resorting to Africa and to the purity of African tradition safeguarded by her *terreiro* as an explanation for the fact that it was safe from police persecution, the *mãe-de-santo* is obviously hiding reasons that are linked, for example, to her network of social relations, to points of support that she had among the "whites," and she is making use of a rhetoric that was widely propagated at the time among educated whites, at least in northeastern Brazil, and gaining advantages from her African uniqueness. For the other *terreiros*, which enjoyed the fame of practicing magic and sorcery, attending their clientele was an extremely risky enterprise, for in the city, the prohibition of the *terreiros*' functioning had been made in the name of the fight against witchcraft and quackery. Such zeal in extirpating curative practices that did not merge with the orthodoxy of science takes on greater strength in Laranjeiras, for the local *intendente* was a doctor and, as such, participated in a form of knowledge that had been constructed and codified within the academy to disqualify popular wisdom and to claim for itself a monopoly over treatment of the body.

It is interesting to observe that police persecution of the *terreiros* served to intensify the stigma of witchcraft attributed to the *torés* and to some of them in particular, renewing persecution that was occasionally intensified according to alliances with local politicians.[9]

The following example is elucidative. In defiance of police prohibition, a *terreiro* gathered its members and performed a ritual that was violently interrupted by the local police commissioner. The *pai-de-santo* swore revenge and, a few days later, the police officer was killed in an accident. The death was attributed to the *torezeiro*'s evildoing, and the *torezeiro* himself transformed into a great sorcerer through the collective belief in the power of magic (Lévi-Strauss, 1967: 193–213). He was the leader of an African *terreiro* that had joined the Toré, and his reputation as a sorcerer is further consolidated and highlighted when contrasted with the "pure Nagô," regarded as opposed to the practice of Evil. Inasmuch as the stigma of sorcery and quackery did not weigh upon it, the Nagô was afforded greater freedom to act even during the period of police repression and, by enjoying the freedom of this consent, he was able to increase his clientele.

If the Toré's reputation as a center for any type of service, irrespective of the ethics involved, would attract, especially to the better known ones, a clientele anxious to see their own desires fulfilled, even if this meant a concourse of the forces of Evil, the same movement also intensifies the client flow to the Nagô *terreiro*. Represented as a *terreiro* exclusively dedicated to the practice of Good, it also attracted those who, believing themselves the targets of the witchcraft of the torés, needed to neutralize their action and undo the magic. According to the *mãe-de-santo*:

> ". . . Lots of these folks who come looking for me go from toré to toré, and catch all this bad stuff and then come looking for me to undo it. I don't enjoy doing this sort of work. But I get a lot of it."
> (Bilina)

Underlying the dynamics of sorcery and counter-sorcery is the idea that "pure" Africa has greater magical efficacy than "mixture," and is able to "undo" the magic of the latter. This external assessment of the power and *força* of *terreiro* leaders is a key element in their success, for it is by means of this rhetoric that the "outsiders" responsible for a significant part of their earnings are attracted to Candomblé.

Although many authors present the wealth of Candomblé as being maintained by the *filhos de santo* themselves,[10] I agree with Leni Silverstein when she declares that such a "point of view represents a romantic and unrealistic assessment of the needs of Candomblé and of the individuals that compose it" (Silverstein, 1979: 156), usually the poor (who would not be able to afford the expenses of Candomblé).

The Nagô *terreiro* of Laranjeiras consists of a low-income congregation. They place work, goods, and (on a much lesser scale) money at the *mãe-de-santo*'s disposal. They agree, however, that expenses incurred by the *terreiro* greatly exceed the application of goods supplied to the *mãe-de-santo* by the congregation's members. Since in recent times the latter has exercised no other activities beyond the magical-religious — for the fixed income she receives from renting out some property is quite modest — one may conclude that the resources employed in the *terreiro* are also external. They are principally furnished by clients. Occasionally, the reason for seeking out the *terreiro* is euphemistically stated as the need to "fulfill a promise or vow."

Promises, which are a form of delaying payment for graces granted by the *orixás* through the *mãe-de-santo*'s intermediation (albeit more common in the *orixá-mãe-de-santo* relationship), also occur in the relationship with the clients, especially with certain clients who maintain closer ties with the *mãe-de-santo*. Oftentimes, they are middle- or upper-class individuals (farmers, professionals, politicians) who, making use of the magical services rendered by the *terreiros*, repay them through endowments presented not as retribution for the *mãe-de-santo*'s work as an agent of the supernatural, but as a counterpart to the *orixá*'s gifts, whose rituals will be enriched by such donations, allowing for greater quantities of food to be made available to those present.

Concealed behind this language of promise are alliances that were established between the *mãe-de-santo* and people whose class position ensures not only the *terreiro*'s material survival but the brilliance of its rituals and facilitates its relationship with the institutional level.

A comparison is imposed with regard to the way that the alliance with people who occupy positions within the social structure allows them to dispense resources and the way that protection upon Candomblé was resolved by the "pure Nagô" of the states of Sergipe and Bahia. In the latter, the inclusion of people from the upper classes occurred through the growth of the *"família de santo"* through the figure of the *ogã* who, in certain *terreiros*, is legitimized by way of Africa through the incorporation of the *Obás de Xangô*,[11] an "African tradition" introduced during the 1930s. In Bahia, where the *ogã* occupies a clear position within the structure of the religious group, mechanisms were created for those who wished to publicly occupy his position. These mechanisms involve prominent participation in public rituals; this is useful because Candomblé's power of legitimization confers social prestige and distinction upon those who protect it.

In Laranjeiras, protectors are not included within the religious group's formal hierarchy but are camouflaged behind the clientele's informality and fluidity. Their financial contributions are expressed through a language that, borrowed from the Catholic Church, attempts to conceal the *mãe-de-santo*'s relationship with the protector, inasmuch as (within the context of Catholicism) "promise fulfillment" is a direct contract between the *mãe-de-santo* and the worshipper who normally dispenses with the mediation of the religious specialists.

The differences in language that express (or rather, conceal) the *pai-de-santo*'s relationship with his support from the upper social strata may be related to Candomblé's degree of public recognition and the transformation of religious content into merchandise to be consumed by laymen, aspects visibly differentiated in cities like Salvador and Laranjeiras. Included among the city's most legitimate traditions and valued for its "African purity," the Nagô *terreiro* of Laranjeiras has resisted proposals to present itself outside its religious context or to allow its sacred dances to be transformed into spectacle for the appreciation of strangers. The group's history records only one displacement (to "perform at the University" in Aracaju) during the early 1960s. On the same occasion, the Nagô *terreiro* of Laranjeiras that had mixed with the Toré was also performing, along with another *terreiro* from Aracaju. Confrontation with the rival *terreiro*—which had largely adopted the Bahian model of dances and colorful ritual costumes—had a negative result for the "pure Nagô." It was clearly less prepared to please a broader public, eager for a visually beautiful show of powerful emotions aroused by spirit possessions, then offered mostly by its antagonist. Nor, on the other hand, did it satisfy the specific interests of students who were concerned with identifying the two *terreiros'* African components, most visible in its rival, once the students' standard of reference was Afro-Brazilian literature, wrought in the Nagô candomblés of Bahia and whose model it had partly copied. With such an experience, the Nagô must have perceived that, in order to advantageously be part of this model, it would be necessary to update its repertory of ritual features, in other words, to give up what was considered and presented as fidelity to Africa. The option chosen was to protect the *terreiro*'s "purity" by turning down requests that became more frequent and aggressive during the 1970s, when the state, in its search for popular legitimacy through its tourist agency, begins to support and promote, along with the Federations of Umbanda and Afro-Brazilian cults, the festivals of Iemanjá and Oxum, with the relocation of hundreds of *terreiros* to the beach. The refusal to align itself with the "mixed ones" is made in the name of Africa and, simultaneously, becomes an additional sign, used to invoke its African distinction, which is also repeated in a refusal to become affiliated with the Federations, as announced in Chapter 2.

As several scholars have shown, the Federations have not only allowed politicians to institutionalize the religious domination exercised in the *terreiros* to be used for electoral purposes, but also, by replacing the police in inspecting the cults, to clearly take over the function of control and integration with the social order and dominant values (Brown, 1974; Silva, 1976; Velho, 1975; Ortiz, 1978).

Federalization is the process that legally permits the existence of the *terreiros*, which must affiliate themselves to a Federation and appoint a board of directors, organized according to the law. This bureaucratic intermediation, established by the Federations is peremptorily rejected by the Nagô *terreiro*, in the name of its African "purity." Responding to regents of the Federation who were threatening her with police intervention should she not become affiliated, the *mãe-de-santo* said: "Africa was never proscribed and we're not about to mix with Federations now."

While intermediation by means of the Federation is, in principle, based on a rational bureaucratic model,[12] the intermediation used by the Nagô *terreiro* is more traditional, based on personal access to prestigious individuals in the dominant sectors. It is by making use of this informal intermediation that the Nagô *terreiro* allows itself to refuse the intermediation from the Federations without being disturbed. Although the two types of intermediation are not incompatible,[13] the efficiency of the traditional model and, on the other hand, its appropriateness to the style of the *terreiro* lead the *mãe-de-santo* in her relationship with the ruling class, having two possible paths before herself. There is the legal path, declaring that the Federation will afford everyone the same rights and the same guarantees in the eyes of the law, and the non-legalized path, through which the individual moves through life according to the personal manipulation of social resources (Fry, 1978), allowing her to choose the second type of intermediation, which constitutes itself as a consequence of the "ideology of favor" (Schwarcz, 1977). It should be noted that adoption of this model still functions as a powerful diacritical sign, establishing boundaries with regard to the city's other possession cult groups, since it is the only *terreiro* in the town that never resorted to bureaucratic intermediation.

The mystique of African purity is thus consolidated and adoption of this model allows the *mãe-de-santo* to use the language of Africa as a survival strategy to face the dilemma in which she finds herself: the supernatural base of her mystical strength comes from her ability to uphold a heritage received from her "unmixed" ancestors or, rather, from the reproduction of tradition, a task that becomes thankless as capitalism penetrates the lives of the cults and attempts to transform them into merchandise. The dilemma becomes even more crucial when one knows that it is among the middle and upper levels of society at large—those therefore more committed to the circulation of capital and interested in its political use, and often making cultural nationalism a mechanism for domination—that it will seek out the resources necessary for its survival.

The solution found by the *mãe-de-santo*—incorporating resources from the upper classes that have come to her through her clientele, keeping "protectors" outside the boundaries of the "familia de santo" and, therefore, of ritual public spaces (associated with tourism's relative unimportance in the city)—have allowed her, thus far, to enjoy the resources of the dominant classes without entering the circuit of candomblé as spectacle and without giving up what are presented as signs of her loyalty to Africa. It is open for debate how long her successor will be able to keep up this twofold strategy. What is certain is that tradition and "African purity" are used by the *terreiro* in different ways at two different moments of the group's history and its relationship to society at large, both of which ultimately have the same objective: the group's survival.

During the 1930s, when under the influx of the appreciation of Africa intellectuals focused on the "purest" Africans, using the categories of religion and magic, Good and Evil, and privileging them in the process of legitimacy and legalization, the Nagô *terreiro* used its "African purity" in order to rid itself of police persecution and dispose of a space that would give it advantages in its competition with the *torés*, who were then in expansion, albeit subject to strong stigma and repression. This strategy, which reflects a much broader movement on a local (or at least regional) level, extends over the following decade and resonates in the city's cult of its past, represented by wealth constructed with the concourse of the African.

In order to assess how efficient the language of Africa was at that moment in the search for a survival space or, at least, for a survival free of police harassment, Nagô—which had updated itself according to the Bahian model and incorporated the *caboclo* tradition (thus becoming at least doubly traditional) in attempting to escape police persecution by registering itself at a notary public as a civil organization—does so by using the language of Africa (Chapter 3).

At a later moment—which in terms of Sergipe would appear to begin during the 1960s, when the legitimacy obtained by Umbanda in the South reaches the Northeast, following the very movement of expansion of that religious form that exalts the *caboclo*—the legitimacy of the cults previously circumscribed by "African purity" grows and comes to encompass the torés as well. Such a movement coincides with the culture industry's better outfitting and greater efficacy in transforming exotic religions into "lucrative national institutions," from both an economic standpoint and a political one (Fry, 1977a).

Within this new context, if the language of "African purity" is no longer needed to ensure legality, now also recognized and extended to the "mixed" ones through the Federations, it is undeniable that the discourse of fidelity to Africa confers uniqueness and greater legitimacy upon it within local Afro-Brazilians. By including the dominant ideological repertory on the participation and signification of ethnic groups in the making of nationality, specifically in the city's history, Nagô participants use the language of African purity as an instrument with which to guarantee the *terreiro*'s survival strategy, maintaining the temple with the resources of the dominant classes and attempting to avoid inclusion in tourist exploitation.

It is in this sense that fidelity to a tradition considered African does not constitute an "explanation" in itself, for tradition as a cultural "product" is

> "like dead labor in Marx's conception — it is efficient only insofar as it is activated by living labor, that is, absorbed and recreated within concrete social action. Culture is, therefore, a process according to which men organize and confer meaning upon their actions through a symbolic manipulation which is the fundamental attribute of all human practice." (Durham, 1977: 34)

Thus, the language of Nagô ethnicity at least makes way for a survival space within society at large, a space in which tradition does not possess a univocal meaning in itself but allows for a polysemics that expresses and updates itself in social practice.

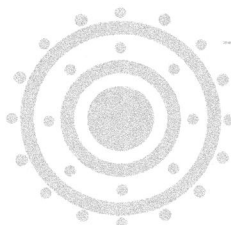

Conclusion

Throughout this work Nagô hegemony has been an ever-recurring problem. In their attempts to come to grips with it, Brazilian black studies scholars have resorted to various factors. Nina Rodrigues, who initially explained it through the numerical predominance of the Nagôs over the other African peoples introduced here, amplified his schema to include diffusion of the language and organization of Nagô priesthood as factors of this hegemony (Rodrigues, 1977: 215).

This point of view is much more elaborately proposed by Édison Carneiro. Taking economic, demographic, social, and cultural factors into account, he argues that, as a consequence "of the social status they had attained in Africa," where Nagô gods were "already almost international" deities, and as a result of the high regard in which they were held in Brazil, the Nagôs of Bahia became a sort of elite, imposing their religions upon other slaves. Internal traffic was an important element in the religious interchange between the African peoples who gathered here, and the concentration of Nagô blacks in Bahia during the late eighteenth century provided the final touches to the construction and hegemony of the religious model that emerges there, above all in urban centers, where blacks possessed the money and freedom indispensable to the existence of organized religion. From Bahia (and, to a lesser degree, from Pernambuco and Maranhão), the model irradiated to the rest of Brazil, reproduced in one way or another depending upon the vigor of already established local cults. This allowed for demarcations of different areas in which Afro-Brazilian religions, in the form in which they are found, "follow [the] trajectories of slave dispersion (internal traffic) all the way to the abolition [of slavery], although the later (and especially the current) movements of the Brazilian population are already slowly amplifying, complicating and transforming this schema" (Carneiro, 1964: 137).

Without dismissing the importance of internal migrations and other significant factors in the analysis of the cultural dynamic, it is clear that—at least since the nineteenth century—intellectuals played a meaningful role in Nagô hegemony. The movement to legitimize Candomblé *terreiros*—which began with evolutionist intellectuals presenting Nagô as the most advanced form of African religions, contrasting it with the magic of other peoples—closely follows the movement of mythical approximation to Africa, of which Nagô would be the "purest," most authentic representation. In notarizing the "purity" and "authenticity" of Nagô Candomblé with the rubber stamp of science, intellectuals are making an alliance with producers of black culture—one that extrapolates the boundaries of the academy (Vogt & Fry, 1982). This has repercussions for expanding the religious model throughout Brazil, to the point of interference with procedures of police repression that, at least temporarily, adjusted the axis of legality/illegality to the axis of Religion/ Magic. In my opinion, this alliance not only affected the expansion of the Nagô model but its very configuration, as crystallized in outlines and selections of cultural traits Bahian *terreiros* deemed and authenticated as the "purest" by intellectuals.

In transforming "Nagô purity"—a native category used by *terreiros* to mark their differences and rivalries—into an analytic category, anthropologists (through the construction of the Nagô model) contributed to a crystallization of cultural contents that came to be regarded as the highest expression of Africanness. However, the existence of *terreiros* that define their link to Africa—especially to the "purest Nagô tradition" recognized by the rest—by calling upon a repertory of cultural traits that differs from the Bahian Nagô model indicates that the standardization of "Nagô purity" based on the crystallization that took place in Bahia through the contribution of intellectuals is, if not arbitrary, at least complicated when identity is considered to be something constructed in the process of social interaction through boundaries established by the group rather than a given that is fused with a reified cultural unit.

On the other hand, the idea of purity has a great deal to do with the power structure of society (Douglas, 1976). Significantly, the demarcation of the outlines of "purity" by the Nagô of Laranjeiras associates the language of orthodoxy to the sharing of common domains of a past dualistically divided between Good and Evil and Order and Disorder. This is how the degeneration of the pure Nagô does not result of any combination, but of combinations with religious forms socially defined as inferior, and the schema of society's symbolic forces is thus incorporated in the configuration of pure/impure.

Inasmuch as it presupposes the existence of an original state, in being transformed into an analytical category, the ideology of purity privileges the search for origins and "Africanisms" and strengthens the methodological orientation according to which the meanings of cultural elements are considered to have been inscribed in their origins. It is as though it were necessary to forge the identity of Brazilian blacks anew so that they would always be *foreigners*, beings linked to Africa. In fact, the debate on Africa (which begins in the academic community just as blacks are given the legal status of citizens) acquires a fully recognized legitimacy in the 1930s (when African heritage is at the center of regionalist and nationalist concerns), extended over time and continuing even today to echo Sílvio Romero's 1888 cry of warning that Africa should be studied in Brazil.

The long journey "back to Africa"—a longer and stormier return than the one endured by the slave ships that sailed from Africa to Brazil in a few short months—has lasted almost a century.

The trail initially blazed by Nina Rodrigues grew wider in the 1930s, with the attempted legalization/legitimization of Candomblé, initially outlined according to criteria of "Africanness"—that is to say, in conformity with the Nagô model. In this process of searching for legitimacy it is possible to identify three discourses that are now juxtaposed and then succeed one another; nevertheless, they are ultimately intertwined: the discourse on possession, the discourse on religion versus magic, and, finally, the discourse on the primitivism, exoticism, and beauty of Candomblé.

The first two draw their ability to persuade—their *força* (or "strength"), to use a term that is quite common in the world of Candomblé—from science. Possession is initially interpreted by psychiatry; nevertheless, social and cultural factors are highlighted, and education and mental hygiene become key concepts. This interpretation is better attuned to the anthropology that had proscribed race as a factor of social interpenetration and makes culture its slogan. It is under the sign of the culturalist explanation (specifically that of cultural relativism) that possession will later be freed from the stigma of "pathological phenomenon" in which it had been imprisoned by psychiatrists when they attempted to situate the cults outside the reach of the Law.

The discourse on religion and magic, the latter negatively connoted as an earlier, inferior state of the former (or even as a degenerate form of it), alludes to the evolutionist anthropology of the nineteenth century and to evolutionary schemas that, under diverse formulations, return to an everyday positivism in which the ideas of progress and absolute belief in science eventually relate to the idea of morality. Through science, the "purest Nagô" Candomblé is presented as a true religion, an ideal romantically transformed into a haven of "cleanliness and morality" in opposition to the magical, amoral world of *catimbós, torés, caboclo* Candomblés, low spiritist sessions, and so on.

At the theoretical level, the prominent position assigned to the Nagô cult by intellectuals was thus a corollary of its recognition as a more evolved Afro-Brazilian religious form through which its resistance and hegemony in Brazil could be explained. At the level of practice and organization, such an assumption reinforced the orthodoxy and need for control over the purity of religion, in an attempt to prevent its degeneration into magic.

In this search for the legitimacy of the more Africanized Candomblé, the discourse of art is associated to the rational discourse of science and the primitive-exotic Candomblé becomes beautiful. In this process of association between the exotic and the aesthetic, beauty became one of the predicates of black religion, establishing itself as a particular form of romanticizing and idealizing the subaltern.

The search for Candomblé's legitimacy (and particularly for that of a more Africanized Candomblé) undertaken in the Northeast, analyzed in this work above all during the 1930s and 1940s, presents some commonalities with regard to the process of Umbanda's legitimization in the Southeast (Brown, 1974; Ortiz, 1978).

At the organizational level, for example, there were attempts to create organizations that replaced or intermediated police control (Federations of Cults, Mental Health Services) or, at the ideological level, an attempt to "cleanse them" of the stigma of sorcery, exploitation, and amorality—characteristics firmly rejected and regarded as components of the opposite pole's identity that are thus disqualified and invalidated: Quimbanda in opposition to Umbanda and Toré or Candomblé in opposition to Africanized Candomblé.

In my opinion, the role reserved for Africa constitutes the main difference between the process of legitimizing Umbanda and Candomblé. In the latter, African heritage, above all the "purest Nagô," is glorified and presented as true religion, whereas in Umbanda it is proscribed and identified with sorcery, thus relegated to the dominions of Quimbanda.

The glorification of Africa in the Northeast and its negation in the Southeast, at the same historical moment and within the same symbolic field—that of religion—seems to articulate it with demographic, historical, and economic variations of the regional structures and the specific mode of black inclusion in those structures. The high concentration of blacks in the Northeast and their permanence in the lower classes of the regional structure points more strongly in the direction of Africa as a subject of high ideological potentiality. The celebration of African cultural heritage, used in the Northeast as a regional diacritical sign, had allowed the local elites to justify the underdevelopment of the Southeast through the black man's solid presence (now as a free laborer) in which emotion and sentiment are superimposed on the rationality needed for success in the supposedly egalitarian and democratic competitive social order. This order takes elements of black African culture and transforms them into symbols that distinguish not only a region but the country itself from the rest of the world and Europe in particular.

Within the context of the 1930s and 1940s, celebration of the "purest" African cultural heritage resembled the mythical appreciation of the Indian, ideally romanticized and elevated to the position of aesthetic object and mythical ancestor in the nineteenth century. The Indian's transformation into a symbol of national identity occurred through a process of transfiguration of reality, which concealed the expropriation of his lands and the many different types of pressure to which Indian communities were submitted. Similarly, almost a century later, despite the many differences that certainly exist and the glorification of a mythical Africa and its reified cultural heritage, as occurred in the Northeast, Brazilian blacks were confined to a cultural ghetto isolated from life's flow and its position within the structure of society, concealing inequalities through an emphasis upon symbolic forms of integration.

On the other hand, this incessant search for "Africanisms" implies the recognition that Brazilian black identity is something inexorably tied to cultural traits that allude to the existence of an authentic African culture, "pieces" of which are continually sought out as treasures to be carefully guarded and preserved because they certify black identity.

Although Africa is a source of powerful symbols for Brazilian blacks, it must be emphasized that cultural traits, whether real or supposedly originated in Africa, in and of themselves do not confer ideological autonomy upon blacks, since origin does not necessarily define the meaning and function of cultural forms. Like identity, these are constructed and take on meaning in the real process of social life.

Glossary

Adaru Vegetable-based ritual food made from cooked corn and beans served with rice and prepared with coconut milk.

Adiborô-pegan Nagô *terreiro* ritual sequence in which *filhos de santo* mimic "working" with a short hoe.

Água do pé do santo Water contained in clay jars and placed at the foot of an altar.

Alumiada [Literally, enlightened.] One to whom supernatural powers are attributed.

Alumiar os santos [Literally, to light the saints.] Keeping the place in which the *orixá*'s stones may be found artificially lit whenever natural lighting is insufficient.

Angola A Candomblé nation.

Axé See *Força*.

Baixar o santo One who is in a state of trance induced by the *orixá*; the same as *manifestar* and *descer*.

Bará See *Lebará*.

Bastão See *Exó*.

Batalhão [Literally, battalion.] A gathering of people to carry out a common task.

Batismo [Literally, baptism.] Name used by the Nagô *terreiro* of Laranjeiras to indicate the initiation ritual through which one's link to an *orixá* is established. Initiation ritual.

Bebemiô Closing ritual in festivities of the Nagô *terreiro*. The leavetaking of the *orixás*.

Beg Title given to the elder chiefs of a Nagô *terreiro*.

Caboclo Supernatural being generally represented as an Indian.

Candomblé Term usually employed in Bahia to designate the set of Afro-Brazilian religions, but also the place of worship and religious feasts. It corresponds to the Xangô of Pernambuco, Alagoas, and Sergipe.

Casa de santo [Literally, house of the saint.] The same as *terreiro*.

Catimbó A ritual to which Indian origin has been attributed, it deals basically with problem-solving.

Centro [Literally, center.] Place of worship. The same as *terreiro*.

Choro [Literally, cry.] Traditional Nagô funeral rite.

Confirmação A confirmation ritual in which a saint is received through family heritage or initiation.

Consulta [Literally, consultation.] Ritual in which *terreiros* resort to *orixás* or other spirits in order to solve clients' problems.

Corpo limpo [Literally, cleansed, purified body.] A body without impurities, one that has been cleansed. In order to keep the body clean, one must observe rules prescribed for different occasions.

Corpo sujo [Literally, soiled, impure body.] An impure body. Impurity stems from the non-observance of ritual practices.

Corte do inhame [Literally, cutting of the yam.] Annual rite that marks the offering of the new yam to the *orixás*.

Dar água aos santos [Literally, to give water to the saints.] The periodic renewal of water in ceramic vessels devoted to various saints and kept upon an altar.

Dar comida aos santos [Literally, to give food to the saints.] Setting food consecrated to each of the entities upon an altar.

Dar contas [Literally, to give beads.] The giving of necklaces with the symbolic colors of the *orixás*.

Despacho An offering to the *orixá* made with intentions as various as appeasement, assistance, bringing harm, etc.

Dogum The metal sword that is *Ogum*'s insignia.

Dono do santo A person who has obligations to an entity because he/she has submitted to initiation or received it as a family heritage.

Encantados [Literally, enchanted ones.] Spirits identified with Indians.

Enrolado A *terreiro* that resorts to various different ritual traditions. The same as *misturado* (mixed).

Esquerda [Literally, left.] The side of Evil, the side of *Exu*.

Exó A metal rod used in rituals by the Nagô *mãe-de-santo* as a symbol of group leadership.

Exu A spirit who serves Good and Evil indiscriminately. In Laranjeiras, it is his evil nature that is highlighted and he is identified with the Devil.

Feitorio de santo [Literally, making of the saint.] The set of ritual practices through which a *mãe* or *pai-de-santo* links someone to a given *orixá*. It is an initiation ritual.

Fereguim Processional rite of a Nagô *terreiro*.

Festejo Group of rituals that necessarily includes animal sacrifices and dancing. Their public nature connotes a feast.

Filho(a) de fé [Literally, faithful son or daughter.] The same as *filho(a) de santo*.

Filho(a) de santo [Literally, son or daughter-of-saint/children-of-saint.] Person linked to a *terreiro*.

Força [Literally, force or strength.] Mystical power attributed to certain people and objects.

Fundamento Knowledge regarding the rituals and doctrines of one's "nation."

Guenguê Ritual food that is distributed to cult participants in the Nagô *terreiro* at the end of festivities. It is a corn mash regarded as the "food of the dead."

Iansã *Orixá* that protects against lightning bolts. Identified as Saint Barbara in the Nagô *terreiro*, where she appears as *Insã*.

Iaô One who has undergone an initiation ritual.

Iguê Rite of the dead that takes place on the third day of a seven-day festival.

Ijexá Candomblé nation.

Iluminada (alumiada) [Literally, enlightened.] A person to whom any supernatural gift is attributed.

Insã *Iansã*'s name in a Nagô *terreiro*.

Irmandade [Literally, brotherhood.] Term used in some *terreiros* in order to designate its members as a group.

Jeje Candomblé nation.

Ketu Candomblé nation.

Lavagem de cabeça [Literally, washing of the head.] Part of the initiation ritual.

Lavagem da pedra do santo [Literally, washing of the saint's stone.] The same as *lavagem de santo*.

Lavagem dos santos [Literally, washing of the saints.] Rite for removing dust accumulated on the stones of the *orixás* in order to replenish the "power" contained within them.

Lebará [In the Nagô terreiro of Laranjeiras.] Regarded as an entity that casts out *Exu* and protects against Evil. Elsewhere, he is regarded as a Dahomeyan *Jeje* entity that corresponds to the Ioruba Nagô *Exu*. The entity is also known as Elegbará and Elegbá.

Levar o ebó The taking of food to *Exu* at the opening of the festivities and, at their end, all the leftover ritual foods to throw into the river, the domain of Olokum.

Levas Insignias of the *orixás.*

Limpeza [Literally, cleansing.] Purification ritual.

Lokum (Olokum) River spirit.

Mãe-de-santo [Literally, mother-of-saint.] Female *terreiro* chief.

Malê Black African Muslim.

Malungo Comrade. Term used by slaves to designate comrades who came over (to Brazil) on the same ship.

Manifestação de santo [Literally, manifestation of the saint.] A spirit's descent (and entry) into the body of the follower.

Mariô Palm leaf that has been unwoven for ritual purposes.

Matança [Literally, slaughter.] Animal sacrifices.

Misturado [Literally, mixed.] *Terreiro* that follows diverse ritual traditions.

Nação [Literally, nation.] Refers to the set of beliefs and ritual practices presented as the *terreiro*'s tradition.

Nagô Term generically applied in Brazil to Africans from southern and central Dahomey and from southeastern Nigeria. One of the "nations" of Candomblé. Denomination of one of the *terreiros* of the city of Laranjeiras identified as "pure African" by opposition to *torés* (who are allegedly of Indian and/or mixed origin).

Obrigação Ritual obligation.

Ogã An individual who may perform ritual functions or simply mediate the *terreiro*'s relationship with society at large. A sort of protector of the *terreiro.*

Ogodô The most important of all the *orixás* in a Nagô *terreiro*, equivalent to the Blessed Sacrament. Elsewhere (in Bahia, for instance), *Ogodô* is considered to be one of the Xangôs.

Ogum the *orixá* of war and of iron.

Omolu the *orixá* of skin diseases.

Oô Ritual food prepared with a mashed yam base and dedicated to Lebará.

Orixás Deities of African origin who possess men and women.

Orixás de frente *Orixás* who practice Good.

Pai da costa Ancestral spirit worshipped in Nagô *terreiros.*

Pai-de-santo [Literally, father-of-saint.] Male *terreiro* chief.

Patrão [Literally, boss.] Name given in Nagô *terreiros* to the slaughterer of animals.

Pegê Sanctuary. The place of stones of the saints and their ritual paraphernalia.

Primeira roda See *Roda.*

Quarto de santo [Literally, saint's chamber.] The same as *Pegê*.

Reparos [Literally, repairs.] Consultations or divination in which cowries are used to propose solutions for any number of problems.

Roda [Literally, wheel or circle.] Ritual dance. In addition to the placement of the dancers, it indicates ritual sequences: the circle of virgins, the first circle, and the circle of the *orixás*.

Roda das virgens [Literally, wheel or circle of virgins.] The first of the dances in a Nagô *terreiro*, danced by women and children.

Salvar as entradas Greeting the spirits that guard or protect doors and other means of entry and passage: Lebará and Exu.

Santo [Literally, saint.] One of the names given to supernatural beings. The same as *orixá*.

Santo forte [Literally, strong or powerful saint.] An *orixá* to whom great supernatural powers are attributed.

Santos da Costa [Literally, saints from the coast.] *Orixás* or the stones in which they dwell.

Santos de pedras [Literally, stone saints.] Stones in which the *orixás* dwell.

Santos que não descem [Literally, saints who do not descend.] Saints who do not possess the faithful. In many cases, this is because there are no initiates consecrated to them.

Ta A particle that precedes references to the name of Africans belonging to the female sex, indicating respect. Masculine: Ti.

Taieira A group of dancers that performs at the feasts of Saint Benedict and Our Lady of the Rosary in Laranjeiras.

Tambor [Literally, drum.] A ritual instrument.

Tambor-mestre [Literally, master drum.] By virtue of the special mystical qualities attributed to it, this is the drum that opens all ritual ceremonial percussion.

Terreiro The temple or house of worship. The group of people who make up a congregation under the leadership of a *pai-* or *mãe-de-santo*.

Tí Particle that precedes reference to the names of African elders of the male sex; indicative of respect. Feminine: *Ta*.

Tirar iaô do quarto [Literally, to bring the initiate out of the room.] One of the final stages of the initiation ritual at a *terreiro*; it includes the *feitorio de santo* (or reclusion of the initiate).

Toadas *Orixá* chants.

Toque Drumbeats. Candomblé festivity.

Toré A *caboclo terreiro* in which various ritual traditions are mixed.

Torezeiro A follower of the Toré.

Trabalhar com a esquerda [Literally, to work with the left.] To work with *Exu*. To do Evil.

Trabalho [Literally, work.] Ritual activity. The term is more generally employed to designate private activities.

Umbanda Religious form of possession to which a mixture of Bantu African, Indian, and spiritualist components are attributed.

Xangô African *orixá* associated with lightning, thunder, and storms. By extension, the term designates the place and group of religious ceremonies in (the Brazilian states of) Pernambuco, Alagoas, and Sergipe. In the latter state, its meaning is equivalent to that of Candomblé in Bahia.

Xerê A small ritual rattle.

Zelador de santo [Literally, caretaker of the saint.] One who looks after a domestic sanctuary that has almost always passed down by deceased family members.

Zelar os santos [Literally, to care or look after the saints.] To keep the saints in a clear, well-lighted place, and to give them food and water.

Notes

INTRODUCTION

1. The term Afro-Brazilian has been the object of criticism, denounced as an ideological connotation associated with evolutionist and racist assumptions (Velho, 1975). I continue to use it because I have not found an alternative term that satisfies me. Black cults or black religions have the inconvenience of inscribing, a priori, meanings that may not have correspondence in the social practice of these religious groups; possession cults (including Protestant religious forms) broaden the field of observation too much. In light of these difficulties, I continue to employ the term Afro-Brazilian, thus running risks similar to those incurred by the use of the term "primitive," which, despite its strong ideological connotations, continues to be used in anthropology due to difficulties in finding a replacement.

2. Nagô tradition encompasses the beliefs and ritual practices through which a connection is intended between certain *terreiros* and the religious traditions of African groups from Dahomey and Nigeria.

3. *Terreiro* is a term that designates both the place of worship and the religious group and its practices, according to which traditionalism (or, in other words, fidelity to Africa) is assessed. In Salvador, the Gantois or Ilê Iyá Omi Axé Iyamassê, the Engenho Velho or Ilê Axé Iya-Nassô, the São Gonçalo do Retiro, better known as Axé Opô Afonjá, and, less often, the Alaketu or Ilê Maroialaji are invariably considered the most traditional *terreiros* by scholars ranging from Nina Rodrigues in the nineteenth century to Juana Elbein dos Santos in the present day. Many other studies of Candomblé have resulted from the observations in these *terreiros*. And so it was that Nina Rodrigues and Artur Ramos worked in the Gantois. In preparing "Os candomblés da Bahia," Édison Carneiro regarded the Engenho Velho as a model *terreiro*. Roger Bastide used data about traditional *terreiros* previously published by his predecessors, and was accepted as a member of the Axé Opô Afonjá, which more currently serves as a source for studies by Juana Elbein dos Santos, even as the Alaketu has been studied by Jean Ziegler (Lima, 1977: 49–50).

4. Xangô is the term generally employed in Pernambuco, Alagoas, and Sergipe to designate those religious practices known in Bahia as Candomblé.

5. Emic refers to the native perspective, supported by the subject's own conceptual terms and categories (Harris, 1968).

CHAPTER I

1. Various researchers have highlighted the difficulty of ascertaining an exact number of *terreiros* and their locations in any given city (see, for example, Mott,

1976: 28). Although I was working in a small town, I, too, came across such difficulties, above all with regard to smaller or recently founded *terreiros*. Similarly, the mobility of the centers of worship (some of which have moved to the capital) and the ephemeral nature of others have led me to pursue many a false lead. Although it is extraneous to my purposes to know the exact number of the city's *terreiros*, that number is surely much greater than the one mentioned in the informational brochures on Laranjeiras that emphasize, above all else, the presence of the black man (Laranjeiras, Turismo, 1976). For the state of Sergipe, the number is undoubtedly large. I do not possess reliable data for the number of *terreiros* registered in this state. In 1974, a local newspaper (*Gazeta de Sergipe*, March 6, 1974) estimated nearly 1,200 *terreiros* in the state, all of them affiliated to one of the five Federations "operating" at that time. I was unable to confirm that number and it seemed exaggerated to me. Claiming that their archives were being organized, two of the Federations denied the researcher access. In 1974, according to files in the other three Federations considered to be of lesser importance, 259 *terreiros* were registered.

2. In this chapter, the concept of a religious market developed by Pierre Bourdieu (1974) is applied restrictively to agencies of Afro-Brazilian cults which, offering the same services, compete with one another for followers and clients. Within the context of Xangô, the term "client" has a restricted meaning, indicating those who seek magical services for the solution of immediate problems, thus differing from those in the congregation (*filhos de santo, filhos de fé*) who maintain lasting relationships of affiliation and commitment to Xangô.

3. Vivaldo Costa Lima notes that the succession of *terreiro* leadership most frequently occurs in accordance with the lineage of a saint than through family lineage (Lima, 1977). In the present case, I do not know if there was any correspondence between the two.

4. Students were asked to write a composition about "*caboclo*, Nagô, Xangô, Candomblé, Umbanda, and Toré *Terreiros*." As for the cult leaders, as far as the interviews are concerned, I did not establish any category and, whenever necessary, I used the categories determined by them: Nagô and *caboclo*.

5. From a total of fifty-two student compositions, fourteen (26 percent) dealt with the distinction between Nagô and Toré.

6. The Manicheistic perspective that associates Toré with Evil and Nagô with Good appears in those compositions that deal with the differences between them. In others, the cults (including the Toré) appear as ambivalent, working to do Evil as well as to cure people.

7. It is the Nagô *terreiro* that deals most specifically with the differences, for it needs to distinguish itself and clearly demarcate its boundaries.

8. See table 1.

9. When asked to list the city's most important *terreiros*, some cult leaders chose not to do so, while the others came up with the following enumeration:

Virgin Santa Bárbara *terreiro*—mentioned eight times (four times in first
place; four in second, after the Filhos de Obá and the Ulufan).

Filhos de Obá *terreiro*—mentioned seven times (four in first place; twice in
second, after the Virgin Santa Bárbara; once in third, after the Ulufan).

Ulufan *terreiro*—mentioned three times (once in first place).

São José and São Jerônimo 2 *terreiros* (each mentioned once, and neither
time in first place).

10. The director of the Virgin Santa Bárbara *terreiro* passed away in late 1974
and the house was under a temporary leadership until 1979 (when it was confirmed). After the death of their old leader in 1976, the Filhos de Obá *terreiro* remained under the leadership of a *filha de santo* who also died and was replaced by
another one in late 1979.

11. The Santa Bárbara and São Jerônimo 2 *terreiros* claim to have fully initiated
members, but the initiation process does not include a period of seclusion such
as the one observed by the Filhos de Obá. According to its leaders, initiation takes
place at the foot of the altar and is not preceded by a period of seclusion.

12. According to "outsiders," the *terreiros*' scale of prestige was established according to a ranking of *terreiros* presented by twenty-two interviewees whom I
asked to list three *terreiros* in order of importance. The result was the following:

Virgin Santa Bárbara *terreiro*—mentioned nineteen times (ten times
in first place, eight in second, and once in third).

Filhos de Obá *terreiro*—mentioned fourteen times (seven in first place,
six in second and once in third).

Ulufan *terreiro*—mentioned eight times (twice in first place, three times
in second and three times in third).

São José *terreiro*—mentioned six times (twice in first place, once in second
and three times in third).

Ogum de Ronda *terreiro*—mentioned four times (once in first place, once
in second and twice in third).

São Jerônimo 2 *terreiro*—mentioned three times (once in second place,
twice in third).

São Jerônimo 1 and São Sebastian *terreiros*—mentioned once each, always
in third place.

According to [the] "outsiders," the *terreiros*' scale of importance is: Virgin Santa
Bárbara, Filhos de Obá, Ulufan, São José, Ogum de Ronda, São Jerônimo 2. Ac-
cording to "insiders," it is: Virgin Santa Bárbara, Filhos de Obá, Ulufan, Saint José,
Saint Jerônimo 2.

13. People often speak of the *santos fortes* of the old Nagôs, occasionally to accuse
individuals who unduly appropriated them, and sometimes to lament the waste-
fulness of those who are entrusted with saints yet do not know how to take proper
care of them.

CHAPTER 2

1. Vivaldo Costa Lima observes that, in the search for an "ideal of orthodoxy" that permeates the Candomblé *terreiros* of Bahia, "at great cost, the *povo de santo* remained faithful to its ancestral beliefs and to the genetic myths of their groups; a fidelity that has led some religious leaders to complicated genealogical rationalizations and fanciful interpretations with which a history and a map of ritual behavior are recreated." (Lima, 1977: 19).

2. From 1972 to 1974, the *mãe-de-santo* was invited to perform rituals in four domestic sanctuaries. Declaring that, in the past, this number had been much higher, in a single breath she rattles off five more such sanctuaries, in addition to those which had been kept in the *terreiros* (see note 4). At the beginning of the twentieth century, Nina Rodrigues wrote of Bahia: "It is almost impossible to count the number of private shrines. In the opinion (which I do not believe to have been exaggerated) of leaders I consulted, this number reaches the thousands" (Rodrigues, 1935: 60).

3. The ritual designated as *despacho dos santos pra Costa* in Laranjeiras consists of casting the saints into a stream; in this way, they will reach Africa by sea. Generally speaking, the rite's form and purpose repeats Nina Rodrigues's observation regarding early-twentieth-century Bahian Candomblé *terreiros*: "If the *orixá* cannot find anyone who will take on the religious responsibilities of the deceased, or if he cannot find anyone worthy of this honor among those present, late at night the insignias and ornaments as well as the idols and their altars are taken, in mysterious procession to running water so that the brook, river, or ebb tide will lead them to Africa where the Negros are certain they will inevitably end up" (Rodrigues, 1935: 352). The execution of such rituals is costly, particularly because of their demand for animal sacrifices. This has required people in Laranjeiras who do not have the resources to *despachar os santos* to turn to the alternative of putting them inside "holy crosses," small rural chapels that usually house ex-votos. Thus, a ritual considered to be African is replaced by another one from popular Catholicism.

4. *Santos da Costa* that do not find caretakers within the family circle of their former owners are taken to the *terreiro de Insã* located some 300 meters away, a sort of extension of the matrix *terreiro*. This is where the *mãe-de-santo*'s family saints and those of the *terreiro*'s founders are kept while the other, made up of two small adjoining houses, accommodates the *santos de muitos donos* (saints with many owners). An old man lives there who occupies a prominent position within the hierarchy of the cult center. He looks after the saints and ensures their physical integrity. Once a year, some of these saints receive sacrifices and special feasts for which their owners (even when they are physically absent) provide the necessary resources. Such is the case, for instance, of one of the altars that belonged to the ancestors of a "battalion sergeant." Having moved south, he entrusted the *mãe de santo* to collect rent from one of his properties in Aracaju, said rent to be used to fund the saint's festival. For many years, however, other altars receive only the

ministrations of *alumiar* and *dar água* because their owners, due either to inability, loss of interest, or even death, do not sponsor a feast for the saints that would necessarily include animal sacrifices and dancing.

5. Abundantly transcribed in this chapter and the next, the Nagô *mãe-de-santo's* statements have been drawn from thirteen interviews held in 1972 and 1973.

6. On this subject, see Lima (1977: 125–45).

7. The black cart driver from whom I took this statement emphasizes that he was never a slave.

8. His name appears on the list of notaries presented by Oliveira (1942: 201).

9. He lived in Laranjeiras from 1863 to 1877 (cf. Oliveira, 1942: 127, 162).

10. See Carneiro (1964: 8) on slaves for rent.

11. See, among others, G. Freyre (1964) and O. Ianni (1962). Whereas the former uses such elements to "demonstrate" the thesis of the mildness of slavery in Brazil, the latter regards paternalism as a subtle form of domination.

12. The figure of the grandmother is present in various interviews as an important part of her life history.

13. Contrary to what has been observed by Carlos Rodrigues Brandão in Goiás — to wit: that blacks do not identify themselves as descendants of a "people" or even of "defined ethnic groups," but simply as the descendants of slaves, people who are "devalued" in Laranjeiras, not only in the congregation but in the city's other black groups—there is a constant reference to Africa and, occasionally, to specific ethnic groups. Another difference to be recorded is that, in Goiás, blacks do not have a discourse about Africa whereas, in Laranjeiras, this discourse is an elaborate one, resembling representations that the whites of Goiás have of Africa (Brandão: 1977: 146).

14. Manoel Querino records a ritual performed during the feast of the yam at Bahian candomblé *terreiros* from the beginning of the twentieth century in which "the mother of the *terreiro* flogs the backs of cult members with a small liana. It is a disciplinary rite intended to forgive bad deeds practiced during the year" (Querino, 1955: 53).

15. In other contexts wealth is linked to the supernatural. See chapter 3.

16. This very same ambiguity has been detected and masterfully analyzed by Roberto Schwarz in the characters of Machado de Assis (Schwarz, 1982).

17. On this subect, see Vivaldo Costa Lima (1977: 61–104).

18. Because it is a group in which the number of participants becomes impossible to specify, in light of the flexibility of the criteria required to define the group members and the circumstance that not all of those defined as such always took part in the festivities, I have adopted the practice of listing all those who attended at least one of the ritual cycles that took place during the research stage and who acted according to behaviors expected of group members. Fifty-eight such individuals presented themselves and, although this was the totality of the group, the number represents a meaningful enough parcel of the same, perhaps quite near to its total, seeing as how I observed seven different *festejos* that took place over

a period of one and a half years, attendance at which is among the most serious "obligations" demanded of the faithful.

19. From 1972 to 1976, the period during which I closely followed the life of the *terreiro*, only one person was submitted to the ritual of baptism, which indicates the group's reduced proselytizing action.

20. The ethnography of the *terreiro*'s rituals may be found in Dantas (1976a).

21. A description of this rite may be found on pages 42–43.

22. Spirits worshipped in the temple, listed by alphabetical order: Abacossô, Abaluaiê, Acedá, Agongote, Aramilá, Bara-Ugudi, Beide-Oró, Chaocô (Orixaokô), Dadá, Efá, Iá-Xangô, Iansã (Insã), Ibeji, Iemanjá, Iguê, Irelodê, Lebará, Lokum, Nanã, Obá, Ogodô, Oguidibô, Ogum, Oiá, Omolu, Oroco, Orixá, Oxalá, Oxoce, Oxum, Teô, Xapanã, e Xangô. Based on studies carried out in *terreiros* in Bahia and Pernambuco, it would be possible to reduce several of these deities to a single one. For instance, in the literature on Afro-Brazilian cults, Abacossô is presented as a laudatory form of Xangô, and Ogodô as another name for the same *orixá* (Ribeiro, 1952). Such an idea is unacceptable to the Nagô *mãe-de-santo*.

23. See the transcript of this myth on pages 79–80.

24. The existence of two "seats" for Lebará and an emic view of the entity remind us of what Maupoil says about Dahomey, where two Legbás are customarily "seated" in each temple: "There is no conflict whatsoever between the Legbá of the gate and the indoor one. The latter protects the entire *terreiro* against misfortune, and especially against evildoings. The former prevents misfortune from entering the premises; it guards against external influences, while the indoor Legbá maintains harmony between the people of the house" (in Barreto, 1977: 64). Do these conceptual and ritual similarities between Legbá and Lebará point to a Jeje influence in the Nagô *terreiro* of Laranjeiras? Although the Nagô *mãe-de-santo* does not acknowledge the influence of other African traditions, comparison with ethnographic data regarding the (state of) Maranhão's Casa das Minas—of recognizably Jeje tradition (Pereira, 1979; Barreto, 1977)—allows us to identify a few more similarities between the two houses of worship. For example: virginity as a requirement for cult leadership; the presence of a *Pai da Costa*—an ancestral spirit reminiscent to the Dadá-Hô-Uussu (the father of all) of the Minas Jeje of Maranhão; the importance assigned to Santa Bárbara; as well as resemblances at the organizational level. Evidently, I am not trying to establish links between the two houses of worship, but merely suggesting the presence of a possible Jeje component within the pure Nagô of Laranjeiras.

25. The highly stylized use of the body in *orixá* dances has been emphasized by various Candomblé scholars who show how they are choreographed according to strict standards that exteriorize the features and personalities of the *orixás*. See Bastide (1971) and Carneiro (1967c: 104), among others.

26. Analyzing Exu's position in Umbanda-Quimbanda, Renato Ortiz draws attention to the fact that "global society functions as a model for classification and black magic is identified with the magic of the black man," at the core of the logic that identifies Exu with the Devil or attempts to domesticate him as a baptized

Exu, concluding that Exu is "what is left of blackness, of Afro-Brazilian," of "tradition" in "modern" Brazilian society and that Umbanda's attempt to eliminate Evil (Exu) is an attempt to "do away with old Afro-Brazilian values, so as to become more fully integrated into class society" (Ortiz, 1978: 122).

CHAPTER 3

1. Zé Sapucari was the African chief who led the Malês of Laranjeiras in the late nineteenth century and, whereas the *mãe-de-santo* highlights his wealth and wickedness, his obituary in a local newspaper emphasizes skills that elevated the deceased in the eyes of "civilized" society: "The highly-regarded African José Sapucari died here on the seventh day of this month. Beloved by all, the deceased could read and write in his native tongue and was a consul and business representative among his countrymen" (*O Cotinguiba*, March 12, 1899 — Laranjeiras).

2. The Chegança of Laranjeiras develops themes associated with maritime life ("Embarque," "Anau Perdido," "Rezinga Grande," "Contrabando dos Guarda-Marinhas," "Rezinga do Gajeiro") and with the fight against the Moors known as the *Combate* or *Mourama*. In the latter performance the "extras" are divided into two opposing groups: Christians and Moors. The latter send ambassadors to the Christians proposing conversion to Mohammed's religion in exchange for riches and marriages to Turkish princesses. The embassies are rejected. Struggles ensue. The Moors are vanquished and taken prisoner until they accept baptism, a sign of their conversion to Christianity. United in belief, everyone dances and sings praises to the Virgin of the Rosary (Dantas, 1976b).

3. The same occurs in the *Cavalhada* and in the *Congada*. On this subject, see Carlos Rodrigues Brandão (1974, 1977).

4. Spirits such as Iara and Jaguaracy (traditionally considered *caboclo*) are among the guides of his *terreiro*.

5. Alexandre's statement (the old leader of the Filhos de Obá *terreiro*) was recorded in Laranjeiras in 1964 under the supervision of Prof. Josefina Leite Campos.

6. Near the end of her life, Bilina became more tolerant toward the *terreiro*, which was attempting to reestablish its Nagô identity. In turn, the *terreiro* continues to uphold a policy of approximation toward leaders of the "pure Nagô" *terreiro*.

7. It is interesting to observe that the origin of the *caboclo terreiros* (whose existence is already noted in late-nineteenth-century Bahia [Rodrigues, 1977: 221] and may be influenced by the movement of Indian glorification that succeeded [Brazilian] Independence) is reported by the Nagô *terreiros* of Bahia and Sergipe. They not only specifically point out people responsible for their introduction in the area but also situate it sometime during the 1920s or 1930s. The information about Bahia that is supplied by Ruth Landes (Landes, 1947) must be added to information regarding Laranjeiras and mentioned in this work.

8. Regarding transference of the romantic idealized vision of the Indian to Afro-Brazilian cults, see R. Ortiz (1978: 66) and P. Birman (1980: 23).

9. The earliest attempts at creating the Federation of Umbanda in Sergipe date back to 1958. However, it was not until 1966, with the support of an influential politician, that the Saint Lazarus Federation of Spiritualist Temples and Brotherhood of Umbanda came into being. Internal dissent generated new associations and, although the state currently numbers five Federations, only three of them are active. On this subject, see A. Oliveira (1978: 20).

10. We must acknowledge the role of the sound recorder as an instrument for the reproduction (albeit inadequately, according to the *mãe-de-santo*'s evaluation) of knowledge — in this case, the chants (which are held to be exclusive and serve as markers of difference). People linked to the Federations record the chants and later attempt to reproduce them. Although she is annoyed by the presence of strangers recording her *toadas*, the *mãe-de-santo* believes that this would in no way affect the distinction of the Nagô for, as she declares, even those who copy them will sing them differently, the result being that difference is irreducible.

11. As they attempt to increase their memberships, the Federations pressure *terreiros* to become affiliated. The great argument is that the police will close down those who are not registered. This pressure is also exerted upon people who give readings and, in order to justify their inclusion in the Federations, their leaders encourage the realization of at least one annual festival at the center, with the presence of *pais* and *filhos de santo* and drums from other *terreiros* in an activity that eventually increases the number of houses considered to be Umbanda centers.

12. The other *terreiros* in the city of Laranjeiras are affiliated to a single Federation, with the exception of the São José *terreiro*, which, intent on being recognized as Nagô, recently split from the Federation, alleging that "Nagô doesn't have dealings with Umbanda."

13. An identical attitude by *pais-de-santo* in Recife's *terreiros* regarding Catholic baptism as a prerequisite for cult initiation has been recorded by Roberto Mota (Mota, 1979).

14. This account aggregates various elements present in the Catholic myth of Saint Barbara. The daughter of a wealthy pagan, she refused a marriage that had been proposed to her and her father locked her away from the world in a tower. One day, before leaving on a journey, the father ordered a bath house with two windows to be built. Barbara asked that, instead, it be built with three windows symbolizing the Holy Trinity. The father denounces her as a Christian and Barbara is tortured and condemned to death, executed by her own father (cf. *Encyclopedia Britannica*). In the *mãe-de-santo*'s account, São Jerônimo is portrayed as having the temper and character of the African *orixá* Xangô — violent and prone to amorous conquests that lead him even to incest — while Saint Barbara, unlike the *orixá* with whom she is identified (Xangô's wife Iansã, according to Yoruba mythology), appears not only as the keeper of order (rejecting the incestuous relationship) but also represents the glorification of virginity and sexual restraint.

15. The terms "mixture" and "combination" do not have the same sense as they do in chemistry, one which has been transposed, by certain authors, to the analy-

sis of religion. See, for example, Pedro Ribeiro Oliveira, who uses the terms "mixture" and "syncretism" analogously to those of "mixture" and "combination" in chemistry. To the author, "mixture" is the practice of acts or adhesion to beliefs of different religious systems, which occur at an individual level without affecting the religious systems involved, whereas "syncretism" is the combination of two religious systems in order to produce a new system (Oliveira, 1977). In this work, use of the terms "mixture" and "combination" is not restricted to semantic differences but to the need to differentiate emic ("mixture") and ethical ("combination") terms.

16. Regarding the disharmony attributed to hybrids, see Poliakov (1975) and Ramos (1961, vol. 3: 7–24).

CHAPTER 4

1. According to Oliveira's research (which attempts to reconstitute the history of black cults in Sergipe), the influence of Bahia is thought to have been more or less recent. He establishes five phases of dominant tendencies in Sergipe's Candomblé. The first is thought to have been marked by the Nagô as a survivor of the African slaves; the second that of the Toré or *caboclo* brought from Alagoas in 1924/25; the third, a consequence of the preceding one, further characterized by a predominance of Quimbanda (working with the left). During the 1930s, Sergipe's *terreiros* incorporated the full initiation practiced by *pais-de-santo*. The current phase is regarded as a mixture of various nations (Oliveira, 1978: 8).

2. Artur Ramos, for example, divides black studies into three phases: the pre-Nina Rodrigues phase, which encompasses the fragmented contribution of chroniclers of the colonial period, the linguistic contributions and observations of sociological and anthropological oriented João Ribeiro and Sílvio Romero; the Nina Rodrigues phase, which marks the beginning of the use of the comparative method in the study of African cultures and their "survivals" in Brazil, a method that would be followed by his disciples; and the third phase, initiated by his disciples, beginning around 1926 with new research on the black man and the publication of the works of Nina Rodrigues (Ramos, 1961: 10–11).

3. Thanks to Mariza Correa of Unicamp's Department of Social Studies for having drawn my attention to the fact that Nina Rodrigues's interest in black religious sentiment was subordinated to a broader interest in proving the thesis of black (and especially *mestiço*) inferiority, a problem central to the author.

4. See the evolutionary model of religions in Brazil according to Nina Rodrigues on pages 89–92.

5. In addition to works on psychoanalysis, psychiatry, social psychology, and education, in which he often deals with blacks, Ramos wrote the following: *O negro brasileiro* (The Brazilian Negro), ed. Civilização Brasileira, 1934, reprinted in 1940 by Editora Nacional in the Brasilianas collection and edited a third time in 1959 by the same publisher; *O folclore negro no Brasil* (Black Folklore in Brazil), published in 1935 by Civilização Brasileira, reprinted by Livraria da Casa do

Estudante do Brasil in 1954; *As culturas negras no novo mundo* (Black Cultures in the New World), published in 1937 by Civilizaçao Brasileira, reedited in 1946 by Editora Nacional (it was also published in Mexico [1943] and in Zurich [1947], having previously appeared in Washington as *The Negro in Brazil* and, later, in Brazil, under the title *O negro na civilização brasileira* [The Negro in Brazilian Civilization], published by Casa do Estudante do Brasil); *A aculturação negra no Brasil* (Black Acculturation in Brazil) was published by Editora Nacional in 1942; and *Introdução à Antropologia brasileira* (Introduction to Brazilian Anthropology), two heavy volumes dealing with Indians, blacks, and Europeans in Brazil, were published by Casa do Estudante do Brasil, the first in 1943 and the second in 1947, both reprinted in 1960. In the 1970s, Casa do Estudante do Brasil began to republish Ramos's works. The author's work on the black man includes many articles published in Brazil and abroad.

6. See propositions expressed in the Regionalist Manifesto and read at the Brazilian Congress of Nationalism, which met in Recife in 1926, organized by the self-named "Modernist-Traditionalist-Regionalists" (Freyre, 1976).

7. Various authors refer to repression in Alagoas (Ramos, 1951: 126), in Baha (Landes, 1947: 70; Ramos, 1951: 121–25), and in Pernambuco (Fernandes, 1937; Ribeiro, 1952). In Sergipe, the oral tradition of old *terreiro* leaders attests to violent police activities during this period.

8. In a paper presented at the 1934 Afro-Brazilian Congress of Recife, Édison Carneiro says: "It is known that blacks have supplied a large contingent of members to the ranks of the Brazilian Communist Party" (Carneiro, 1935: 240). But he does not refer specifically to Candomblé. With regard to the Bahian *terreiros* of the 1930s, Ruth Landes observes that "the cult groups were accused of being nests of communist propaganda" and that "the blacks and the intellectuals were being made scapegoats of the administration's anxieties." Drawing a parallel with the South, she adds: "Nor were the Rio blacks notorious as 'communists'; rather they were feared as magicians, and glamorized as street vagrants, since they were very poor. But in Bahia they were taken seriously in all ways—and, if the intellectuals were communists, why not the blacks with whom they associated?" (Landes, 1947: 61–62). It should be noted that most of the scholars who researched northeastern Candomblé during the 1930s had trouble with the police because they were accused of being communists. In 1934, when he was a member of the Democratic Left, Gilberto Freyre was arrested for having organized the First Afro-Brazilian Congress (Mota, 1977: 70). In 1935, Ulysses Pernambucano de Melo, leader of a group of specialists on the Xangô of Recife, attempting to "scientifically control" cults through the use of psychiatry (see page 105), was also arrested under the same charge (Cerqueira, 1978), as was Édison Carneiro, a Bahian Candomblé scholar who organized the Union of Afro-Brazilian Sects in Salvador in 1939 (Landes, 1967). Although, with regard to the post–World War II period, there is some (albeit unilateral) information on the Communist Party's Candomblé-related activity (Ziegler, 1972) and black movements in Brazil (Nascimento, 1981: 189–92), insofar as the 1930s are concerned such activity would appear not to have

been an object of study in this country, despite the fact that, since then, blacks have been the target of special attention by the Communist Party, not only in Africa but also in America (Nascimento, 1981: 61–72).

9. For a discussion on attempts to establish boundaries between the categories of sorcerers, fortune tellers, witch doctor, and priest from a legal perspective, see Barreto (1972: 33–52).

10. Nina Rodrigues transcribes various newspaper articles on the persecution of *terreiros* in Salvador (Rodrigues, 1977: 239–50), as does Artur Ramos, with items on Rio, Belém, Maceió, and Salvador in the 1920s, 1930s, and 1940s (Ramos, 1951: 121–26, 147, 155, 158, 190).

11. The idea that blacks were incapable of abstraction was explained by a certain branch of European psychiatry which believed that Africans did not possess the upper part of the cortex, ruled more by sentiment than by reason (Fanon, 1979).

12. On this subject, Mariza Correa's doctoral thesis (1982) on the school of Nina Rodrigues and anthropology in Brazil provides crucial reading.

13. Actually, although he criticized the Penal Code for being anachronistic, Nina Rodrigues himself wound up admitting that, in any event, the guarantee of the country's social order lay in its application.

14. Roger Bastide makes explicit use of the opposition between religion and magic to characterize traditional Afro-Brazilian cults of the Northeast and the disaggregated cults of the Southeast. Starting with the religious practice of Candomblé (above all in northeastern Jeje-Nagô Candomblé—characterized as a means to social control, an instrument of solidarity and communion)—he moves on to the individualized magical practices of Macumba, of Catimbó, and so on, making room for "exploitation, social parasitism and moral laxity." Magic is thus portrayed as cultural decadence and associated with black social disorganization in the urban-industrial world. Considering that, to the author, religious syncretism occurs by juxtaposition and magical syncretism takes place by addition, it follows that Candomblé (above all the "purest," most Africanized Candomblé) is a locus of religion, with ethical and social aims, whereas magic, incorporating disparate cultural elements, including those of whites, became perverse and dedicated to the exploitation of popular credulity and leaning toward crime (Bastide, 1971: 376–417). This stance leads to a romantic idealization of the "purest cults."

15. Rodrigues and Ramos were *ogãs* of the Gantois *terreiro* (Ramos, 1951: 63). According to Landes (1947: 42), Édison Carneiro was an *ogã* of the Axé Opô Afonjá, a version he presents in the following terms: "Eu era então disputado como ogã pelo Engenho Velho e pelos candomblés de Aninha e de Procópio, mas não me 'confirmei' em nenhum." My own translation would be: "In those days, I was very much in demand as an *ogã* at Aninha and Procópio's *terreiros*, although I had been 'confirmed' at neither one" (Carneiro, in Landes, 1947: 162). "Confirmation" implied submitting to initiation rituals and establishing a permanent protective tie to a *filha de santo*. Unconfirmed *ogãs* are the protectors and sources of money and prestige for Candomblé, although their positions in group organization are merely honorific.

16. The Mental Health Service of Pernambuco, whose projects and initial considerations were "written up under the supervision of Ulysses," included the following:

1. Services for non-hospitalized mental patients: a) outpatient;
   b) open hospital.
2. Services for hospitalized mental patients: a) hospital for acute illnesses;
   b) colony for the chronically ill
3. Asylum for the criminally insane.
4. Mental health services: a) service for the prevention of mental illness;
   b) Institute of psychology (Sá, 1978: 20).

17. The ideas of Nina Rodrigues clearly influenced Ulysses Pernambucano's work on Recife's Xangôs, which Gilberto Freyre claims to have eradicated and replaced by a Boazian view of culture. Writing about the common concerns that bound them (in addition to kinship ties, for they were cousins), Freyre says: "After we became acquainted I felt obliged to challenge him, given the manner in which he initially presented this interest of his, through Africological investigations he undertook himself, assisted by the competent Anita Paes Barreto. He based himself, however, on the illustrious Raimundo Nina Rodrigues, a Bahia-based native of Maranhão for whom blacks were biologically inferior, and whose presence, for this very reason, in Brazil's ethnic-social and sociocultural development was and continues to be more negative than positive. This was precisely the anthropological disorientation that I (a recent disciple of anthropologist Franz Boas at the University of Boas [sic]) was preparing myself to attack. On this subject, our exchange of information and criteria (from the conceptual to the methodological) was intense. I believe it to be nothing but honorable that, in Ulysses Pernambucano [. . .]" (Freyre, 1978: 133).

Such rejection does not appear to have been total, to judge from a statement by Gonçalves Fernandes, a disciple of both men who, in depicting the close collaboration between Freyre and Ulysses Pernambucano, situates the interpretation of possession as a point of disagreement between the two: "From the perspective of Mental Medicine, the concept of the pathology of possession was an idea that could hardly be eradicated from the (strictly) medical background of psychiatrists in those days, even those such as Ulysses Pernambucano who was as existential a psychologist, as social a psychiatrist, as innovative as anyone had ever been. Although to a somewhat rigid group possession was regarded as a pathological syndrome that merited careful observation by the Mental Health Service, professor Gilberto Freyre attempted to dissuade them, presenting states of possession not as taught but as the expression of a cultural past which took place under certain circumstances, favored by a reflex action. In those days, the concept tacitly accepted nowadays by cultural anthropologists was one of the things Master Ulysses Pernambucano did not accept from his dear friend and collaborator" (Gonçalves Fernandes, in Freyre, 1959: xxii).

18. Regarding the intermediation of the MHS, Waldemar Valente has written:

"On one hand, Ulysses would submit practitioners of the African religion to mental examinations while, on the other hand, the police committed to allowing them to operate subject to calendar and operating hours previously informed by the religious groups. The Xangôs were allowed to operate (albeit under certain restrictions) thanks to the diplomatic actions of Ulysses" (Valente, 1978: 123).

19. Pernambuco psychiatrist Abaeté de Medeiros recently published an article in a specialized journal warning about the dangers of Xangô as a disseminator of mental illness and demanding control of the mentally ill by the Mental Hygiene Services (Medeiros, 1974).

20. This authorization has repercussions in the *terreiros* of Alagoas, whence some *pais-de-santo* fled persecution to seek refuge in Recife, where "the *terreiros* enjoyed medical and police protection" (Bastide, 1973: 165).

21. It is interesting to observe how this discourse (appropriated by intellectuals in an attempt to retrieve the "pure African") is constantly repeated by *terreiro* leaders who proclaim themselves African. See the example of Sergipe in Chapter 2. For Bahia, see Landes (1947) and Pierson (1971). On Pernambuco, see also Lima (1937).

22. In those days, the *terreiros* of Pai Anselmo and Pai Adão's were considered to be the most Africanized in Recife. Pai Adão is known to have traveled to Africa to ensure his own orthodoxy. See Fernandes (1967) and Lima (1937: 39, 57).

23. The Axé Opô Afonjá was registered as a civil society as early as 1936 (Lima, 1966: 8).

24. Carneiro's bibliographical data may be found in the Introduction to *Religiões negras e negros bantus* (Carneiro, 1981).

25. Carneiro's theoretical position with regard to Afro-Brazilian cults and to working class cultural manifestations generally changed in the sense that he freed himself from the search for roots and culturalism and brought a more sociological bias to his analyses. Whereas his concerns with the social situation of blacks in Brazilian society and his attempts to explain it through historical materialism are remote (Carneiro, 1935) — possibly due to the difficulty of finding a theoretical-methodological focus in the writing of Marx — he pauses in his analysis of culture to identify the cultural items of *terreiros*. Living in Rio de Janeiro in the 1950s, he was influenced by a small group of intellectuals who regarded black studies from a more social than cultural angle (see, for example, Guerreiro Ramos, 1957). Along with Ramos and Abdias do Nascimento, Édison Carneiro organized the First National Black Congress (1950), which led to a split between a more Africanist current and one that was focused on the problem of class (see Nascimento, 1981: 198–205; Carneiro, 1964: 116). However, certain constants may be observed in his work. So it was that, although the Carneiro of the 1950s reviewed his positions regarding the search for Africa in Candomblé (see the article "Os estudos brasileiros do negro" [1953], published in Carneiro, 1964: 103–18), he never quite freed himself from the omnipresence of the Nagô model as an analytical schema of the cults. Consequently, in attempting an overview of African cults in Brazil that seeks to incorporate elements of historical materialism, he begins his analy-

sis with the existence of a Nagô model of worship that started in Bahia and spread to the rest of the country, and was copied to one degree or another in its many regions, depending on the vigor of the cults already established in each place (Carneiro, 1964: 121–42). This article, titled "Os cultos de origem Africana no Brasil," was published by the Biblioteca Nacional in 1959 and has been translated into French. It was reprinted in 1964 in *Ladinos e Crioulos* with slight adaptations that do not affect the hypothesis of the Nagô model's expansion in 1972 in *Revista Planeta*, n. 1, Editora Três.

26. Carneiro was one of the great articulators of the organization that received the support of the participants of the Afro-Brazilian Congress of Bahia (Carneiro 1964: 101). He was elected secretary of the short-lived organization (Lima, 1977: 38; Landes, 1947: 30).

27. See Landes (1967), Amado (1940), and Carneiro (1967b: 437) on Martiniano Bonfim.

28. Another obstacle to the legalization of the "purest" African *terreiros* is the alleged presence of communist intellectuals. Centers are thus occasionally targeted by police persecution as supposed centers of political subversion. See note 8 and Dantas (1984).

29. Papers presented at the Recife Congress were published in two volumes: *Estudos afro-brasileiros* (1935) and *Novos estudos afro-brasileiros* (1937). The Bahia Congress resulted in the publication of *O negro no Brasil* (1940).

30. This idea that dance is "impregnated in the blood" of blacks is a recurrent one, often invoked to explain Africa's remarkable contribution to Brazilian popular dances — and not only dance but also other typical features of "Brazilian culture." According to Freyre: "The Brazilian game of football is like a dance. This is certainly due to the influence of African-blooded Brazilians or of those whose culture is markedly African: they tend to reduce everything to dance — be it work or play — a trend which appears to be growing in Brazil, rather than remaining characteristic of an ethnic or regional group" (Freyre, 1947: 172).

31. Such as the ones by João do Rio, Xavier Marques, Graça Aranha, Herman Lins, and the one in Jorge Amado's *Jubiabá*.

32. Also in the 1940s, Pierre Verger settles in Bahia and intellectuals begin to travel from Salvador to the western coast of Africa; many would follow this route in search of Africanisms.

33. The bibliography available to the public during the 1930s included works by Rodrigues: *Os africanos no Brasil* (1932); Ramos: *O negro brasileiro* (1934), *As culturas negras no Novo Mundo* (1937); Carneiro: *Religiões negras* (1936), *Negros bantus* (1937); and Gonçalves Fernandes: *Xangôs do Nordeste* (1937).

34. See Ortiz (1980a) on the merchandising of religious products.

35. In an interesting work that focuses on Candomblé's articulation with the whole of Bahian society in recent years, Leni Silverstein notes that "artists representative of the group influenced by Candomblé [include] sculptors and painters Mário Cravo, Carybé and Emanoel Araújo; songwriters Dorival Caymmi, Gilberto

Gil, and Caetano Veloso; writer Jorge Amado: *Jubiabá*, *Shepherds of the Night*, *Tent of Miracles*, and *Sea of Death*, among other works; and filmmakers Glauber Rocha (*Antonio das Mortes* and *The Tuning Wind*) and Nelson Pereira dos Santos (*Tent of Miracles* and *Amuleto de Ogum*)" (Silverstein, 1979: 165–66).

36. In some cases this intention is explicit: "With the publication of *O leque de Oxum*, the author hopes to contribute to the dissemination of the beauty, fascination, and refinement preserved in the best Bahian candomblés, and to call attention to the splendid source material they offer to writers of fiction" (Maia, n.d.)

37. Brown sugar is a type of dark sugar considered to be of inferior quality that must be whitened and purified through a refining process.

38. Carlos Hasenbalg demonstrates the fallacy of this affirmation and the regional differences in racial inequalities (Hasenbalg, 1979).

39. The purpose of the Afro-Brazilian Congress that took place in Campinas in 1938 was also to fight racism and assess the global situation of blacks (Nascimento, 1981: 184).

CHAPTER 5

1. According to the census, in 1872 there were in Sergipe 1506 Africans, of which 412 (or 41 percent) were located in the Parish of Laranjeiras. The local slave population represented 12 percent of the slave population in the entire province, one of the highest concentrations.

2. Social differentiation is exemplified in the following table:

Professional Activities in the Parish of Laranjeiras for the Year 1854

Farmers	750	Public servants	14
Traders	115	Goldsmiths	13
Tailors	88	Priests	12
Carpenters	86	Saddlemakers	11
Shoemakers	61	Painters	6
Proprietors	54	Cigar manufacturers	6
Master sugar refiners	52	Pyrotechnists	6
Masons	41	Barbers	4
Musicians	35	Tinkers	4
Salesmen	34	Caulkers	4
Fishermen	25	Physicians	3
Sugar refiners	25	Lawyers	2
Blacksmiths	19	Apothecaries	2
Boatmen	16	Sextons	2
Bricklayers	15		

Source: Free and Slave Population Statistics for the Province of Sergipe, as organized in the year 1854—Public Archive of the State of Sergipe, 286 (in Dantas, 1976a).

3. Researching in the state of Goiás, in a city whose history presents similarities with Laranjeiras, Carlos Rodrigues Brandão observed that "as a paradigm for knowledge of the present, resorting to earlier times is part of the core of the society's ideology" (Brandão, 1977: 106).

4. In 1937, the local vicar launches a reconstitution of the city's past called *Laranjeiras a Católica* (Laranjeiras the Catholic), expanded and reprinted in the following decade as *Registro de fatos históricos de Laranjeiras* (A Register of the Historical Facts of Laranjeiras) (Oliveira, 1942).

5. The newspapers *Vida Laranjeirense* (1931, numbers 70, 75, and 77), (1933, numbers 126, 127, and 135), (1935, number 172), (1936, number 252), (1937, number 272), and *O Perigo* (1931, number 30), also published in Laranjeiras.

6. Basing himself on historical documents and Congada chants, Édison Carneiro draws attention to the Reis do Congo's "overseeing function": "At first the election (or rather, the choice) was made directly by the Brotherhood, but police approval soon became necessary. For example, confirming the election of Antonio de Oliveira (1748), the police of Pernambuco entrusted him with certain other highly un-monarchical duties — and the aforementioned king was obliged to inspect, maintain order, and subordination among his black subjects. The same thing happened in Rio de Janeiro, although documents are not as explicit as the one discovered by Pereira da Costa. Melo Morais Filho tells how Caetano Lopes dos Santos and Maria Joaquina of the Cabundá nation (1811) were crowned king and queen in the chapel of Lampadosa after being elected and licensed by the Honorable Police Intendant. The express function of [slave] foreman, which the Congo Kings had may still be seen today in *congadas*: 'Our kings tell everyone what to do / Everyone works for us'" (Carneiro, 1965: 39–40).

Nonetheless, other documents indicate that, more than once, the institution of the *reinado* had acquired a "revolutionary content, one that would be the cause of yet another deplorable incident which included bloody confrontations." Impugning the reelection of the king of the Black Brotherhood of the Rosary of his parish, in 1711, the Vicar of Mariana (in the state of Minas Gerais), lists a series of documents to prove the "abusive use of the titles of king and queen." One of these documents tells how "on the occasion of the king's appearance at the jail to release some prisoners, defying the jailer and asking after the judge's warrant, responded that he didn't care about the judge; as king, *he* was in charge. Disobeying the jailer, he sent the king off to fetch axes and assault the jail (which had wooden bars in those days), and the jailer had to hold this fury in check with men and weapons" (Freyre, 1968: 413–16).

7. Although the *terreiro* was also the object of scientific study, the presence of scientists is a good deal more recent than that of primary school teachers and priests. According to the methodological orientation of the day, it was only in the 1950s that anthropologists went there in search of Africanisms and concluded that the group represented a travesty of Nigerian clans dedicated to worshipping the gods of agriculture (Bezerra, 1954).

8. This would appear to corroborate Perdo A. Ribeiro de Oliveira's hypothesis, according to which the coexistence of religions "is only possible when it does not affect the religious power of the Catholic clergy," and religious permissiveness would apply only to "religious goods for individual, privatized consumption," while the Church would zealously protect its exclusivity at the public level, attempting to maintain the monopoly of the "rites of integration of individual biography within civil society," among which would be baptism and other rites of passage (Oliveira, 1977).

9. *Terreiro* leaders openly linked to local parties and political bosses were exposed to the most violent repression when the opponent rose to power. The intensity of the persecution against the Filhos de Obá *terreiro* at certain times is considered by the townspeople as being associated with the *pai-de-santo*'s explicit political link to one of the local political leaders. The role of politics in *terreiro* life was thus expressed by an informant: "this business of Candomblé and Xangô is like a match. Politics and the police go when they want to go. When they don't want to go, they have everything closed down, because they always have a way to get us."

10. This position is quite explicit in Édison Carneiro: "Candomblé is the home of the *filhas*—it is they who support it—economically and religiously. With her money, each daughter must pay for the rich garments of her respective Orixá and the sacred foods to be placed at their feet, on the days consecrated to them. Candomblé's external beauty is in the hands of the *filhas* who must dress appropriately, decorate the room, clean house, tend to guests, dance and sing satisfactorily, be respectful at public ceremonies, and occasionally cook leftover ritual foods for distribution among the audience. They are the present and the future of candomblé." (Carneiro, 1967c: 141–42).

11. *Obás de Xangô* are a body of para-religious dignitaries who serve as counselors to the *mãe-de-santo* in the Opô Afonjá *terreiro* in Salvador, Bahia.

12. See Yvonne Velho (1975) on the rational bureaucratic model in Afro-Brazilian cults.

13. Yoshiko T. Mott shows how, in Marília, in the state of São Paulo, despite the fact that they belong to the Federations, the older and more prestigious *terreiros* more often settle their problems with the police by appealing to the help of friends and support from the city's influential individuals than by the Federation's intermediation (Mott, 1976: 95).

Bibliography

NEWSPAPERS

O Cotinguiba (Laranjeiras), 1899
Diário Oficial do Estado de Sergipe (Aracaju), 1947
Gazeta de Sergipe (Aracaju), 1974
O Perigo (Laranjeiras), 1931
Vida Laranjeirense (Laranjeiras), 1931–37

BOOKS, ARTICLES, ESSAYS, AND PAPERS

Almeida, Mauro W. B. "Linguagem Regional e Fala Popular." *Revista de Ciências Sociais*, Fortaleza, vol. 8, 1977.
Amado, Jorge. "Elogio de um Chefe de Seita." In *O Negro no Brasil*, Nacional. São Paulo, 1940.
Arantes Neto, Antonio Augusto. "Cultura Popular Conservadora." *Revista de Ciências Sociais*, Fortaleza, vol. 8, 1977.
Araújo, Waldenir Caldeira. "Parentesco Religioso no Grande Recife." M.A. diss., UFRJ, 1977.
Auzias, Jean-Marie. *A Antropologia Contemporânea*. São Paulo: Cultrix, 1978.
Bakhtin, Mikhail. *Marxismo e Filosofia da Linguagem*. São Paulo: Hucitec, 1979.
Barreto, Djalma. *Parapsicologia, Curandeirismo e Lei*. Petrópolis: Vozes, 1972.
Barreto, M. Amália Pereira. *Os Voduns do Maranhão*. São Luís, 1977.
Barreto, Paulo (João do Rio). *As Religiões do Rio*. Rio de Janeiro: Simões, 1951.
Barth, Fredrick. *Ethnic Groups and Boundaries*. Boston: Little, Brown, 1969.
Bastide, Roger. *As Religiões Africanas no Brasil*. São Paulo: Pioneira/USP, 1971.
———. *O Candomblé da Bahia (Rito Nagô)*. São Paulo: Nacional, 1978.
———. "O Estado Atual da Pesquisa Afro-Americana na América Latina." *Boletim Sárepegbé*, 1975.
———. *Estudos Afro-Brasileiros*. São Paulo: Perspectiva, 1973.
———. *Imagens do Nordeste Místico em Branco e Preto*. Rio de Janeiro: O Cruzeiro, 1945.
Berger, P., & Luckmann, T. A. *A Construção Social da Realidade*. Petrópolis: Vozes, 1974.
Bezerra, Felte. "Notas sobre um Folguedo em Aracaju." *Boletim da Comissão Catarinense de Folclore*, 1954.
Birman, Patrícia. "Feitiço, Carrego e Olho Grande, os Males do Brasil São." M.A. diss., UFRJ, 1980.

Bourdieu, Pierre. "Gênese e Estrutura do Campo Religioso." In *A Economia das Trocas Simbólicas*. São Paulo: Perspectiva, 1974.

Brandão, Carlos Rodrigues. *Cavalhada de Pirenópolis—um Estudo Sobre Representações de Cristãos e Mouros em Goiás*. Goiânia: Oriente, 1974.

—. *Os Deuses do Povo—um Estudo sobre Religião Popular*. São Paulo: Brasiliense, 1980.

—. *Peões, Pretos e Congos—Trabalho e Identidade Étnica em Goiás*. Goiânia: Editora Universidade de Brasília, 1977.

Brandão, Maria de Azevedo. "Conversa de Branco: Questões e Não Questões da Literatura Sobre Relações Raciais." *Revista Vozes*, 1979.

Brown, Diana De G. "Umbanda: Politics of an Urban Religious Movement." Ph.D. diss., Columbia University, 1974.

Carneiro, Édison. "Candomblé da Bahia." In *Antologia do Negro Brasileiro*. Rio de Janeiro: Ouro, 1967a.

—. *Candomblés da Bahia*. Rio de Janeiro: Ouro, 1967c.

—. *Dinâmica do Folclore*. Rio de Janeiro: Civilização Brasileira, 1965.

—. *Ladinos e Crioulos—Estudos Sobre o Negro no Brasil*. Rio de Janeiro: Civilização Brasileira, 1964.

—. "Martiniano do Bonfim." In *Antologia do Negro Brasileiro*. Rio de Janeiro: Ouro, 1967b.

—. *Religiões Negras e Negros Bantos*. Rio de Janeiro: Civilização Brasileira/ INL-MEC, 1981.

—. "Situação do Negro no Brasil." In *Estudos Afro-Brasileiros*. Rio de Janeiro: Ariel, 1935.

Cascudo, Luiz da Câmara. *Dicionário do Folclore Brasileiro*. Rio de Janeiro: Ouro, 1969.

—. "Notas sobre o Catimbó." In *Novos Estudos Afro-Brasileiros*. Rio de Janeiro: Civilização Brasileira, 1937.

Cavalcanti, Pedro. "As Seitas Africanas do Recife." In *Estudos Afro-Brasileiros*. Rio de Janeiro: Ariel, 1935.

Cerqueira, Luís. "Ulysses Pernambucano, Meu Mestre." In *Ciclo de Estudos Sobre Ulysses Pernambucano*. Recife, 1978.

Chauí, Marilena. *Cultura e Democracia—O Discurso Competente e Outras Falas*. São Paulo: Moderna, 1980.

Cohen, Abner. *Custom and Politics in Urban Africa*. London: Routledge and Kegan Paul, 1969.

Copans, Jean. "Da Etnologia à Antropologia." In *Antopologia—Ciência das Sociedades Primitivas?* Lisboa: Edições 70, 1974.

Correa, Mariza. "As Ilusões de Liberdade—a Escola de Nina Rodrigues e a Antropologia no Brasil." Ph.D. diss., USP, 1982.

Cunha, Manuela Carneiro da. "Etnicidade: da Cultura Residual mas Irredutível." *Revista de Cultura e Política*, 1979.

—. "Religião, Comércio e Etnicidade: uma Interpretação Preliminar do Catolicismo Brasileiro em Lagos, no Século XIX." *Religião e Sociedade*, 1977.

Dantas, Beatriz Góis. "Chegança." *Cadernos de Folclore*. Rio de Janeiro: MEC-FUNARTE, 1976b.

———. "De Feiticeiros a Comunistas, Acusações Sobre o Candomblé." *Dédalo*, 1984.

———. "Estudo de Um Grupo Afro-Brasileiro de Laranjeiras, Sergipe." (manuscript) 1976a.

———. "Repensando a Pureza Nagô." Religião e Sociedade, 1982.

———. *A Taieira de Sergipe*. Petrópolis: Vozes, 1972.

Douglas, Mary. *Pureza e Perigo*. São Paulo: Perspectiva, 1976.

Durham, Eunice Ribeiro. "A Dinâmica Cultural Na Sociedade Moderna." *Ensaios de Opinião*, 1977.

Fanon, Franz. *Os Condenados da Terra*. Rio de Janeiro: Civilização Brasileira, 1979.

Fernandes, Gonçalves. "Pai Adão." *Antologia do Negro Brasileiro*, 1967.

———. *Xangôs do Nordeste*. Rio de Janeiro: Civilização Brasileira, 1937.

Ferraz, Aydano do Couto. "Volta à África." *Revista do Arquivo Municipal de São Paulo*, 1939.

Freyre, Gilberto. *Casa Grande e Senzala— Formação da Família Brasileira sob o Regime da Economia Patriarcal*. Rio de Janeiro: José Olympio, 1964.

———. *Interpretação do Brasil*. Rio de Janeiro: José Olympio, 1947.

———. *Manifesto Regionalista*. Maceió: UFAL-DAC-MEC, 1976.

———. *Nordeste—Aspectos da Influência da Cana Sobre a Vida e a Paisagem do Nordeste do Brasil*. Rio de Janeiro: José Olympio, 1967.

———. "O que Foi o 1º Congresso Afro-Brasileiro do Recife." In *Novos Estudos Afro-Brasileiros. Rio de Janeiro*: Civilização Brasileira, 1937.

———. *Problemas Brasileiros de Antropologia*. Rio de Janeiro: José Olympio, 1959.

———. *Sobrados e Mocambos— Decadência do Patriarcado Rural e Desenvolvimento do Urbano*. Rio de Janeiro: José Olympio, 1968.

———. "Sobre Ulysses Pernambucano." In *Ciclo de Estudos Sobre Ulysses Pernambucano*. Recife, 1978.

Fry, Peter. "Feijoada e Soul Food." *Ensaios de Opinião*, 1977a.

———. "Manchester, Século XIX e São Paulo, Século XX. Dois Movimentos Religiosos." *Religião e Sociedade*, 1978.

———. "Mediunidade e Sexualidade." *Religião e Sociedade*, 1977b.

Fry, Peter, et al. "Mafambura e Caxapura: na Encruzilhada da Identidade." *Dados. Revista de Ciências Sociais*, 1981.

Goffman, Erving. *A Representação do Eu na Vida Cotidiana*. Petrópolis: Vozes, 1975.

Gramsci, Antonio. *Literatura e Vida Nacional*. Rio de Janeiro: Civilização Brasileira, n.d.

———. *Os Intelectuais e a Organização da Cultura*. Rio de Janeiro: Civilização Brasileira, 1978.

Harris, Marvin. *A Natureza das Coisas Culturais*. Rio de Janeiro: Civilização Brasileira, 1968.

Hasenbalg, Carlos A. *Discriminação e Desigualdades Raciais*. Rio de Janeiro: Graal, 1979.

Herskovits, Melville. "Pesquisas Etnológicas na Bahia." *Afro-Ásia*, 1967.

———. "The Social Organization of the Afrobrazilian Candomble." *Phylon*, 1956.

———. "Some Economic Aspects of the Afrobahian Candomblé." In *Miscellanea P. Rivet*. Mexico, 1958.

Hollanda, Sérgio Buarque de. "Negros e Brancos." In *Cobra de Vidro*. São Paulo: Perspectiva, 1978.

Ianni, Octávio. *As Metamorfoses do Escravo*. São Paulo: Difusão Européia do Livro, 1962.

Landes, Ruth. *City of Women*. New York: Macmillan, 1947.

Leach, Edmund. *Political Systems of Highland Burma*. Boston: Beacon Press, 1954.

Leclerc, Gérard. *Crítica da Antropologia—Ensaio Acerca da História do Africanismo*. Lisbon: Estampa, 1973.

Leite, Dante Moreira. *O Caráter Nacional Brasileiro—História de uma Ideologia*. São Paulo: Pioneira, 1969.

Lévi-Strauss, Claude. "O Feiticeiro e sua Magia." In *Antropologia Estrutural*. Rio de Janeiro: Tempo Brasileiro, 1967.

Lima, Vicente. *Xangô*. Recife: Jornal do Comércio, 1937.

Lima, Vivaldo Costa. "A Família de Santo nos Candomblés Jejes-Nagôs da Bahia—um Estudo de Relações Intragrupais." M.A. diss., UFBa, 1977.

———. "O Conceito de 'Nação' nos Candomblés da Bahia." *Afro-Ásia*, 1976.

———. "Os Obás de Xangô." *Afro-Ásia*, 1966.

Lucena, José. "Ulysses Pernambucano e sua Escola de Psiquiatria Social." In *Ciclo de Estudos Sobre Ulysses Pernambucano*. Recife, 1978.

Luz, Marco Aurélio, & Georges Lapassade. *O Segredo da Macumba*. Rio de Janeiro: Paz e Terra, 1972.

Maia, Vasconscelos. *O Leque de Oxum*. Salvador: Carlito Ed., n.d.

Medeiros, Abaeté. "Xangô, Enfoques de Higiene Mental." Revista de Psiquiatria, 1974.

Mendonça, Renato. *A Influência Africana no Português do Brasil*. Rio de Janeiro: Civilização Brasileira, 1973.

Menezes, Eduardo Diatahy. "Elitelore versus Folclore, ou de como a Cultura Hegemônica tende a Devorar a Cultura Subalterna." In *Seminário de Cultura Brasileira-ANPOCS*. Minas Gerais, 1980.

Mota, Carlos Guilherme da. *Ideologia da Cultura Brasileira*. São Paulo: Ática, 1977.

Mota, Roberto. "Protesto e Conformismo no Xangô do Recife." *Ciência e Trópico*, 1979.

Mott, Yoshiko Tanabe. "Caridade e Demanda—um Estudo de Acusação e Conflito na Umbanda em Marília." M.A. diss., UNICAMP, 1976.

Nascimento, Abdias. *O Quilombismo*. Petrópolis: Vozes, 1980.

Nascimento, Elisa Larkin. *Pan-Africanismo na América Do Sul — Emergência de uma Rebelião Negra.* Petrópolis: Vozes, 1981.

Nascimento, Maria Beatriz. "Culturalismo e Contracultura." *Cadernos de Estudos Sobre a Contribuição do Negro na Formação Brasileira,* 1976.

Oliveira, Agamenon Guimarães de. "Candomblés Sergipanos — Subsídios para sua História." *Cadernos de Folclore Sergipano,* 1978.

Oliveira, Pedro A. Ribeiro. "Coexistência das Religiões no Brasil." *Revista Vozes,* 1977.

Oliveira, Philadelpho Jonathas de. *Registro de Fatos Históricos de Laranjeiras.* Aracaju: Ávila, 1942.

Oliven, Ruben George. "As Metamorfoses da Cultura Brasileira." In *Antropologia e Movimentos Sociais.* UNICAMP, 1981.

Ortiz, Renato. "Cultura Popular e Memória Nacional." *Cadernos do CERU,* 1980b.

———. *A Morte Branca do Feiticeiro Negro.* Petrópolis: Vozes, 1978.

———. "Religiões Populares e Indústria Cultural." *Religião e Sociedade,* 1980a.

Pereira, Nunes. *A Casa das Minas.* Petrópolis: Vozes, 1979.

Pernambucano, Ulysses. "Alguns Dados Antropológicos da População do Recife." In *Novos Estudos Afro-Brasileiros.* Rio de Janeiro: Civilização Brasileira, 1937.

Pierson, Donald. *Brancos e Pretos na Bahia (Estudo de Contato Racial).* São Paulo: Nacional, 1971.

Poliakov, Léon. *Hommes et Bêtes — Entretièns sur le Racisme.* The Hague: Mouton, 1975.

Querino, Manuel. *A Raça Africana e os seus Costumes.* Salvador: Progresso, 1955.

Ramos, Artur. *Introdução à Antropologia Brasileira.* 3 vols. Rio de Janeiro: Casa do Estudante do Brasil, 1961.

———. *O Negro Brasileiro — Etnografia Religiosa.* São Paulo: Nacional, 1951.

———. *O Negro na Civilização Brasileira.* Rio de Janeiro: Casa do Estudante do Brasil, 1971.

Ramos, Guerreiro. *Introdução Crítica à Sociologia Brasileira.* Rio de Janeiro: Andes, 1957.

Ribeiro, René. "Cultos Afro-Brasileiros do Recife — um Estudo de Ajustamento Social." *Boletim do Instituto Joaquim Nabuco de Pesquisas Sociais,* 1952.

Rodrigues, Nina. *O Animismo Fetichista dos Negros Bahianos.* Rio de Janeiro: Civilização Brasileira, 1935.

———. *Os Africanos no Brasil.* São Paulo: Nacional, 1977.

Russell, Bertrand. "The Superior Virtue of the Oppressed." *Nation* (June 26, 1937): 731–32.

Sá, João Marques de. "Abertura do Ciclo de Estudos sobre Ulysses Pernambucano." In *Ciclo de Estudos Sobre Ulysses Pernambucano.* Recife, 1978.

Sahlins, Marshall. *Cultura e Razão Prática.* Rio de Janeiro: Zahar, 1979.

Santos, Juana Elbein dos. *Os Nagôs e a Morte.* Petrópolis: Vozes, 1976.

Schwarcz, Roberto. "As Idéias Fora de Lugar." In *Ao Vencedor as Batatas.* São Paulo: Duas Cidades, 1977.

————. "A Velha Pobre e o Retratista." *Novos Estudos Cebrap*, 1982.

Serra, Ordep. "Na Trilha das Crianças — Os Erês num Terreiro de Angola." M.A. diss., Universidade de Brasília, 1978.

Silva, Anaíza Vergolino e. "O Tambor das Flores — Uma Análise da Federação Espírita Umbandista e dos Cultos Afro-Brasileiros do Pará." M.A. diss., UNICAMP, 1976.

Silverstein, Leni M. "Mãe de Todo Mundo — Modos de Sobrevivência nas Comunidades de Candomblé da Bahia." *Religião e Sociedade*, 1979.

Skidmore, Thomas. *Preto No Branco (Raça e Nacionalidade no Pensamento Brasileiro)*. Rio de Janeiro: Paz e Terra, 1976.

Souza, Ailton Benedito de. "Uma Contribuição ao Enfoque do Problema Negro." *Revista Vozes*, 1978.

Szasz, Thomas. *O Símbolo Sagrado da Psiquiatria*. Rio de Janeiro: Zahar, 1978.

Valente, Waldemar. "Educador e Reformador do Ensino Primário em Pernambuco." In *Ciclo de Estudos Sobre Ulysses Pernambucano*. Recife, 1978.

Velho, Yvonne. *Guerra de Orixá (um Estudo de Ritual e Conflito)*. Rio de Janeiro: Zahar, 1975.

Vogt, Carlos, & Fry, Peter. "A Descoberta do Cafundó, Alianças e Conflitos no Cenário da Cultura Negra no Brasil." *Religião e Sociedade*, 1982.

Ziegler, Jean. *O Poder Africano*. São Paulo: Difusão Européia do Livro, 1972.

Index

Economy: of Laranjeiras, 44, 134–36
Elderly: seniority of, 49; in Virgin
    Santa Barbara *terreiro*, 50
Elegbá. *See* Lebará
Elegbará. *See* Lebará
Elites: repression of cults by, 96–98
Emic criteria: in classification of *terrei-
    ros*, 7, 15, 16; definition of, 161 (n. 5);
    in prestige of *terreiros*, 21, 27
Encantados, 10, 156
Engenho Velho *terreiro*, 113
Enrolado, 11, 12, 156
Esquerda, 156
Ethnicity: boundaries of, 4; and con-
    ceptions of Nagô purity, 86–87; and
    culture, relationship between, 3–4,
    53; hierarchy of, 93; traditional aca-
    demic approaches to, 3–4
European immigration, 129–30
Evil: *caboclo terreiros* associated with,
    17–18, 73–74, 162 (n. 6); Exu iden-
    tified with, 61–64, 166–67 (n. 26);
    Good and, dualism of, 64, 82–83;
    magic as, 110; Malê associated with,
    65–68, 83; mixture with, 83–84
Evolutionist perspective, 88–90,
    92–93, 103
Exó (stick), 6, 46, 156
Exoticism, 118–22, 153
Exu (spirit): definition of, 156; iden-
    tified with Evil, 61–64, 166–67
    (n. 26); in Nagô versus *caboclo terrei-
    ros*, 17–18, 60–64, 73–74, 86

Family life, 107, 109
Feast of Saint Benedict, 137, 138
Federation of Brasília, 76
Federations of Umbanda, 75–77, 146–
    47, 168 (nn. 9–12)
Feitorio de santo, 85, 86, 156
Feliciano, José Amaro, 109
Fereguim, 57, 156
Fernandes, Gonçalves, 172 (n. 17)
Ferraz, Aydano do Couto, 123, 124
Festejo (ritual cycle): definition of, 157;

in domestic cult of *orixás*, 33; dura-
    tion of, 56; as marker of difference,
    56–59
Festivals: as markers of difference, 58
Fetishism, 91, 92, 101, 103
Fidelity to Africa: cultural features as
    proof of, 86–87; Nagô purity based
    on, 36, 56, 85; as sign of north-
    eastern regionalism, 8; as sign of
    self-identity, 2; in Virgin Santa
    Barbara *terreiro*, 36, 57
Filadelfo (priest), 139–41
Filhos de fé, 9, 157
Filhos de Obá *terreiro*: Alexandre on
    history of, 68–69; Bilina on differ-
    ences with, 55, 57, 61, 74; Bilina on
    history of, 68–70; classification of,
    12, 13, 14, 16; current status of, 28–
    29; influence of, on other *terreiros*,
    13, 19; leaders on prestige of, 18–25,
    163 (n. 9); link with Africa, 68–70;
    mission of, 69; number of members
    of, 23; origins of, 68–69; outsiders
    on prestige of, 25, 163 (n. 12); police
    persecution of, 68–69, 177 (n. 9);
    rivalry with Virgin Santa Barbara
    terreiro, 68, 74; seniority of, 20, 20–
    21; succession of leaders of, 19, 163
    (n. 11); traits and abilities of leaders
    of, 22. *See also* Alexandre
Filhos de santo, 9, 157
Finances: of Umbanda, 75–76; of Vir-
    gin Santa Barbara *terreiro*, 144–45
Folklore, 136
Football, 174 (n. 30)
Força: definition of, 22–23, 26, 157;
    demonstration of, 26; in prestige
    of *terreiros*, 19, 21–28; in success of
    terreiros, 26–28
Freedom of religion, 100, 115
Freyre, Gilberto, 93–96; in Afro-
    Brazilian Congress of Recife, 116–
    18; arrest of, 170 (n. 8); on Brazilian
    society, 125; on Pernambucano, 172
    (n. 17); and regionalism, 89, 93–96

Irmandade, 157
Islam, 66. *See also* Malê(s)
Isméria (grandmother of Bilina), 34–36, 40–44

Jaguaracy (spirit), 167 (n. 4)
Jeje (Candomblé nation): definition of, 157; influence of, 166 (n. 24)
Jeje-Nagô: disappearance of, 101; in hierarchy of religions, 101, 102; as purist model, 23, 56, 87, 90; repression of, 100–102
Jerônimo, São, 80, 168 (n. 14)

Kachin, 30–31
Ketu, 157
Kinship succession of leaders, 13, 35, 162 (n. 3)

Labor market: in Laranjeiras, decline of, 44, 134–35; relationships in, 45
Land, 44
Landes, Ruth: on communism, 170 (n. 8); on intellectuals' relationship with blacks, 127; on press coverage, 119; on use of term black versus African, 88; working in Bahia, 109–16, 125–26
Language: of purity, 142; religious tradition as, 69
Laranjeiras (city): black population of, 134, 135, 175 (n. 1); Catholic traditions in, 139–42; as center of Nagô tradition, 9; cult of past in, 134–36; cultural tradition of, 134–36; domestic cult of *orixás* in, 33–34; economy of, 44, 134–36; establishment of, 135; location of, 6, 9; Malês in, 65–68; methodological approach to, 6–8; Nagô purity in, conceptions of, 85–86; police persecution in, 136–37, 143; popular tradition of, 136–39; population of, 9; rhetoric of purity in, 142; slavery in black identity in, 165 (n. 13); smallpox in,

45, 46–47; social differentiation in, 134, 175 (n. 2)
Laranjeiras *terreiros*, 9–29; current status of, 28–29; differences among, 10, 16–18; functions of, 10; Indian versus African origins of, 16–17; leaders on classification of, 11–18, *12*, *14*; leaders on prestige of, 18–25, *20*, 162–63 (n. 9); links between, 11–16, *14*; methodological approach to, 6–8; number and location of, 9, 161–62 (n. 1); outsiders on classification of, 10–11, 17; outsiders on prestige of, 25–26; reasons for success of, 26–28. *See also specific terreiros*
Lavagem de cabeça, 157
Lavagem de pedra do santo, 157
Lavagem dos santos, 56, 157
Law, 98–116; dialogue between science and, 102–16; versus science, repression of cults through, 98–102; on witchcraft, 98–99
Leach, Edmund, 30–31
Leaders, religious: classification of *terreiros* by, 11–18, *12*, *14*; on differences among *terreiros*, 17–18; former, in criteria for prestige, 19–20; genealogies of, 30; on history of *terreiros* as myth, 30–32, 164 (n. 1); intellectuals' books read by, 123–24; and magic, 110–12; on prestige of *terreiros*, 18–25, *20*, 162–63 (n. 9); rivalries among, 47–50; succession of, 13, 34–36, *38*, 162 (n. 3); and success of *terreiros*, 26–28; traits and abilities of, in prestige of *terreiros*, 21–28; visits to Africa by, 122–28. *See also specific leaders*
Lebará (deity), 56, 62–63, 157, 166 (n. 24)
Left: Nagô versus *caboclo terreiros* working with, 17–18
Legitimacy: of religious practices, 74, 107